Studies in German Literature, Linguistics, and Culture

STUDIES IN GERMAN LITERATURE, LINGUISTICS,
AND CULTURE

Editorial Board

Frank Banta, Donald Daviau, Gerald Gillespie, Ingeborg Glier, Michael Hamburger, Gerhart Hoffmeister, Herbert Knust, Wulf Koepke, Victor Lange, James Lyon, Erika Metzger, Michael Metzger, Hans-Gert Roloff, John Spalek, Eitel Timm, Frank Trommler, Heinz Wetzel, A. Leslie Willson

Managing Editors

James Hardin and Gunther Holst
(South Carolina)

Johann Hellwig: A Descriptive Bibliography

Portrait of Johann Hellwig at age forty-six (1655),
by Jacob Sandrart after a painting by Georg Christoph Eimart, d. J.
National Library of Medicine

Johann Hellwig

A Descriptive Bibliography

Compiled and with an
Introduction and Notes
by
Max Reinhart

CAMDEN HOUSE

Copyright © 1993 by
CAMDEN HOUSE, INC.

Published by Camden House, Inc.
Drawer 2025
Columbia, SC 29202 USA

Printed on acid-free paper.
Binding materials are chosen for strength and
durability.

All Rights Reserved
Printed in the United States of America
First Edition

ISBN:1-879751-46-1

Library of Congress Cataloging-in-Publication Data

Reinhart, Max, 1946-
    Johann Hellwig : a descriptive bibliography / compiled with an introduction and notes by Max Reinhart.
    p. cm. -- (Studies in German literature, linguistics, and culture)
    Includes bibliographical references and index.
    ISBN 1-879751-46-1
    1. Hellwig, Johann, 1609-1674--Bibliography. I. Title.
    II. Series: Studies in German literature, linguistics, and culture (Unnumbered)
Z8395.58R45   1993
[PT1737.H52]
016.831,5--dc20   92-42474
                                                                                                 CIP

Acknowledgments

COPIES OF works by Johann Hellwig are scattered across Europe and North America and, although relatively few in number, present the descriptive bibliographer with sizable difficulties. The task of compiling his works could not have been accomplished without generous assistance from many librarians and interested colleagues. Although I personally visited as many holding sites as resources would allow, I often had to rely on the assistance of others in the form of correspondence that exacted considerable time and effort on their part. For that assistance my gratitude is greater than I can possibly express.

First, I wish to acknowledge the repositories that responded with helpful information, sometimes in great detail, about their copies of Hellwig materials:

Amberg: Staatliche Provinzialbibliothek
Augsburg: Staats- und Stadtbibliothek
Bamberg: Staatsbibliothek
Basel: Universitätsbibliothek
Berkeley: Bancroft Library
Berlin: Staatsbibliothek zu Berlin - Preussischer Kulturbesitz
Berlin: Stadtbibliothek
Berlin: Universitätsbibliothek
Bethesda: National Library of Medicine
Chicago: University of Chicago Library
Coburg: Landesbibliothek
Darmstadt: Hessische Landes- und Hochschulbibliothek
Darmstadt: Zentralarchiv Evangelische Kirche
Donaueschingen: Fürstliche Fürstenbergische Hofbibliothek
Dresden: Sächsische Landesbibliothek
Edinburgh: National Library of Scotland
Eichstätt: Katholische Universität, Universitätsbibliothek
Einsiedeln: Stiftsbibliothek
Erlangen: Universitätsbibliothek
Firenze: Biblioteca Nazionale Centrale
Frankfurt a. M.: Senkenbergische Bibliothek
Freiburg: Universitätsbibliothek
Glasgow: University Library
Gotha: Forschungsbibliothek

Göttingen: Niedersächsische Staats- und Universitätsbibliothek
Greifswald: Ernst-Moritz-Arndt-Universitätsbibliothek
Heidelberg: Universitätsbibliothek
Innsbruck: Universitätsbibliothek
Krakow: Uniwersytet Jagielloński, Biblioteka Jagiellońska
Laubach: Gräflich Solms-Laubachsche Bibliothek
Leipzig: Universitätsbibliothek
Lodz: Biblioteka Uniwersytecka
London: British Library
Lüneburg: Ratsbücherei
Madison: University of Wisconsin Memorial Library
Mainz: Universitätsbibliothek (Medizinhistorisches Institut)
Marburg: Universitätsbibliothek
Munich: Bayerische Staatsbibliothek
Munich: Stiftsbibliothek Abtei St. Bonifaz
Munich: Universitätsbibliothek
New Haven: Beinecke Rare Book and Manuscript Library
Nuremberg: Archiv des Pegnesischen Blumenordens
Nuremberg: Germanisches National Museum
Nuremberg: Landeskirchliches Archiv
Nuremberg: Stadtbibliothek
Oslo: Universitetsbiblioteket
Oxford: Bodleian Library
Oxford: Queen's College Library
Padua: Museo Civico Biblioteca
Paris: Bibliothèque Nationale
Philadelphia: The Library Company
Philadelphia: Thomas Jefferson University (Jefferson Medical College)
Prague: Národní v Praze
Princeton: University Library
Regensburg: Fürst Thurn und Taxis Zentralarchiv, Hofbibliothek
Regensburg: Staatliche Bibliothek
Rome: Biblioteca Apostolica Vaticana
Rome: Pontificia Università Gregoriana (Kircher Collection)
St. Petersburg: Biblioteka Akademii Nauk
Salzburg: Universitätsbibliothek
Schwerin: Mecklenburgische Landesbibliothek
Strasbourg: Bibliothèque Nationale et Universitaire
Tübingen: Universitätsbibliothek
University Park: Pennsylvania State University Library
Uppsala: Universitetsbibliotek
Vienna: Österreichische Nationalbibliothek

Acknowledgments   ix

Vienna: Universitätsbibliothek
Winterthur: Stadtbibliothek
Wolfenbüttel: Herzog August Bibliothek
Wroclaw: Biblioteka Uniwersytecka
Würzburg: Universitätsbibliothek
Zurich: Zentralbibliothek
Zwickau: Ratsschulbibliothek

A number of persons and institutions are due special mention for extraordinary assistance: the Bayerische Staatsbibliothek, Munich; the Bibliothèque Nationale et Universitaire, Strasbourg; Maristella Casciato, Universita di Roma, Rome; Wernhilt Dietel, Fürst Thurn und Taxis Zentralarchiv, Hofbibliothek, Regensburg; Gerlinde Frank, Universitätsbibliothek, Erlangen; Irene Friedl, Universitätsbibliothek, Munich; Volker Gentejohann and Richard Hamilton, both of the University of Georgia, Athens; the Herzog August Bibliothek, Wolfenbüttel; Irmgard Hofmann, Staatsbibliothek, Bamberg; the Interlibrary Loan Department, University of Georgia; W. A. Kelly, National Library of Scotland, Edinburgh; Susanne von Lennep-Reeder, Nuremberg; Otto Mazal, Österreichische Nationalbibliothek, Vienna; Annamarie Müller, Landeskirchliches Archiv, Nuremberg; David L. Paisey, British Library, London; John Roger Paas, Carlton College, Northfield, Minn.; Susan Rankin, University of Georgia; Jill Rosenshield, University of Wisconsin Memorial Library, Madison; Christa Sammons, Beinecke Rare Book and Manuscript Library, New Haven; Eberhard Slenczka, Germanisches National Museum, Nuremberg; the Universitätsbibliothek, Leipzig; Andrea Wölbing, Stadt- und Universitätsbibliothek, Frankfurt a.M.

I wish to thank the Vice-President for Research at the University of Georgia for seeding the research in the form of a Junior Faculty Research Grant. Betty Stowe of the Department of Germanic and Slavic Languages, University of Georgia, deserves appreciation for helping to translate the abracadabra of advanced Word Perfect.

Finally, I owe special debts of gratitude to Harry Vredeveld of The Ohio State University, Columbus, who introduced me to Johann Hellwig; and to James Hardin, University of South Carolina, Columbia, to whom this volume is dedicated, for reminding me regularly that he would be satisfied with nothing less than "a really complete bibliography."

For Jim Hardin

Contents

Frontispiece	iv
Acknowledgments	vii
Preface	xiii
Plates	xiv
Abbreviations	xv
Bibliographical Resources	xix
General	xix
Special Collections	xxxi
Catalogues of Occasional Verse and Letters	xxxiii
Contemporary Works	xxxiv
General Introduction	1
Johann Hellwig: Life and Works	1
Editorial Practice	21
A Descriptive Bibliography of the Works of Johann Hellwig	25
Independent Works	27
Translations	52
Occasional Verse	69
Manuscripts	104
Letters	108
Other Publications	110

Annotated Bibliography 115

Supplemental Bibliography 137

Index of Libraries 147

Index of Names 151

Preface

THIS BOOK represents the first attempt ever to compile, organize and describe the complete works of Johann Hellwig (1609-1674). Although Hellwig is remembered chiefly for only one work, *Die Nymphe Noris* (1650), he was in his day an avid contributor to the literary life of Nuremberg, and his writings are extensive enough to warrant systematization. They are treated here in six categories: 1) independently printed books (four); 2) translations (three); 3) occasional poems (285, including verse inserts); 4) manuscripts (one); 5) personal letters (three); 6) other publications (three). With two exceptions all of his publications were single printings. These are widely scattered in some seventy-three repositories throughout Europe and North America. In the chapter, A Descriptive Bibliography of the Works of Johann Hellwig (short: Descriptive Bibliography), the works are presented in chronological order, beginning with a photograph of the title page.

Insofar as the editor was unable to view firsthand every copy in every library, some lacunae persist. They are not of a substantive nature, however, and in no way prevent the reconstruction of ideal texts. In all instances of works not inspected *in situ*, the holding library has at least been identified. The purpose is to describe every work succinctly but thoroughly. Full details of editorial method are outlined in the second chapter of the General Introduction under the rubric, "Editorial Practice."

The first chapter of the General Introduction gives a biography of Hellwig. By comparison with biographies of better known figures this one will necessarily seem somewhat uneven. Because so little was previously known about Hellwig the editor has not been chary of documentation. In other words, the biography seeks to be as rigorous as possible in pursuit of a relatively obscure figure. All references are keyed by identifying word or short-title to a list with full-title information in the Bibliographical Resources, which immediately precede the General Introduction. An additional list of monographs relevant to the life and works of Hellwig is provided in the Supplemental Bibliography. The Annotated Bibliography provides a survey of notice and opinion on Hellwig's life and works from 1634 to the present. Two indexes are located at the end of the book: an Index of Libraries (compiled from the Descriptive Bibliography) and an Index of Names (compiled from the General Introduction and the Descriptive Bibliography).

Plates

Portrait of Hellwig (1655)	iv
Title page, *Alphabeton Iatrikon* (1631)	26
Title page, *Die Nymphe Noris* (1650)	31
Title page, *Prodromus Apologeticus* (1662)	40
Title page, *Observationes Physico-Medicæ* (1680)	44
Title page, *Ormund* (1648)	51
Title page, *Ormund* (1666)	56
Title page, *Neunhof* (1648)	59
Title page, *Neunhof* (1758)	62
Title page, *Christlich Vernünftiges Bedenken* (1660)	65
Epicedium for Elena Kob (1629)	71
Epicedium for Georg Nößler (1650)	79
Title page, "Sacrarium Bonæ Memoriæ Noribergensium" [n.d.]	103
Recto of letter to Athanasius Kircher (1655)	107

Abbreviations

THIS LIST contains only abbreviations of words and sigla. Short-titles are given in the Bibliographical Resources. Abbreviations pertaining only to Section C (Occasional Verse) of the chapter, Descriptive Bibliography, are listed separately there (pp. 69-70).

a.k.a. = also known as
ant. = antiqua
approx. = approximate(ly)
b. = born
B = binding
bet. = between
bl. = blank
c = correct
C = condition
ca. = approximately
cf. = compare
col., cols. = column(s)
coll. = collection
com. = commendatory
comp., comps. = compiler(s)
CW = catchword(s)
ded. = dedicatory; dedication
dep. = departure
diss. = dissertation
[E] = examined
ed. = edition; edited by
eds. = editors
engr., engrs. = engraving(s)
esp. = especially
exc. = excellent
f.c. = front cover

fig. = figure
fl. = flourished, lived around
f.m. = front matter
fn., fns. = footnote(s)
foll. = following
fp. = frontispiece
Frak. = Fraktur
Ger. = German
hdwr. = handwritten
HT = half-title
incl. = including
ital. = italics
l., ll. = line(s)
Lat. = Latin
max. = maximum
MS = manuscript
M/S = marks and stamps
[n.d.] = no date
no., nos. = number(s)
[n.p.] = no place; no publisher; no printer
[NR] = not reported
orig. = original
orn., orns. = ornament(s); ornamental
p., pp.; P., Pp. = page(s)
P = paper
parch. = parchment
P.Bl.O. = Pegnesischer Blumenorden
port. = portrait
pt. = part
r. = right
reb. = rebound
ref., refs. = reference(s)
resp. = respectively
rpt. = reprint
RT = running title
s. = see
S = source
ser. = series
sig. = signature
supp. = supplement
t.p. = title page

tr. = translation
trans. = translator
V = variants
viz. = namely
vol., vols. = volume(s)

Sigla:

> = becomes

† = died

| = end of line

∞ = married

|| = page break

+ = plus

? = uncertain; undetermined; unknown

Bibliographical Resources

PRESENTED HERE in full are the works referred to by key-word below in the General Introduction, the Descriptive Bibliography, and the Annotated Bibliography. A related selection of works is provided in the Supplemental Bibliography. The Bibliographical Resources are organized under four categories: I: General (Bibliographies, Compilations, Encyclopedias, Studies); II: Special Collections; III: Catalogues of Occasional Verse and Letters; IV: Contemporary Works. (*MVGN* = *Mitteilungen des Vereins für Geschichte der Stadt Nürnberg*)

I: General

Adler   Adler, Jeremy. "Pastoral Typography: Sigmund von Birken and the 'Picture-Rhymes' of Johann Helwig." *Visible Language* 20.1 (1986): 121-135.

Adler—Ernst   Adler, Jeremy, and Ulrich Ernst. *Text als Figur: Visuelle Poesie von der Antike bis zur Moderne*. 2nd ed. Weinheim: VCH, 1988.

Auktionspreise   *Jahrbuch der Auktionspreise für Bücher, Handschriften und Autographen*. Hamburg: Hauswedell, 1956 ff.

Bauer   Bauer, Johann Jacob. *Bibliotheca Librorum Rariorum Universalis: Oder vollständiges Verzeichniß rarer Bücher, aus den besten Schriftstellern mit Fleiß zusammen getragen und aus eigener vieljährigen Erfahrung vermehret....* Vol. 1. Ed. Georg Andreas Will. Nürnberg: Bauer, 1770.

Biedermann   Biedermann, Johann Gottfried. *Geschlechtsregister des Hochadlichen Patriciats zu Nürnberg*. 1748. Rpt. Neustadt a.d.A.: Verlag für Kunstreproduktionen, 1982.

Bischoff	Bischoff, Theodor. *Georg Philipp Harsdörfer: Ein Zeitbild aus dem 17. Jahrhundert. Festschrift zur 250jährigen Jubelfeier des Pegnesischen Blumenordens.* Nürnberg: Schrag, 1894.
Bosl	*Bosls Bayerische Biographie: 8000 Persönlichkeiten aus 15 Jahrhunderten.* Regensburg: Pustet, 1983.
Bünger	Bünger, C. *Matthias Bernegger: ein Bild aus dem geistigen Leben Strassburgs zur Zeit des dreissigjährigen Krieges.* Strassburg: Trübner, 1893.
Daly	Daly, Peter M. *Literature in the Light of the Emblem: Structural Parallels between the Emblem and Literature in the Sixteenth and Seventeenth Centuries.* Toronto: University of Toronto Press, 1979.
Dencker	Dencker, Klaus-Peter. *Text Bilder visuelle Poesie international.* Köln: Schaubert, 1972.
D'Ors	D'Ors, Miguel. *El caligramma, de Simmias a Apollinaire.* Pamplona: Ediciones Universidad de Navarra, 1977.
Dülmen	Dülmen, Richard van. "Sozietätsbildungen in Nürnberg im 17. Jahrhundert." In *Gesellschaft und Herrschaft: Forschungen zu sozial- und landesgeschichtlichen Problemen vornehmlich in Bayern.* Ed. R. v. Dülmen. München: Beck, 1969.
Dünnhaupt	Dünnhaupt, Gerhart. *Bibliographisches Handbuch der Barockliteratur.* 3 vols. Stuttgart: Hiersemann, 1980-1981.
Ehrenberg	Ehrenberg, Richard. "Die alte Nürnberger Börse." *MVGN* 8 (1889): 69-86.
Eloy	Eloy, N. F. J. *Dictionnaire Historique de la Médecine Ancienne et Moderne.* Vol. 2. 1778. Rpt. Bruxelles: Editions Culture et Civilisation, 1973.

Elsener	Elsener, Ferdinand. "Die Doktorwürde in einem Consilium der Tübinger Juristenfakultät des 18. Jahrhunderts." *Mélanges Philippe Meylan. Recueil de travaux publiés par la Faculté de droit.* Vol. 2: *Histoire du Droit.* Lausanne: Imprimerie Centrale, 1963: 25-40.
Emrich	Emrich, Wilhelm. *Deutsche Literatur der Barockzeit.* Königstein/Ts.: Athenäum, 1981.
Ernst	Ernst, Ulrich. "Europäische Figurengedichte in Pyramidenform aus dem 16. und 17. Jahrhundert." *Euphorion* 76 (1982): 247-328.
Ersch—Gruber	Ersch, Johann Samuel, and Johann Georg Gruber. *Allgemeine Encyclopädie der Wissenschaften und Künste.* Part 2/5. 1829. Rpt. Graz: Akademische Druck- und Verlagsanstalt, 1978. Article by K. Huschke.
Fletcher	Fletcher, John E. "Georg Philipp Harsdörffer, Nürnberg, und Athanasius Kircher." *MVGN* 59 (1972): 203-210.
Frank z. D.	Frank zu Döfering, Karl Friedrich von. *Die Kressen: eine Familiengeschichte.* Wien: Gistel, 1936.
Franz	Franz, Albin. *Johann Klaj: Ein Beitrag zur deutschen Literaturgeschichte des 17. Jahrhunderts.* Beiträge zur deutschen Literaturwissenschaft, 6. 1908. Rpt. New York: Johnson Reprint Corp., 1968.
Freher	Freher, Paul. *Theatrum virorum eruditione clarorum. In quo vitae & scripta theologorum, jureconsultorum, medicorum & philosophorum, tam in Germania superiore & inferiore, quam in aliis Europae regionibus ... à seculis aliquot, ad haec usque tempora, florentium.* 4 parts. Nürnberg: Hofmann, 1688.
Freytag	Freytag, Friedrich Karl. "Deutsche Uebersetzungen." *Trost der Philosophie aus dem Lateinischen des Boethius mit Anmerkungen und Nachrichten....* Trans. F. K. Freytag. Riga: Hartknoch, 1794: 32-38.

Garber/ 1966	Garber, Klaus. "Nachwort." *Pegnesisches Schäfergedicht 1644-1645*. Deutsche Neudrucke. Reihe Barock, 8. Tübingen: Niemeyer, 1966: 3*-27*.
Garber/ 1974	Garber, Klaus. *Der locus amoenus und der locus terribilis: Bild und Funktion der Natur in der deutschen Schäfer- und Landlebendichtung des 17. Jahrhunderts.* Literatur und Leben, 16. Köln and Wien: Böhlau, 1974.
Garber/ 1977	Garber, Klaus. "Vergil und das 'Pegnesische Schäfergedicht': Zum historischen Gehalt pastoraler Dichtung." *Deutsche Barockliteratur und europäische Kultur*. Eds. Martin Bircher and Eberhard Mannack. Dokumente des Internationalen Arbeitskreises für deutsche Barockliteratur, 3. Hamburg: Hauswedell, 1977: 168-203.
Garber/ 1982	Garber, Klaus. "Martin Opitz' *Schäferei von der Nymfe Hercinie*: Ursprung der Prosaekloge und des Schäferromans in Deutschland." *Daphnis* 11 (1982): 547-603.
Garber/ forthcom.	Garber, Klaus. "Der Hirten- und Blumenorden an der Pegnitz." Chapter 1 of the MS, "Arkadien und Gesellschaft: Ein Beitrag zur Sozial- und Mentalitätsgeschichte bürgerlich-gelehrter Dichtung in der Frühen Neuzeit" (forthcoming: Metzler, Stuttgart).
Georgi	Georgi, Theophil. *Allgemeines Europäisches Bücher-Lexicon*. Part 2. Leipzig: Georgi, 1742.
Gervinus	Gervinus, Georg Gottfried. *Geschichte der Deutschen Dichtung*. Vol. 3. 4th ed. Leipzig: Engelmann, 1853.
Goedeke	Goedeke, Karl. *Grundriß zur Geschichte der deutschen Dichtung*. Vol. 3: *Vom dreißigjährigen bis zum siebenjährigen Krieg*. 2nd ed. Dresden: Ehlermann, 1887.

Gottsched	Gottsched, Johann Christoph. "Severini Boethii Christlich vernünftiges Bedenken...." *Beyträge zur Critischen Historie der Deutschen Sprache, Poesie und Beredsamkeit* 7 (1741). Rpt. Hildesheim: Olms, 1970: 491-501.
Graesse	Graesse, Jean Georg Théodor. *Trésor de Livres Rares et Précieux: ou Nouveau Dictionnaire Bibliographique.* 6 vols. + supp. Dresden: Kuntze, 1859-1869.
Gran	Gran, Ulf. "Studier i manierism." MA Thesis. Lund University. Lund (Sweden) 1981.
Grotto dell'Erri	Grotto dell'Erri, Luigi I. *Della Università di Padova: Cenni ed iscrizioni.* Vol. 3. Padua: Crescini, 1841.
Hammer	Hammer, William. *Latin and German Encomia of Cities.* Diss. Chicago University 1937. Chicago: University of Chicago Libraries, 1937.
Hefner	Hefner, Otto Titian von, et al. *Die Wappen bürgerlicher Geschlechter Deutschlands und der Schweiz.* Part I [= Siebmacher, vol. 5: Nürnberg 1857, 1873, 1888]. Rpt. Neustadt a.d.A.: Bauer & Raspe, 1971.
Helmont	Helmont, Francis Mercurius van. "Nachricht von einem verteutschten Werke *Boëthii,* dessen vollständiger Titel: Des vortrefflichen hochw. *Severini Boëthii,* weiland Bürgermeisters zu Rom, *Consolatio Philosophiæ,* oder Christlich-Vernunftgemässer Trost und Unterricht in Widerwärtigkeit und Bestürtzung über den vermeinten Wohl- oder Uebelstand der Bösen und Frommen: verteutschet, und mit beygefügten kurzen Anmerkungen über etliche dunkele Oerter desselben zum andern male aufgeleget." Lüneburg: Lipper, 1697:)(2^r.
Herdegen	Herdegen, Johann. *Historische Nachricht von deß löblichen Hirten- und Blumen-Ordens an der Pegnitz Anfang und Fortgang....* Nürnberg: Riegel, 1744.

Heyse	Heyse, Karl W. Ludwig. *Bücherschatz der deutschen National-Literatur des XVI. und XVII. Jahrhunderts*. Berlin: Stargardt, 1854.
Higgins	Higgins, Dick. *Pattern Poetry: Guide to an Unknown Literature*. Albany: State University of New York Press, 1987.
Hirsch	Hirsch, August. *Biographisches Lexikon der hervorragenden Ärtzte aller Zeiten und Völker*. 3 vols. 3rd ed. München: Urban & Schwarzenberg, 1962.
Hofmann	Hofmann, Hanns Hubert. "Nobiles Norimbergenses: Beobachtungen zur Struktur der reichsstädtischen Oberschicht." *Untersuchungen zur gesellschaftlichen Struktur der mittelalterlichen Städte in Europa: Reichenau Vorträge 1963-1964*. Vorträge und Forschungen, 11. Konstanz and Stuttgart: Thorbecke, 1966: 114-150.
Holzmann	Holzmann, Michael, and Hanns Bohatta. *Deutsches Pseudonym-Lexikon: Aus den Quellen bearbeitet....* 1906. Rpt. Hildesheim: Olms, 1961.
Jaitner	Jaitner, Klaus. "Der Pfalz-Sulzbacher Hof in der europäischen Ideengeschichte des 17. Jahrhunderts." *Wolfenbütteler Beiträge* 8 (1988): 273-394 + appendix.
Jöcher	Jöcher, Christian Gottlieb. *Compendiöses Gelehrten-Lexicon*. 4 vols. Leipzig: Gleditsch, 1715.
Jöns—Laufhütte	Jöns, Dietrich, and Hartmut Laufhütte, eds. *Sigmund von Birken: Prosapia / Biographia*. Sigmund von Birken: Werke und Korrespondenz, 14. Tübingen: Niemeyer, 1988.
Kayser	Kayser, Wolfgang. *Die Klangmalerei bei Harsdörffer: Ein Beitrag zur Geschichte der Literatur, Poetik und Sprachgeschichte der Barockzeit*. Palaestra, 179. 2nd ed. Göttingen: Vandenhoeck & Ruprecht, 1962.

Kestner	Kestner, Christian Wilhelm. *Medicinisches Gelehrten-Lexicon: Darinnen Die Leben der berühmtesten Aerzte, samt deren wichtigsten Schrifften...*. Jena: Meyer, 1740.
Kirchner	Kirchner, Gottfried. *Fortuna in Dichtung und Emblematik des Barock: Tradition und Bedeutungswandel eines Motivs*. Stuttgart: Metzler, 1970.
Knod	Knod, Gustav C. *Die alten Matrikeln der Universität Strassburg 1621 bis 1793*. Vol. 2. Strasbourg: Trübner, 1897.
Koberstein	Koberstein, August. *Geschichte der deutschen Nationalliteratur vom Anfang des siebzehnten bis zum zweiten Viertel des achtzehnten Jahrhunderts*. Vol. 2. 5th ed. Ed. Karl Bartsch. 1872. Rpt. Nendeln: Kraus, 1974.
Kosch	Kosch, Wilhelm. *Deutsches Literatur-Lexikon*. 3rd ed. Eds. Heinz Rupp and Carl Ludwig Lang. Bern and München: Francke, 1979 ff.
Krebs	Krebs, Jean-Daniel. *Georg Philipp Harsdörffer (1607-1658): Poétique et Poésie*. Vol. 1. Publications Universitaires Européennes. Série 1: Langue et littérature allemandes, 642. Bern, Frankfurt a.M., and New York: P. Lang, 1983.
Kühlmann	Kühlmann, Wilhelm. "Kunst als Spiel: Das Technopaegnium in der Poetik des 17. Jahrhunderts." *Daphnis* 20/3-4 (1991): 505-529.
Linden	Linden, Johann Antonida. *De scriptis medicis libri duo*. Continuation by Georg Abraham Mercklin. Nürnberg: Endter, 1686.
Lohmeier	Lohmeier, Anke-Marie. *Beatus ille: Studien zum "Lob des Landlebens" in der Literatur des absolutistischen Zeitalters*. Hermaea, N. F., 44. Tübingen: Niemeyer, 1981.

Lotter	Lotter, Johann Georg. "Fortsetzung des Verzeichnißes von deutschen Uebersetzungen der meisten alten Lateinischen Scribenten." *Beyträge zur Critischen Historie der Deutschen Sprache, Poesie und Beredsamkeit* 3 (1732). Rpt. Hildesheim: Olms, 1970: 447-453.
Maché—Meid	Maché, Ulrich, and Volker Meid, eds. *Gedichte des Barock*. Universal-Bibliothek, 9975. 2nd ed. Stuttgart: Reclam, 1986.
Maltzahn	Maltzahn, Wendelin von. *Deutscher Bücherschatz des sechzehnten, siebenzehnten und achtzehnten bis um die Mitte des neunzehnten Jahrhunderts*. 1875-1882. Rpt. Hildesheim: Olms, 1966.
Mannack	Mannack, Eberhard, ed. *Die Pegnitz-Schäfer: Nürnberger Barockdichtung*. Universal-Bibliothek, 8545. 2nd ed. Stuttgart: Reclam, 1988.
Martino	Martino, Alberto. *Daniel Casper von Lohenstein: Geschichte seiner Rezeption*. Vol. 1. Trans. Heribert Streicher. Tübingen: Niemeyer, 1978.
Mayer	Mayer, Moritz Maximilian, trans. and ed. *Wilibald Pirkheimer's Aufenthalt zu Neunhof von ihm selbst geschildert. Nebst Beiträgen zu dem Leben und dem Nachlasse seiner Schwestern und Töchter*. Nürnberg: Campe, 1828.
Menzel	Menzel, Wolfgang. *Geschichte der Deutschen Dichtung von der ältesten bis auf die neueste Zeit*. Vol. 2. 2nd ed. Leipzig: Zander, 1875.
Meyer	Meyer, Heinrich. *Der deutsche Schäferroman des 17. Jahrhunderts*. 1928. Rpt. Hannover-Döhren: Harro von Hirschheydt, 1978.
Müller	Müller, Günther. *Deutsche Dichtung von der Renaissance bis zum Ausgang des Barock*. Handbuch der Literaturwissenschaft, 16. Potsdam: Athenaion, 1927.

Mummenhof	Mummenhof, Ernst, et al., eds. "Geschichtliches zur Heilkunde in Nürnberg." In *Nürnberg: Festschrift dargeboten den Mitgliedern und Teilnehmern der 65. Versammlung der Gesellschaft Deutscher Naturforscher und Ärtzte*. Nürnberg: Schrag, 1892: 73-96.
Neubecker	Neubecker, Ottfried. *Großes Wappen-Bilder-Lexikon der bürgerlichen Geschlechter Deutschlands, Österreichs und der Schweiz*. München: Battenberg, 1985.
Newald	Newald, Richard. *Die deutsche Literatur vom Späthumanismus zur Empfindsamkeit 1570-1750*. Vol. 5 of *Geschichte der deutschen Literatur von den Anfängen bis zur Gegenwart*. 2nd ed. München: Beck, 1957.
Newman/ 1983	Newman, Jane Ogden. "Institutions in the Pastoral: The Nuremberg Pegnesischer Blumenorden (1644)." Diss. Princeton University 1983.
Newman/ 1990	Newman, Jane Ogden. *Pastoral Conventions: Poetry, Language, and Thought in Seventeenth-Century Nuremberg*. Baltimore and London: Johns Hopkins University Press, 1990.
Omeis	Omeis, Magnus Daniel. *De Claris Quibusdam in Orbe Literato Norimbergensibus*. Altdorf and Nürnberg: Meyer, 1708.
Paas	Paas, John Roger. *Effigies et Poesis: An Illustrated Catalogue of Printed Portraits with Laudatory Verses by German Baroque Poets*. Vol. I: A-I. Wiesbaden: Harrassowitz, 1988.
Panzer	Panzer, Georg Wolfgang. *Verzeichnis von Nürnbergischen Portraiten aus allen Staenden*. Nürnberg: [n.p.], 1790.
Peignot	Peignot, Jerome. *Du caligramme*. Paris: Chêne, 1978.
Petit	Petit, Marc, trans. and ed. *Poètes baroques allemands*. Paris: Maspero, 1977.

Reicke	Reicke, Emil. *Geschichte der Reichsstadt Nürnberg von dem ersten urkundlichen Nachweis ihres Bestehens bis zu ihrem Uebergang an das Königreich Bayern (1806)*. 1896. Rpt. Neustadt a.d.A.: Schmidt, 1983.
Reinhart/ 1987	Reinhart, Max. "An Annotated Edition of Johann Hellwig's *Die Nymphe Noris* (1650)." Diss. Ohio State University 1987.
Reinhart/ 1988	Reinhart, Max. "The Privileging of the Poet in Johann Hellwig's *Die Nymphe Noris*." In *Sprachgesellschaften — Galante Poetinnen*. Eds. Erika A. Metzger and Richard E. Schade. *Daphnis* (Sonderheft) 17/3 (1988): 229-243.
Reinhart/ 1990	"Historical, Poetic and Ideal Representation in Hellwig's Prose Eclogue *Die Nymphe Noris*." In *Konstruktion: Untersuchungen zum deutschen Roman der frühen Neuzeit*. Ed. Lynne Tatlock. *Daphnis* (Sonderheft) 19/1 (1990): 41-66.
Reinhart/ 1991	Reinhart, Max. "Poets and Politics: The Transgressive Turn of History in Seventeenth-Century Nürnberg." In *Writing on the Line: Transgression in Early Modern German Literature*. Ed. Lynne Tatlock. *Daphnis* (Sonderheft) 20/1 (1991): 199-229.
Reinhart/ 1992	Reinhart, Max. "*De Consolatione Philosophiae* in Seventeenth-Century Germany: Translation and Reception." In *Translation and Translation Theory in Seventeenth-Century Germany*. Ed. James Hardin. *Daphnis* (Sonderheft) 21/1 (1992): 65-94.
Reinhart/ 1993	Reinhart, Max. *Johann Hellwig's "Die Nymphe Noris" (1650): A Critical Edition*. Studies in Germanic Literature, Linguistics, and Culture. Columbia: Camden House, 1993.
Reinhart/ DB	Reinhart, Max. *Johann Hellwig: A Descriptive Bibliography*. Studies in Germanic Literature, Linguistics, and Culture. Columbia: Camden House, 1993.

Rossetti	Rossetti, Lucia, et al., eds. *Gli Stemmi dello Studio di Padova*. Trieste: Lint, 1983.
Roth	Roth, Johann Ferdinand. *Verzeichniß aller Genannten des größern Raths von den ältesten bis auf die neuesten Zeiten mit historischen Nachrichten*. Nürnberg: Milbradt, 1802.
Rypson	Rypson, Piotr. "La Tradición de la poesia visual." *Arquitecto* 18 (1980): 53-58.
Satzinger	Satzinger, Walter. *Entwicklung, Stand und Möglichkeiten der Stadtkartographie: dargestellt vorwiegend an Beispielen aus Nürnberg*. Deutsche Geodätische Kommission, Reihe C, 71. München: Beck, 1964.
Scholte	Scholte, Jan Hendrik. "Nürnberger Dichterschule." In *Reallexikon der deutschen Literaturgeschichte*. Vol. 2. 2nd ed. Berlin: de Gruyter, 1965: 705-708.
Schultheiß	Schultheiß, Werner. "Woher stammt die Bezeichnung 'Noris'?" *MVGN* 52 (1963/1964): 551-553.
Schwaiger	Schwaiger, Georg. *Kardinal Franz Wilhelm von Wartenberg als Bischof von Regensburg (1649-1661)*. Münchener Theologische Studien: Historische Abteilung, 6. München: Zink, 1954.
Severin	Severin, Karl. *Fünfundzwanzig Figurengedichte des Barock*. München: Basse & Lechner, 1983.
Siebmacher	Siebmacher, Johann. *Wappenbuch*. Nürnberg: [Siebmacher], 1605.
Steinmeyer	Steinmeyer, Elias von. *Die Matrikel der Universität Altdorf*. 2 vols. Veröffentlichungen der Gesellschaft für fränkische Geschichte. 4th series: Matrikeln Fränkischer Schulen. Würzburg: Stürtz, 1912.

Surgeon General	*Index-Catalogue of the Library of the Surgeon General's Office, United States Army. Authors and Subjects.* 2nd series. Vol. VI. Washington, D.C.: Government Printing Office, 1901.
Szyrocki	Szyrocki, Marian. *Die deutsche Literatur des Barock: Eine Einführung.* Universal-Bibliothek, 9924. 2nd ed. Stuttgart: Reclam, 1979.
Tittmann	Tittmann, Julius. *Die Nürnberger Dichterschule: Harsdörffer, Klaj, Birken.* 1847. Rpt. Wiesbaden: Sändig, 1965.
Trechsel	Trechsel, Johann Martin. *Erneuertes Gedächtnis des Nürnbergischen Johannis-Kirch-Hofs; samt einer Beschreibung der Kirche und Kapelle daselbst.* Ed. Georg Jacob Schwindel. Frankfurt and Leipzig: Felßecker, 1735.
Vogt	Vogt, Johannis. *Catalogus Historico-Criticus Librorum Rariorum.* Hamburg: Herold, 1753.
Vredeveld	Vredeveld, Harry. "Zur Herkunft des Wortes 'Noris'." *MVGN* 71 (1984): 208-211.
Waller	*Bibliotheca Walleriana: A Catalogue of the Erik Waller Collection.* 2 vols. Comp. Hans Sallander. Stockholm: Almquist and Wiksell, 1955.
Warnock—Folter	Warnock, Robert G., and Roland Folter. "The German Pattern Poem: A Study in Mannerism of the Seventeenth Century." In *Festschrift für Detlev W. Schumann zum 70. Geburtstag.* Ed. Albert R. Schmitt. München: Delp, 1970: 40-73.
W.D.	W.D. "Nymphe 'Noris' lebt nur in der Phantasie." *Nürnberger Nachrichten*, 27 August 1985.
Will/ *BNW*	Will, Georg Andreas. *Bibliotheca Norica Williana. Kritisches Verzeichniß aller Schriften, welche die Stadt Nürnberg angehen....* 7 vols. Altdorf: Meyer, 1772.

Bibliographical Resources xxxi

Will/ *NGL*	Will, Georg Andreas. *Nürnbergisches Gelehrten-Lexicon oder Beschreibung aller Nürnbergischen Gelehrten beyderley Geschlechtes nach Ihrem Leben / Verdiensten und Schrifften....* Part 2 (H-M). Nürnberg and Altdorf: Schüpfel, 1756.
Will—Nopitsch	Will, Georg Andreas. *Nürnbergisches Gelehrten-Lexicon.* Ed. and enlarged by Christian Conrad Nopitsch. Altdorf: Nopitsch, 1805.
Zedler	Zedler, Johann Heinrich. *Grosses Vollständiges Universal-Lexikon.* 64 vols. 1732-1750. Rpt. Graz: Akademische Druck- und Verlagsanstalt, 1961-1964.

II: Special Collections

Adler—Ernst	Adler, Jeremy, and Ulrich Ernst, comps. Exhibit: "Text als Figur" (Wolfenbüttel: Herzog August Bibliothek, 1 Sep. 1987 — 23 May 1988).
BaySb	Bayerische Staatsbibliothek, München
Dieterichs	Dieterichs, Georg Septimus, comp. Pamphlet coll. in National Library of Scotland, Edinburgh.
Faber du Faur	Faber du Faur, Curt von, comp. *German Baroque Literature: A Catalogue of the Collection in the Yale University Library.* 2 vols. New Haven: Yale University Library, 1958 and 1969.
GNM	Germanisches National Museum, Nürnberg
H-A-B	*Deutsche Drucke des Barock 1600-1720 in der Herzog August Bibliothek Wolfenbüttel.* Ed. Martin Bircher. Abteilungen A-D + Register. München, New York, London, and Paris: Saur, 1977-1989.
Jantz	Jantz, Harold, comp. *German Baroque Literature: A Descriptive Catalogue of the Collection of Harold Jantz and a Guide to the Collection on Microfilm.* 2 vols. New Haven: Research Publications, Inc., 1974.

xxxii   Johann Hellwig: A Descriptive Bibliography

Kaathoven   Kaathoven, Cornelius Wilhelm Hendrik von. *Portraits de médicins et gravures ayant rapport à l'histoire de la médecine....* National Library of Medicine, Bethesda, Maryland. Described in *Catalogue of the Library of the Surgeon General's Office, United States Army.* Vol. 3. Washington: Government Printing Office, 1882.

LkAN   Landeskirchliches Archiv, Nürnberg

LkAR   Landeskirchliches Archiv, Regensburg

Manheimer   *Sammlung Victor Manheimer: deutsche Barockliteratur von Opitz bis Brockes.* Introduction and notes by Karl Wolfskehl. 1927. Rtp. Hildesheim: Olms, 1966.

NUC   *National Union Catalogue*

P.Bl.O.   Pegnesischer Blumenorden, GNM

Spahr   Spahr, Blake Lee, ed. *The Archives of the Pegnesischer Blumenorden: A Survey and Reference Guide.* University of California Publications in Modern Philology, 57. Berkeley and Los Angeles: University of California Press, 1960.

Sammons   Sammons, Christa, comp. Exhibit: "German Baroque Literature"; exhibit 8: "Pattern Poetry." (New Haven: Beinecke Rare Book & Manuscript Library, 8 Nov. — 21 Dec. 1988).

SB-PK   Staatsbibliothek zu Berlin - Preußischer Kulturbesitz

StAN   Stadtarchiv, Nürnberg

StAN/ Lochner   *Personenregister zu Lochners "Regesta Norica" und zum Urkundenzugangsverzeichnis (1883-1926),* StAN.

StAN/ Rep.   *Repertorium B7/III. Stadtgericht der Reichsstadt Nürnberg. Grundverbriefungsbücher (Libri Litterarum).* Vol. 3, parts 113-180, StAN.

StAN/ Sig.	Sig(naturen), StAN
StBN	Stadtbibliothek, Nürnberg

III: Catalogues of Occasional Verse and Letters

Darmstadt	*Bibliotheka Schottensis Sammlung: Epicedia Ratisponensia.* Zentralarchiv Evangelische Kirche, Darmstadt.
Koch	Herbert Koch: *Die Leichenreden der Universitätsbibliothek Jena.* 2 vols. Jena 1941.
Laubach	Gräflich Solms—Laubachsche Schloß-Bibliothek, Laubach
Leipzig	*Verzeichnis der Leichenpredigten ... in der Universitätsbibliothek zu Leipzig.* Ed. Peter von Gebhardt. Leipzig: Universitätsbibliothek, 1920.
Liegnitz	*Katalog der Leichenpredigten-Sammlungen der Peter-Paul-Kirchenbibliothek und anderer Bibliotheken in Liegnitz. Register 3: Verfasser von Trauer- und Trostgedichten (Epicedien).* Marktschellenberg: Degener, 1938.
Schmidt-Herrling	Schmidt-Herrling, Eleonore. *Die Briefsammlung des Nürnberger Arztes Christoph Jacob Trew (1695-1769) in der Universitätsbibliothek Erlangen.* Erlangen: Universitätsbibliothek, 1940.
Stolberg	*Katalog der fürstlich Stolberg-Stolberg'schen Leichenpredigten-Sammlung.* Vols. I-IV/2. Ed. Friedrich Wecken. Bibliographie familiengeschichtlicher Quellen, 2. Leipzig: Degener, 1927-1928. [Wolfenbüttel]
Tiedemann	*Katalog der Leichenpredigtensammlung der Niedersächsischen Staats- und Universitätsbibliothek in Göttingen.* 3 vols. Göttingen 1954-1955.

Trew	[Trew-Sammlung]. *Gelegenheitsgedichte, Leichenpredigten und Nachrufe im Besitz der Universitätsbibliothek Erlangen. Verzeichnis 1501-1945*. Part 2: *Alphabet der Verfasser, Nachträge, Ergänzungen und Berichtigungen zu Teil 1*. Ed. Agnes Stählin. Schriften der Universitätsbibliothek Erlangen-Nürnberg, 17. Erlangen: Universitätsbibliothek, 1985.

IV: Contemporary Works

"Acta consil."	"Acta consiliario Nicolao Bentzon Rhandrusio-Dano, bibliothecariis Paulo Spindler Vienna-Austrio, Iohanne Hellwigio Norimbergensi a die 12 Septembris anni 1633 ad diem 21 Augusti anni 1634." Rpt. in *Acta Nationis Germanicae Artistarum (1616-1636)*. Eds. Lucia Rossetti, et al. Acta Nationis Germanicae, 1/3. Padua: Antenore, 1967: 346-356.
Alphabeton	[s. Descriptive Bibliography A1]
Bohmer	Bohmer, Johann Christoph. Notary report to Geyger/ *Sequi*, D5^v-6^r.
Christlich vernünftiges Bedenken	[s. Descriptive Bibliography B3]
Epithal. 1635	*Epithalamia v. c. Johannis Helwigii, Philosophiæ et Medicinæ Doctoris, Sponsi et Nobiliß. atque Lectissimæ Virginis Helenæ Viri Nobiliß. Ampliß. ac Prudentiß. Dn. Caroli Schlüsselfelderi à Schlüsselfeldt, Senioris, Senatoris quondam b. m. Spectatissimi Filiæ relictæ, Sponsæ Nuptiis XIV. Calend. Novemb. MDCXXXV*. Nürnberg: Endter, 1635.
Epithal. 1643	*Epithalamia Nuptiis secundis v. cl. Johannis Helwigii Philosophiæ et Medicinæ Doctoris Sponsi, Cum Lectissimâ atque Pudicissimâ Virgine Euphrosyna Integerrimi et Spectatissimi Viri Domini Jacobi Kochii, Mercatoris et Numerosioris Senatus Filia Chariβimâ Sponsa XVIII. Septembris MDCXLIII*. Nürnberg: Dümler, 1643.

Bibliographical Resources   xxxv

Geyger/ Let.   Geyger, Daniel. Letter to a friend. December 1661. Printed version in *Prodromus*: D4ʳ-E2ᵛ.

Geyger/ *Resp.*   Geyger, Daniel. *Responsum medicum defensivum ad Iohannis Helwigii Phil. Med. Prodromum Pseudo-Apologeticum...*. Augsburg: Praetor, 1662.

Geyger/ *Sequi.*   Geyger, Daniel. *Sequitur Instrumentum Retorsionis legitime...*. Geyger/ *Resp.*: D1ʳ-5ᵛ.

GPH/ *Cato*   Harsdörffer, Georg Philipp: *Cato Noricus, sive Meditatio Panegyrica in Obitum ... Domini Johann Friderici Löffelholtze...*. [Nürnberg] 1640.

GPH/ *FG*   Harsdörffer, Georg Philipp. *Frauenzimmer Gesprächspiele*. 8 vols. Ed. Irmgard Böttcher. Deutsche Neudrucke: Barock, 13-20. Tübingen: Niemeyer, 1968-1969.

GPH—Klaj   Harsdörffer, Georg Philipp, and Johann Klaj. *Pegnesisches Schäfergedicht...*. 1644. Rpt. Ed. Klaus Garber. Tübingen: Niemeyer, 1966.

GPH/ Let. 1646   Harsdörffer, Georg Philipp. Letter to Sigmund von Birken, 27 September 1646. Archives of P.Bl.O., sig. C.127.7.

GPH/ Let. 1647   Harsdörffer, Georg Philipp. Letter to Sigmund von Birken, 6 June 1647. Archives of P.Bl.O., sig. C.127.11.

GPH/ *PT*   Harsdörffer, Georg Philipp. *Poetischer Trichter: Die Teutsche Dicht= und Reimkunst / ohne Behuf der Lateinischen Sprache / in VI. Stunden einzugiessen*. Vol. 1. 1647. Rpt. of 2nd enlarged edition (1650) Darmstadt: Wissenschaftliche Buchgesellschaft, 1975.

Hercinie   Opitz, Martin. *Schäfferey von der Nimfen Hercinie*. 1630. Ed. Peter Rusterholz. Universal-Bibliothek, 8594. Stuttgart: Reclam, 1969.

xxxvi   Johann Hellwig: A Descriptive Bibliography

"Hirtengedichte"   "Etliche Hirtengedichte." [s. Descriptive Bibliography F2]

HQ   Historical Quatrains, "Was sich denkwürdigst zu Nürmberg / oder derentwegen zugetragen: imgleichen die namhaftesten Gebäu daselbsten." Included are items of historical, architectural, and artifactual importance to Nuremberg. *Noris*: 28-48. [Each consists of 4 ll. in Ger.]

Knorr   Knorr von Rosenroth, Christian. "Liebe Kinder / etc." Foreword to *Deß Fürtrefflichen Hochweisen Herrn SEVER. BOETII weil. Burgermeisters zu Rom Christlich-Vernunfftgemesser Trost und Unterricht / in Widerwertigkeit und Bestürtzung über dem vermeinten Wohl- oder Ubelstand der Bösen und Frommen / in Fünff Büchern.* Trans. Knorr von Rosenroth and Francis van Helmont. Sulzbach: Lichtenthaler, 1667: A3^r-7^r.

Kreß   Genealogical quatrains on history of the Kreß family. *Noris*: 183-186. [Each consists of 4 ll. in Ger.]

Kreß/ Inscript.   Inscriptions by Johann Wilhelm Kress in personal copies of *Noris*, ca. 1655. [copy 1: s. Frank z. D.; copy 2: in GNM, sig. G.7877^r].

"Lobgedicht"   [s. Descriptive Bibliography F1]

Neunhof 1648   [s Descriptive Bibliography B2.1]

Neunhof 1758   [s Descriptive Bibliography B2.2]

Noris   [s. Descriptive Bibliography A2]

Observationes   [s. Descriptive Bibliography A4]

Ormund 1648   [s. Descriptive Bibliography B1.1]

Ormund 1666   [s. Descriptive Bibliography B1.2]

"Poet. Gedanken"   [s. Descriptive Bibliography B2.1: *Neunhof* 1648]

Prodromus	[s. Descriptive Bibliography A3]
"Sacrarium"	[s. Descriptive Bibliography D1]
"Schauplatz"	[s. Descriptive Bibliography F3]
Schottel	Schottel, Justus Georg. *Ausführliche Arbeit Von der Teutschen HaubtSprache*. Part 2, Book 5. 1663. Rpt. Ed. Wolfgang Hecht. Tübingen: Niemeyer, 1967.
Schröck	Schröck, Lucas. "Lectori Benevolo Salutem!" In *Observationes*. Ed. Lucas Schröck. Augsburg: Goebel, 1680: a4^v-b1^r.
Schröck/ *Memoria*	Schröck, Lucas. *Memoria Welschiana, sive historia vitæ viri celeberrimi, Dr. Georgii Hieronymi Welschii*. Augsburg: Goebel, 1678.
Schröck—Volkamer	Schröck, Lucas, and Johann Georg Volkamer. "Vita Hellwigiana." In *Observationes*. Ed. Lucas Schröck. Augsburg: Goebel, 1680: b1^v-b2^v.
SvB/ *Fortsetzung*	Birken, Sigmund von. *Fortsetzung der Pegnitz-Schäferey....* Nürnberg: Endter, 1645.
SvB/ *Gedächtnis*	Birken, Sigmund von. *Ehren Gedächtnis der Edlen Magdalis / an der Ilmenau.* 1651.
SvB/ *Guelfis*	Birken, Sigmund von. *Guelfis oder NiderSächsischer Lorbeerhayn....* Nürnberg 1669.
SvB/ *Helden-Beut*	Birken, Sigmund von. *Dannebergische Helden-Beut / in den Jetzischen Blum-Feldern beglorwürdigt.* Hamburg: Rebenlein, 1648.
SvB/ *Kriegs*	Birken, Sigmund von. *Floridans Kriegs und Friedens = Gedächtnis.* Nürnberg 1650.

xxxviii　　　　　*Johann Hellwig: A Descriptive Bibliography*

SvB/ *Teutonie*　　　Birken, Sigmund von. *Die Friederfreute Teutonie. Eine Geschichtsschrifft von dem Teutschen Friedensvergleich, was bey Abhandlung dessen, in des H. Röm. Reichs Stadt Nürnberg ... vorgelauffen.* Nürnberg: Dümler, 1652.

SvB/ *Winters*　　　Birken, Sigmund von. *Gottandächtige Winters-Betrachtung: verfasset durch Floridan.*

WAb　　　"Wappen der abgestorbenen Rahtsfähigen Geschlechten." *Noris*: 140-147. [Each consists of 4 ll. in Ger.]

WARG　　　"Wappen der Adelichen Rathsfähigen Geschlechten." *Noris*: 28-48. [Each consists of 4 ll. in Ger.]

WAUG　　　"Wappen der Adelichen, doch unrathsfehigen Geschlechten." *Noris*: 57-61. [Each consists of 4 ll. in Ger.]

WLP　　　"Wolverdiente und lobwürdige Personen des obersten Standes." *Noris*: 121-134. [Each consists of 4 ll. in Ger.]

General Introduction

I

Johann Hellwig

Life and Works

Youth and Education

JOHANN HELLWIG,[1] second of seven children born to Christoph and Maria Hellwig née Mörl,[2] was baptized in the church of St. Sebald in Nuremberg on 30 July 1609, the day after his birth.[3] His father was a merchant of substance who owned a large house "am Zotenberg" in the northeastern quarter of the city[4] and rose to local prominence as a market director[5]; he served as a member of Nuremberg's Greater Council of *Genannte* between 1621 and his

---

[1] The name entered by his father in the baptismal record is spelled with only one *l* (LkAN, *Kirchenbücher/ St. Sebald*, 39ᵛ), but Johann himself commonly doubled it, as in the autograph record of his second marriage (LkAN, *Trauungen/ St. Lorenz*, 569ʳ). The edition follows the apparently preferred usage. Seven spellings of his name, reflecting either dialectical, orthographical, or socio-professional preference, have been documented: Helbig, Hellwig, Hellwigius, Helwich, Helwichius, Helwig, Helwigius.

[2] The other children and their dates of birth: Christoph, 17 November 1607; Hans Georg, 10 November 1611; Georg Andres, 6 September 1613; Maria, 15 September 1615; Magdalena, 10 August 1617; Helena, 27 October 1619 (LkAN, *Taufbücher/ St. Sebald*). Their mother Maria was baptized on 3 January 1580 (LkAN, *Taufbücher/ St. Sebald*, 17ᵛ) and died 15 August 1648 (LkAN, *Bestattungsbücher/ St. Sebald*, 91ᵛ). Her parents, Konrad (also: Cunrad) and Elisabeth Mörl (b. 10 August 1550, LkAN, *Taufbücher/ St. Sebald*, 233ʳ), married on 18 November 1578 in St. Sebald's (LkAN, *Trauungen/ St. Sebald*, 37ʳ). The parents of Johann's maternal grandmother were Matthaeus and Helena Leutkirchner née Hoffmen; Matthaeus was a *Bader* and *Wundartz* in Nuremberg.

[3] Incorrectly as 1600 in Hirsch, 149, and in Bosl, 330, who follows Hirsch.

[4] Zotenberg was situated between Bindergasse and Alte Ledergasse, conveniently adjacent to the Obst Markt (Satzinger, map no. 10). Christoph purchased the house in 1625 for 4500 guilder (StAN/ *Rep.*, 137.108). The house remained in possession of the family until November 1654 when Christoph's daughter Maria sold it (StAN/ *Rep.*, 168.166-168).

[5] On the office of *Marktvorsteher*, s. Ehrenberg, 83-85; cf. Hofmann, 139-141.

death in 1634.⁶ It is unclear whether Christoph was born in Nuremberg, only that he came from an honorable (*erbar*) Franconian family, his father Blasius having been a guardian of the Franconian Circle.⁷ According to St. Sebald marriage records, Christoph married Maria Mörl on 12 August 1600.⁸ In 1621 Christoph and Maria sent Johann, aged twelve, north to school in Erfurt. Ill health forced his return to Nuremberg in 1624 where he completed his secondary education at the recently founded *Ægidianum*.⁹

"Johannes Hellwigius, Norib." is entered in the matriculation register of Altdorf University for 31 July 1627,¹⁰ during the rectorship of Johann Kob. Here he distinguished himself as a student of medicine under Georg Noessler (his adviser, or *Tischrat*)¹¹ and Caspar Hoffmann, as well as in philosophy under Rector Kob, Jacob Bruno, and Georg Mauricius.¹² Upon graduation in 1631 he presented to the Nuremberg elders a printed copy of his *Alphabeton iatrikon*,¹³ a tabular summation of Hippocratic principles, for which he was awarded the coveted *Stipendium Aureum*.

This monetary prize he applied to his cavalier's tour and further education.¹⁴ He enrolled on 11 May 1631 as a student of medicine at Strasbourg University.¹⁵ After five months there he paid brief visits to Basel,

---

⁶ Roth, 114. The Hellwig family belonged to the honorable estate (the *Ehrbare*) of Nuremberg, which was comprised of affluent and professional burghers one rung below and permanently excluded from those privileges, such as service in the Small Council, exclusive to the socalled *Stadtadel*, or patriciate.

⁷ The technical term was *quartein*, or, in German, *Vorsteher*. An inheritance clause on Christoph's behalf speaks of "deß Erbarn Blasius Helwigs des fränkischen Kreis quartein selig hinterlaßner Sohn" (LkAN, *Verkündbuch 1592-1602*, L 51, 318ʳ). The wife of Blasius was Anna. The Hellwig family arms show Justitia with bound eyes, holding a sword and scale (Hefner, plate 87; also Neubecker, 124).

⁸ LkAN, *Trauungen/ St. Sebald*, 38ʳ.

⁹ Freher, 1414b-1415a. Cf. Will/ *NGL*, 86-87; Will—Nopitsch, 86; Knod, 12; Steinmeyer, vol. 2, 280, note 18, cites Knod.

¹⁰ Steinmeyer, vol. 1, 200.

¹¹ Will/ *NGL*, 87; cf. Freher, 1414b: "[...] convictum apud Medicum celebrem *D. Georg. Nöslerum* habuit."

¹² Freher, 1414b; cf. Schröck, b1ᵛ.

¹³ Omeis, 60, erroneously reports its date as 1635.

¹⁴ Eloy, 488, acknowledges the role of Hellwig's father in providing his son "tous les secours possibles pour réussir dans son éducation littéraire."

¹⁵ As "Johannes Hellwigius, Noribergensis Med. Stud." Knod, 12.

Geneva, and Lyon, before taking up medical studies in Montpellier, "wo er sich 2. Jahr aufgehalten, und die vortreflichsten Medicos, Ranchinum, Bellovallium, Delort und Scarpium, mit grossem Nutzen gehöret."[16] On 17 October 1633 he set sail for Genoa with a group of friends. On this voyage Hellwig, "in habitu nigro," found himself in the company of Athanasius Kircher, with whom he shared — as he recollected in a letter to the great polymath twenty-two years later — "colloquii humanissimi ac eruditissimi" amid a stormy sea.[17] Before reaching his destination of Padua he made short stops in Piacenza, Mantua, and Verona.

At the University of Padua he took lectures from some of Europe's foremost medical authorities, among them Benedictus Sylvaticus, Fortunatus Licetus, Johannis Veslingius, Jacobus Tomasinus, and Johannis Rhodius. The high regard in which Hellwig was held by his peers, and specifically by the German contingency, may be inferred from their election of him in 1634 as *Bibliothecarius* and *Consiliarius Bohemicus*.[18] An honorary bronze plaque in Hellwig's name stands in the atrium of the University of Padua; on it he is identified as "Ultramontana," i.e. as having come from trans-Alpine Germany (this may also account for his later sobriquet, "Montano," in the Pegnesischer Blumenorden).[19] In August 1634 he received his doctorate in medicine, with distinction, under his mentor Julius Sala.[20] As it was customary for German graduates to donate scholarly works to the library on behalf of their nation, Hellwig presented two works: the *Consultationes* of Rodericus a Fonseca in two folio volumes; and an unattributed *Licetum de monstris et eorum natura*, in quarto.[21]

---

[16] Herdegen, 242.

[17] Letter, 10 January 1655, from Regensburg to Kircher in Rome. Hellwig was writing in anticipation of the opening in Nuremberg of Kircher's *Oedipus Aegypticus*.

[18] Handwritten record of the Nation of Germany: "Acta consil.," 349: "10 februarii [1634] conventum privatum officiariis nationis indixi, ubi dominus Paulus Spindler, inclytae nationis bibliothecarius, se suo abdicavit officio. Proponebantur duo alii praestantissimi viri: dominus Ludovicus Örber et dominus Iohannes Helwigius; hic vero inclytae nationis bibliothecarius restitit."

[19] Photo and legend in Rossetti, 19, no. 58: "Entro targa, in basso: 'IOHANnes HELLVIG / NORICUS Inclytæ Nationis Germanicæ Artistarum BIBLIOTHECarius ET / CONSiliarius BOHEMicus'. Su cartiglio, in alto: 'ULTRAMONTANA'." Cf. Grotto dell'Erri, 115^r. For the other possible explanation of his society name, s. fn. 42.

[20] Julius Sala is not to be confused with Johannis Sala, likewise a professor of medicine at that time at Padua (Will/ *NGL*, 87; cf. Freher, 1415a). A misprint in Reinhart/ 1988, 649, gives the year of Hellwig's promotion from Padua as 1632.

[21] "Acta consil.," 356.

Hellwig's final half-year in Padua was clouded by the loss of his father in March. Whether his father succumbed to the plague which in 1634 was ravaging Nuremberg at its fiercest is not known.[22] But if Johann had hopes of remaining abroad they must have been dashed by the news, for he returned to his hometown within a month of receiving his degree.[23]

Soon thereafter Hellwig was inducted into the Collegium Medicum[24] under the presidency of Johann Jacob Tetzel, one of Nuremberg's outstanding citizens whom Hellwig would later commemorate in *Die Nymphe Noris*.[25] The following year he joined the private practice of Dr. Sigismund Rüdel, remaining in that service for two years until his superior's death, at which time Hellwig succeeded him as *Medicus ordinarius* at the hospital of the Heiliger Geist.[26] Over the following years Hellwig became one of the city's leading physicians, with a large and devoted roster of patients.[27] By 1647 he had achieved preeminence among his colleagues, for in that year he occupied the first rank in the "Pentagon" of the Collegium Medicum, an elite group of

---

[22] Reicke, 988, reports that more than 2200 plague-related deaths occurred in Nuremberg in 1634 alone. Numerous *Pestordnungen* were issued in the summer and fall of the year (StAN, *Sachregister zu den Mandaten*, 103ff.). The most intensive period was fall, coincidental with Hellwig's return from Italy. Nuremberg's health crisis was exacerbated by the disastrous military turn of events. Nördlingen fell to the emperor's troops on 6 September, leaving Nuremberg, which was allied with the Swedish-Protestant side, politically vulnerable.

[23] Schröck—Volkamer, b1^v. At the time of Christoph Hellwig's death the family resided "neben dem güld Mörßner." He was buried on 15 March (LkAN, *Bestattungsbücher/ St. Sebald*, 48^r) in the inner court of the chapel at St. Johannis Cemetery where he had erected a stone in 1625 (Trechsel, 871).

[24] Will/ *NGL*, 87. On the Collegium Medicum, see Will/ *BNW*, 288-332; Reicke, 539-595. Mummenhof, 79, explains the college's membership policy: "Es sollen ihm beitreten alle von Rat angenommenen Doktoren der Medizin, welche ihm jährlich die gewohnte Pflicht leisten, dann die auf den bekannten Universitäten Deutschlands und anderswo Promovierten und in der 'doctrina Hippocratica et Galenica und derselben praxi' wohl Geübten, wenn sie vom Rat zum Praktizieren angekommen worden sind."

[25] *Noris*, 6 and 133.

[26] Eloy, 488-489; s. also Schröck—Volkamer, b2^r; Freher, 1415a. Kestner, 387, refers to Hellwig as "Hospital-Medicus"; Hirsch, 149, "Hospitalarzt."

[27] Eloy, 488-489: "Il fut d'ailleurs extréement suivi dans cette ville, où sa pratique étoit également brillante et nombreuse," and he gained "l'estime et la confiance de ses concitoyens."

physicians that consisted of Hellwig, Johann Georg Volkamer, Gregor Hilling, Heinrich Heigel, and Christoph Nicolai.[28]

On 19 October 1635 in the church of St. Sebald the twenty-five-year-old doctor was married to Helena Schlüsselfelder, daughter of *Ratsherr* Carl Schlüsselfelder and his wife Catharina née Tucher.[29] The marriage remained childless, perhaps due to Helena's advanced childbearing age, and lasted only until June 1641 when she died.[30] During the five-and-a-half years that they were married the couple resided "gegen dem Güldn Schild uber."[31] On 3 August 1637 Hellwig was granted an official seal. It is of red wax, and around the seal are the words: "JOH. HELLWIG PHIL ET MED D."[32]

At the age of thirty-four Hellwig married again in September 1643, this time twenty-one-year-old Euphrosina Koch,[33] eldest daughter of the prominent merchant Jacob Koch and his first wife Euphrosina,[34] in the church of St. Lorenz.[35] The common theme of the printed epithalamia presented on this occasion was of Johann's revivification. Euphrosina Koch will, one humorous poem promises, "renourish him, as befits the good cook that she is, from their own field":

---

[28] Schröck—Volkamer, b2ʳ. "Primus ille in Societatis Collegii sui Pentagono, quod pro felicibus praxos suæ incrementis An. MDCXLVII. laudatissimo conatu instituit nunquam satis laudatus D. C. Jo. Georg. Volckamerus, cum Excell. Dnn. Gregorio Hillingio, Henrico Magno Heigelio, & Christophoro Nicolai, Professore Aldorfino, agmen duxit, atque frequenti & amica inter eos conversatione pro ægrorum commodis impigro subinde animo excubuit."

[29] LkAN, *Pfarrei-Kirchenbücher/ St. Sebald*, 222ᵛ. Johann and Helena were presented by their friends with a collection of epithalamia dated 14 November: *Epithal.* 1635.

[30] Helena was born in 1595, making her fourteen years older than her husband (Biedermann, Jiii3ᵛ). She was buried on 24 June 1641 (LkAN, *Beerdigungen/ St. Sebald*, 218ʳ).

[31] LkAN, *Beerdigungen/ St. Sebald*, 218ʳ.

[32] It is conserved in StAN/ Lochner, 371, Nr. 1832.

[33] Euphrosina Koch was baptized in St. Sebald's Church on 29 October 1622 (LkAN, *Taufbücher/ St. Sebald*, 219).

[34] Jacob Koch, son of Konrad and Esther Koch, was baptized on 16 November 1591 (LkAN, *Taufbücher/ St. Sebald*, 29ʳ) and buried on 2 June 1658 (LkAN, *Beerdigungen/ St. Lorenz*, 237ʳ). He owned a home on Fischbach and towards the end of his life became senior *Marktvorsteher*. He married Euphrosina Steininger, daughter of the Augsburg *Ratsherr* Johann Steininger, on 30 January 1615 (LkAN, *Trauungen/ St. Lorenz*, 660ʳ). After her death (she was buried on 2 November 1628: LkAN, *Beerdigungen/ St. Lorenz*, 365ʳ) he married Anna Katharina ImHoff, daughter of Wilhelm d.J. ImHoff, on 11 October 1629 (LkAN, *Trauungen/ St. Sebald*, 221ᵛ), and after her death, Margaretha Katharina Kleewein, daughter of Joachim Kleewein, on 13 November 1643 (LkAN, *Trauungen/ St. Sebald*, 46ʳ).

[35] LkAN, *Trauungen/ St. Lorenz*, 569ʳ.

Sie wird von ewrem Feld / und sonst von andern dingen /
Euch Morgends / zu Mittag / und auch deß Abends bringen /
Auff ewren Tisch / was sie mit Kochen angericht /
Glaubt mir / O glaubet mir / ihr werds verachten nicht.[36]

As the wedding poem augured, Hellwig's second marriage proved to be happy and fruitful. Six children were born to this union, two boys and four girls, of whom two daughters preceded their father in death.[37] During these years the Hellwigs owned a house on Fischbach, although it is not known whether they resided there, or whether it was in fact the house of Euphrosine's father, Jacob Koch.[38]

From the dedication page of his 1648 translation of Willibald Pirckheimer's Latin description of the Neunhof estate, it can be inferred that a family relationship existed between Hellwig and the Kolers, former owners of Neunhof; Hellwig speaks there of Georg Seyfried Koler as his *Schwäger*. For their part the Kolers were related to Hellwig's friend Ferdinand Jenisch, recently of Augsburg,[39] through his marriage to Georg Seyfried Koler's sister Maria Sabina.[40] Ferdinand and Maria Sabina Jenisch stood as godparents to Hellwig's daughter Helena Sabina. As a retreat during the 1640s from the demands of his medical practice and the continuing shadow of war Hellwig enjoyed visits to Neunhof. In 1648 he could write of those times with nostalgia:

---

[36] *Epithal.* 1643, no. XIV, "Tisch strew: und Kochbüchlein," by Heinrich Clerford, B3^v; collection presented on 18 September.

[37] Schröck—Volkamer, b2^r. The birth of only one of the children is documented in the LkAN records, Helena Sabina, baptized 14 May 1646 (*Taufbücher/ St. Sebald*, 674^r). Her godparents were Ferdinand Jenisch and his wife Maria Sabina née Koler. The "junge Schäferin" with the initials "H.H." whom Montano mourns in *Noris*, 8, cannot have been his daughter Helena Sabina. "H.H." died, as the lemma indicates, in 1645, whereas his daughter Helena was not born until 1646. We find documented, however, the death on 8 September 1645 of Helena Hellwig, born 1619, sister of Johann (LkAN, *Bestattungsbücher/ St. Sebald*, Bd. 1644-1654, 36^v): "Die Erbar und Tugentreiche Jungfraw Helena, deß Erbar, und Fürnehmen Christoph Hellwigs S[eelig] hinterlaßne Tochter von Obenem Zottenberg." She would have been only twenty-five years old at her death. The "junge Schäferin" for whom Montano weeps is in fact his sister.

[38] Johann and Euphrosina, together with other heirs, sold the house in 1663 (StAN/ *Rep.*, 176.17.22b).

[39] Siebmacher, Tafel 215.

[40] Biedermann, Gggg2^v.

Ich / die ringste Zucht der Musen / hab auch oftmals mich ergetzt /
Mich mit Eurer hohen Gunste / diesen Orts / zur Quell gesetzt /
Mit Gesprech' und külem Trunck' in die Nacht den Tag gestekket /
Nachmals vor dem blassen Mond nach der leichten Dek gestrekket /
Bis ich sänftlich ausgeruhet.[41]

The Pegnesischer Blumenorden and Die Nymphe Noris

In 1645, probably early in the year, Hellwig became the fifth member of the Pegnesischer Blumenorden, joining at about the same time as Johann Sechst (Alcidor), Sigmund Betulius (later von Birken, Floridan), Christoph Arnold (Lerian), Friedrich Lochner (Periander), and Johann Georg Volkamer (Helianthus). As was the order's custom, he was initiated under a pastoral sobriquet (Montano)[42] and — if we are to take the details in Birken's mythifying *Fortsetzung* literally — bestowed with both a character flower ("Feld-Negelein" = *Nelke*)[43] and a monogram ("M").[44] It can be gathered from the introduction to *Noris* that members committed themselves to abide by certain ethical, linguistic, and aesthetic regulations. Hellwig speaks of the committment as a vow ("seinem gethanen Gelübd nach"), although this "Gelübd" probably remained uncodified: "in Ausübung der Teutschen Heldensprache desto mehrers zu üben"; "in den reinen Quellen derselben sich umzuschauen"; "und also anderen mehrern zum Beyspiel mit vorzugehen."[45]

---

[41] *Neunhof* 1648, A2ᵛ.

[42] The source of this pseudonym is uncertain. The first appearance of a pastoral character named Montano seems to be in Boccaccio's *Buccolicum carmen*, Eclogue 4. There Montano, a resident of the mountain town of Volterra, offers rest and temporary shelter in his rustic grotto to the fugitive shepherd Dorus — an obvious allusion to Vergil's first eclogue. But, as noted above, Hellwig was already known in Padua as "Ultramontana" for his trans-Alpine homeland. Cf. fn. 19 above.

[43] SvB/ *Fortsetzung*, 65-66.

[44] SvB/ *Fortsetzung*, 78.

[45] *Noris*, A2ᵛ. Herdegen, 49, confirms only a general regulation under Harsdörffer to practice German. It is doubtful that the obligation mentioned by Hellwig was formally written down.

Under the mentorship of Georg Philipp Harsdörffer[46] and in the heady atmosphere created by Birken and Johann Klaj, Hellwig began to develop a mature German style and to display signs of literary ambition. For his first German-language contribution as a Pegnitz Shepherd he invented a remarkable prosimetric idyll in honor of Harsdörffer in 1645.[47] Borrowing a name coined over one hundred years earlier by Eobanus Hessus, he fitted it to a mythical figure of his own devising, thereby giving birth to a local deity that remains a popular personification of Nuremberg to this day: Noris the nymph.[48] The significance of this small work lies in its formal reproduction in miniature of Opitzian prose eclogue. Obviously, Hellwig had by now studied Harsdörffer and Klaj's *Pegnesisches Schäfergedicht* (1644) and Birken's sequel, *Fortsetzung der Pegnitz-Schäferey* (1645), both of which took Opitz' *Schäfferei von der Nimfen Hercinie* (1630) as their model, for most of the seminal elements are present here: alternation between prose and meter; setting in a pleasance; nature-walk by a shepherd; encounter with a spring nymph at an autochthonic location; transmission of privileged knowledge, accompanied by observation and astonishment; commissioning of a poetic task by the local deity; versified praise of the dedicatee; reentry into nature.

By late 1645 Hellwig had undertaken to create a full-scale prose eclogue, *Die Nymphe Noris*, which in fact amounts to a greatly expanded version of his miniature idyll to Harsdörffer. But in place of a single addressee, scores of names fill the two-book, two-hundred-page work, eloquent testimony that Hellwig's elevated social station in Nuremberg allowed him privileged access to the private archives of families that would have been off limits to most non-patrician chroniclers. Dedicated to the *Stadtrat* of Nuremberg, *Noris* is an erudite historical and poetic appreciation of his hometown, a "Beschreibung seines lieben Vatterlands," as he says in the introduction,

> zu dessen schuldigsten Ehren meisten Theils Er dieses Werklein unter die Hand genommen / indem er nicht allein desselben von Gott reichgesegnet Landsart mit Poetischem Grieffel abreisset / sondern auch zugleich dessen hochrühmliche Regimentsform / benebenst denen Adelichen Geschlechten /

---

[46] Kayser, 238, describes Hellwig's relationship with Harsdörffer as both disciple and friend. That is clearly evident in Hellwig's contributions to the *Frauenzimmer Gesprächspiele* — which suggest that Harsdörffer played a unique role in Hellwig's schooling as a poet in the first place — as well as in the repeated references in other works to Harsdörffer's inspiration and guidance. Faber du Faur, 149b, claims that Birken was his primary guide, and Hellwig's letter of 1650 to Birken, following the publication of *Noris*, expresses gratitude for his younger colleague's contribution of poems to the work. Otherwise, however, Hellwig more often acknowledges Harsdörffer.

[47] In GPH/ *FG*, vol. 5, 46-52.

[48] S. Vredeveld; cf. Schultheiß; also W.D.

denkwürdigsten Begebenheiten / und namhaftesten Gebäuen lebhaft abmahlet / und mit sonderlichen Lehrberichten auszieret / vermeinend / gnugsam gethan zu seyn / so etwas darinnen denen noch kommenden zur Tugendbringender Anmahnung und löblicher Nachfolge dienen solte.[49]

This sounds very much like Harsdörffer's profile of *Noris* in June 1647 in a letter to Birken: "Der Inhalt ist von den hiesigen Geschlechten, vielen Bildheimen, und Beschreibungen der Nymphe Noris Herrlichkeit." Represented in this manner, the work has much in common with the neo-Latin tradition of the *laus urbis* genre which began, in Nuremberg, as early as the mid fifteenth century and culminated in Conrad Celtis and Eobanus Hessus.[50] Hellwig mentions (Johann) Sleidanus, (Nathan) Chytraeus, (Caspar) Peucerus, (Matthaeus) Dresserus, Carl Nützel, and Michael Piccart as predecessors in the tradition of praising nobility in verse form.[51] Peucerus' *Idyllium Patriae* (1594) is of particular interest here in that, like the Romance pastoral novel adapted by Opitz in his *Hercinie* and borrowed by the Nuremberg school, it combines metrical and prose forms.

On the other hand, Hellwig's intentions for *Noris* were not limited to mere description and praise. It is indeed probable that his intentions changed after 1647 to forge a more ambitious program of social and historical commentary.[52] What sets Hellwig's work apart from its models and represents a step beyond them is the degree to which he was able to realize this broader potential of prose eclogue. None surpasses *Noris* for historical breadth and local color; none for comprehension of the dispute between ruling

---

[49] *Noris*, A4ʳ.

[50] The first humanistic praise-of-Nuremberg was the *Chronica Neronpergensium* (1456) by the monk Sigismund Meisterlin; Celtis' *Norimberga* (1495) is less topographical in conception, more cultural and interpretive and with a higher degree of narrative sophistication; the neo-Latin tradition climaxed with Eobanus' *Noriberga Illustrata* (1532). S. esp. Hammer.

[51] In other words, they are all writers who "von den Adelichen Geschlechten schöne Lateinische Verse gemacht haben" (*Noris*, A4ʳ). While Hellwig does not adduce specific works, they would likely include Sleidanus' *Compendium de 4 summis imperiis* (ca. 1550); Chytraeus' *Quenstedt de patriis virorum illustrorum* (ca. 1590); Peucerus' *Idyllium patriae* (1594); Dresserus' *Neues Stamm- und Wappen-Buch* (ca. 1600); Nützel's *Leges Caesaris et Consilii Bellici, de nostri seculi magnatibus Anagrammatissimi* (1604); and Piccart's *Insignia gentilitia familiarum patriciarum inclytae urbis Norimberg* (1614).

[52] Reinhart/ 1990. Harsdörffer assumed that *Noris* was virtually complete as of the date of his letter to Birken, 6 June 1647: "Montano Schäfergedicht ist noch nicht unter der presse, sol aber ehist angefangen werden." Harsdörffer likely did not know that the work would run beyond what in fact turned out to be only Part One. In fact, it seems that historical events after that date motivated Hellwig to create an entire second part of equal length.

and learned-professional interests that was in full swing by mid-century; none for exploitation of the sociocritical implications of the greenworld.[53]

Hellwig must also have been researching around this time a work in Latin titled "Sacrarium Bonæ Memoriæ Noribergensium." The "Sacrarium" is a catalogue of inscriptions commemorating lives of eminent Nuremberg citizens (mostly men but some women as well) who died during the fifteenth and sixteenth centuries, either in Nuremberg or elsewhere in Europe, in the service of their home town.[54] As Hellwig explains in the introduction, he made use of church and other archival records, even mural inscriptions, in Nuremberg and other cities in Germany and abroad.[55] As in *Noris* where the shepherds are led through a secret temple replete with historical and genealogical artifacts, in this sublime shrine the reader is regaled with curious and privileged observations: a six-line epitaph by Conrad Celtis and Sebald Schreyer for Anna Nicodemus Citharæda, 1462, St. Sebald's; a dedication in Altdorf University's *Theatrum Anatomicum* by Nuremberg city fathers to Rector Wilhelm Ludwell and Dean of Medicine Moritz Hofmann, 1550; an epicedium for former *Ratsherr* Sebastian Fütter, 27 July 1560, Paris, Church of St. Severinus. For reasons unknown the "Sacrarium" was never published.

Occasional Poetry

With few exceptions the Pegnitz Shepherds — Hellwig among them — were content to work mainly within a narrow range of shorter forms, venturing beyond them usually only as translators. But within that limited sphere Hellwig's work often displays ingenuity ("sinnreiche Erfindung"), the gift according to Harsdörffer that makes a poet;[56] thus G. A. Will is justified in

---

[53] Before Meyer's study of 1928 *Noris* received only passing notice as a curiosity, an undefinable compilation of topical descriptions and playful sound effects. With Garber's groundbreaking studies in prose eclogue a set of sociocultural criteria became available by which to assess the bucolic repertoire of the German seventeenth century, and in these terms Hellwig's *Noris* has appreciably risen in stature. Cf. Elsener; also Reinhart/ 1991.

[54] Only two bibliographers have commented on the "Sacrarium," Omeis and Will/ *NGL*.

[55] "Continentur autem in hoc SACRARIO non solum ea monumenta, quæ in templis, sacellis, caenobiis, ac coemiteriis inclutæ Urbis Noribergæ, sed et quæ passim extra Urbem inque territorio ejusdem, itemque peregrinis in oris quorumque colligo potuere, de Norica progenie celebrantur, et latine sonant [...]" (A2ᵛ).

[56] GPH/ *PT*, 13 and passim.

describing Hellwig as "ein guter Poet."⁵⁷ With the exception of the older Birken none of the first generation Pegnitz Shepherds cultivated to such a degree the art of occasional verse. From the age of twenty, when as a student at Altdorf he composed the first of his extant poems, until his death forty-five years later, Hellwig contributed verses in both Latin and German (there are a few in Greek), by far the greatest number being epicedian, but also encompassing aphoristic, bucolic, congratulatory, departure, devotional, echo, epithalamic, genealogical, genethliaconic, mythical, onomatopoeic, riddle, utopian, and others — more than thirty thematic varieties in all. Nearly 300 individuals, families, and things or events pertaining to them are subjects of his verse; most addressees belong to the patriciate, the others to the honorable-professional estate.⁵⁸

Poems dutifully composed *per occasionem* often make for dull reading, and Hellwig contributed his share of mediocre verse. But there are also gems to be gleaned here and there, such as the following distichs on the occasion of Harsdörffer's death in 1658:

> NOridos in gemitus Pastores pectora solvunt,
>   Oraque Castalidum luctibus ægra silent.
> Contremuit Pindus, nec Pegnesus arva rigabit,
>   Per loca multivago murmure verna strepens.
> Cur? cecidit, cecidit Magni pars magna Senatus,
>   Stemmatis antiqui stella corusca ruit.
> Pieridum columen, Pastorum insigne levamen,
>   Aonius quotquot conciliavit Amor.
> Germanæ dextræ, patriæque hîc cura loquelæ,
>   Carpoferumque decus morte soluta jacent.
> Ast quæ Cæsareos defessa erexerat Arcus,
>   Artia pro requie Mens petit alta Poli.

---

⁵⁷ Will/ *NGL*, 87. Tittmann, 68, insists that Hellwig's style is "alterthümlicher in Ausdruck und Wendung, kanzleimäßiger und unbehülflicher, als der der übrigen Pegnitzer. Reim, Quantität und Strophenbau erinnern oft noch an den Meistergesang, der doch sonst dem Kreise fern genug lag." This pungent criticism may represent a reaction to the sometimes tedious march of verse inserts constituting much of *Noris*; it ignores Hellwig's superior verses. Of course, Tittmann is also indifferent to the social question of occasionality.

⁵⁸ Under the term "occasional verse" are included the brief — usually four-line — socalled verse inserts, *Verseinlagen*, insofar as they fulfill the basic criterion of having an explicit addressee and occasion. Faber du Faur's claim, 149b, that Hellwig was "one of the most active members of the order" is fully verified there. In Part C3 of Descriptive Bibliography below the verse inserts in Hellwig's larger works are catalogued separately.

Pattern Poetry

Hellwig's fondness for miniature forms extended to figured verse (*technopaegnia*, *Bildgedicht*) as well, an ancient art form that enjoyed a brisk revival among German poets in the seventeenth century. Most critics, from the early eighteenth century on, heaped scorn upon the genre as manneristic nonsense; but just as methodological advances late in this century have cast a favorable light on Hellwig's pastoral work, recent comparativist studies have done the same for his work in pattern poetry. Since 1970 no fewer than fourteen publications on the subject — by American, British, French, German, Polish, and Spanish scholars — have adduced examples in Hellwig's name.[59] Adler—Ernst rate the theoretical statement in *Noris*, 82-83, on figured verse among the most significant of the baroque age. Adler's separate monograph equates Hellwig with Birken, arguing that he was a chief revivalist of the ancient art and unsurpassed in Germany.

Unfortunately, not all of the poems upon which such reasoning is based are unequivocally attributable to Hellwig. Of the twelve (the last ten comprise a set) in *Noris*, his authorship can safely be assumed in only four instances:[60]

1. *Herz*	p. 7	Montano/Hellwig
2. *Pyramis*	p. 8	Montano/Hellwig
3. *Parnassus*	p. 83	Strephon/Harsdörffer
4. *Thurn*	p. 84	Montano/Hellwig
5. *Nußbaum*	p. 85	Helianthus/Volkamer
6. *Reichsapfel*	p. 86	Strephon/Harsdörffer
7. *Oergelein*	p. 87	Helianthus/Volkamer
8. *Schalmei*	p. 88	Klajus/Klaj
9. *Laute*	p. 88	Montano/Hellwig
10. *Quell*	p. 89	Periander/Lochner
11. *Sanduhr*	p. 90	Alcidor/Sechst
12. *Ehrengebäu*	p. 91	Lerian/Arnold

It was not uncommon for a Pegnitz Shepherd in his own publications to include poems by colleagues under their respective pseudonyms. Certainly poems by Hellwig/Montano are verifiable in this way, for example, in Birken's

---

[59] The studies mentioned here begin with that by Warnock—Folter.

[60] The one other figured poem clearly attributable to Hellwig is found in *Ormund* (1648), 116; it is of a *Flammenseule*, and is reprinted by Warnock—Folter, 54.

Life and Works   13

work.⁶¹ The theoretical statement in *Noris* cited by Adler—Ernst is in fact made by Strephon/Harsdörffer. There can be little doubt that Hellwig deserves special credit as a compiler, or aficionado, of pattern poetry. But if we are consistent in attributing authorship to the person behind the *Ordensname* — or at least until the matter of attribution in the Pegnesischer Blumenorden is better understood — Hellwig's status as a practitioner of pattern poetry must remain indefinite.

Translations

Hellwig completed three major German translations:

1. *Ormund*, 1648 (2nd printing, 1666), of Francesco Pona's *L'Ormondo* (1635, Italian);
2. *Neunhof*, 1648 (2nd printing, 1758; poems reprinted in the new translation of 1828), of Willibald Pirckheimer's description of the estate Neunhof (1521, Latin);
3. *Christlich vernünftiges Bedenken*, 1660, of Boethius' *De Consolatione Philosophiae* (ca. 524, Latin).

As late as the second edition of the Szyrocki history of German baroque literature (1979), Hellwig was still mentioned primarily as a translator, thus echoing an opinion first articulated by Justus Georg Schottel (1663).⁶² While he was considerably more than that, it is true that translation seriously occupied his interest at nearly every stage of life, perhaps already in Padua. He shared the belief of the Fruchtbringende Gesellschaft that translations of "hochkluge und vernunftmässige Schriften" contributed to the improvement of national language, intellect, and manners.⁶³ His theory of translation is similar, not surprisingly, to Harsdörffer's, laying greatest stress on the pragmatic categories of meaning, usefulness, and inventiveness.⁶⁴

---

⁶¹ As only one example, Hellwig's "SEyn dann künftig unser' Auen" from *Noris*, 70, is taken up by Birken in *Guelfis*, 127, with slight editorial touches, as "Sind dann künftig unsre Auen." This practice of attribution is followed in Part C of Descriptive Bibliography below.

⁶² Szyrocki, 169; Schottel, 1183. Numerous literary historians, collectors, and bibliographers have categorized Hellwig exclusively, or mainly, as a translator, e.g. Vogt, Bauer, Graesse, Maltzahn, Goedeke, Manheimer, Müller, Kosch, Newald.

⁶³ *Christlich vernünftiges Bedenken*, "Zuschrift,")(7ʳ.

⁶⁴ In recommending Boethius' *Consolatio* for translation in 1643, Harsdörffer emphasized the principles of meaning and usefulness (GPH/ *FG*, vol. III, 60). For a study of Hellwig as translator, based on his *Christlich vernünftiges Bedenken*, s. Reinhart/ 1992.

Italian courtly novels flourished in Germany during the 1640s and 1650s, as attested by the translations of Johann Wilhelm von Stubenberg and others, including Hellwig.[65] Pona's *L'Ormondo* was intended in part as a *roman à clef*,[66] but its popularity doubtless owed more to an adventurous storyline and vividly wrought foreign landscapes than to historical veracity. A typical knightly novel, it relates in indulgent detail the story of a feud between the kings of Scotland and England instigated by an advertised competition for the Princess of Scotland and kept at fever pitch by the passions of love and revenge. Prince Ormund leads the English army. Numerous plots and subplots sustain the adventure, and there is no lack of the requisite battles, imprisonment, separation, shipwreck, and rediscovery. The novel concludes openendedly, with Ormund still separated from his wife Rosidora and an announcement that the story will be continued.

Did Hellwig know the work as a student in Italy? Did he meet Pona, a well known physician living in Padua at the time? However that may be, a note from Harsdörffer to Birken indicates that Hellwig had the translation underway by 27 September 1646: "Montanus [...] translationem Ormundi adornat";[67] it was ready for press by March 1648.[68] Seven commendatory poems by nine colleagues, Harsdörffer, Volkamer, Klaj, Hund, Birken, Sechst, Arnold, and Jakob and Friedrich Lochner, are attached to the front matter. Hellwig himself thought of the work as an *"Icon animorum* und Gemütherspiegel" worthy of a prince's attention, as he makes clear in his dedication to fourteen-year-old Anton Ulrich of Braunschweig-Lüneburg.[69] His translation was successful enough to be reprinted eighteen years later by the Frankfurt publisher Zunner, with certain alterations in conventional usage, such as compound noun form and orthography.

---

[65] Müller, 215.

[66] Hellwig characterizes Pona's original as a "wahre Geschichte mit erdichten Namen" (*Ormund* 1648, (*)11^r).

[67] GPH/ Let. 1646.

[68] Date given in the dedication, *Ormund* 1648, (*)5^r.

[69] *Ormund* 1648, (*)9^v. Whether Hellwig was personally associated with the house of Braunschweig-Lüneburg is not known. It more likely was an indirect relationship owing to Birken, then in Wolfenbüttel serving as a tutor to Anton Ulrich, the young prince having been moved there in 1645. Birken sent enthusiastic reports to Nuremberg about the budding poetic talents of his pupil. Hellwig's introduction appeals to the "hohes belieben" "zu dergleichen Gedichten" of Anton Ulrich, who has already proven himself to be "ein Eyferer über der Mayestetischen Teutschen Sprache," (*)5^r.

Life and Works   15

Hellwig's translation of Pirckheimer's sketch of Neunhof also appeared in 1648.[70] It seems to have been privately commissioned by the Koler family and published only in a very limited quantity. Hellwig probably did not work from the manuscript but rather from Melchior Goldast's edition of Pirckheimer's works.[71] This overlooked little translation contains some of Hellwig's most sensitive writing. It is an unforced imitation, largely successful in capturing the simple bucolic rhythms of Pirckheimer's text, although Hellwig often cannot resist an embellishing touch:

> Praecipue tamen Philomela canora querelas repetit solitas, ac Itim suum voce deflet suaviplora.

> Und sonderlich die singende Nachtigal wiederhohlet zum öftern ihre gewöhnliche Klage, indem sie mit ihrer holdklingenden Kehle, ihren lieben Freund betrauret.[72]

As an appendix Hellwig added a set of eight original poems in German under the title "Poetische Gedanken": six are addressed to individual Neunhof attractions mentioned in the description, while the final two commemorate respectively the Koler and Jenisch family arms. Whereas the 1758 dual language reissue drop the poems, the first six are again taken up in the nineteenth century by Moritz Mayer and appended to his new German translation.[73]

Hellwig's final translation was occasioned by Harsdörffer's death in Fall 1658. He recalls in the introduction the profound desire of his deceased mentor to see Boethius' monumental work in German translation.[74] By more

---

[70] The translation omits small sections from the description made by Pirckheimer for his friend Bernhard Adelmann von Adelmannsfeld.

[71] Frankfurt, 1610; this according to a note in the 1758 reissue of the translation, A1^v: "Dieses Schreiben Herrn Wilibald Pirckheimers, so Er A. 1521. von Neunhof aus an seinen guten Freund den Domherrn zu Augspurg und Eychstett Herrn Bernhard Adelmann von Adelmannsfeld ergehen lassen, ist in *Melchior. Goldasti edi*rten *Operibus Bilibaldi Pirckheimeri*, welche zu Frankfurt 1610. in Fol. gedruckt worden, in denen *Epistolis* p. 232. 233. 234. zu finden."

[72] *Neunhof* 1758, 10-11.

[73] Mayer, 26-31.

[74] *Christlich vernünftiges Bedenken*,)(7^v-8^v: "[Indem] unser hochermeldter Spielende oft gewünscht / solche [sinnreichen und erbaulichen Schriften] in unserer angeborner Muttersprache zu sehen / habe ich Ihm zu Ehren und gehorsamer Freundsfolge [...] / solches Werklein ins Teutsche überzutragen mir belieben lassen [...]." Harsdörffer first recommended the *Consolatio* for translation in 1643 (GPH/ *FG*, vol. 3, 59-61). For a study of Hellwig's translation and its reception, s. Reinhart/ 1992.

modern standards that were beginning to emerge around this time, Hellwig's translation often seems clumsy and recondite. Christian Knorr von Rosenroth rejected it seven years later as unintelligible ("unverständlich").[75] Soon thereafter it passed into oblivion until 1732 when it came to the attention of Johann Georg Lotter, who was reviewing the 1667 Sulzbach translation by Knorr von Rosenroth and Francis Mercurius van Helmont.[76] No copy of the Nuremberg translation could be found until 1741. In that year Johann Christoph Gottsched delivered a withering, if anachronistic, attack on the translation and its author (unknown to him, but presumed to be a member of the Fruchtbringende Gesellschaft):

> Seine Rechtschreibung, Wortfügung, und die übrigen in die Sprache einfließenden Umstände sind meistentheils so beschaffen, daß sie mit den Regeln der Sprachwissenschaft nicht übereinstimmen.[...] Und da er eine grosse Hochachtung gegen diejenigen Muster bezeuget, welche ihm aus der fruchtbringenden Gesellschaft vor Augen lagen, so ist es nicht zu verwundern, daß die meisten ihm den Geschmack gäntzlich verderbet, und er dasjenige für Tugenden angesehen und nachgeahmet, was wir billig nach den Regeln der Sprachlehrer für Fehler und Gebrechen halten. Neugebackene, uneigentliche, und ungewohnte Wörter; kecke, metaphorische, lange und halbe Seiten füllende Perioden; ein hartklingender Gebrauch der Zeitwörter, an statt der Nennwörter; unrichtige Abweichung der Nenn- und Zeitwörter u.s.w. verstellen diese Uebersetzung recht abscheulich.[77]

This wholesale attack is more applicable to the Late Silesian School than to Hellwig — much less the Fruchtbringende Gesellschaft![78] It certainly did not generate new demand for the book; Johannis Vogt's catalogue of 1753 again speaks of its extreme rarity.[79]

---

[75] Knorr, A3^r.

[76] Lotter, 447.

[77] Gottsched, 497-498.

[78] Cf. Martino on early-enlightened attacks on the Baroque, esp. Chapter 3, "Die Kritik der Aufklärung," 291-435.

[79] Vogt, 132.

Life and Works   17

Later Life and Medical Writings

A month after the death of Bishop Albert in April 1649, Bishop Franz Wilhelm von Wartenberg was installed as his successor in Regensburg. It must have been only shortly thereafter that Hellwig was invited to serve the ecclesiastical court as chief surgeon and personal physician to the new bishop.[80] City records show Hellwig still present in Nuremberg on 28 July, resolving financial matters relating to the house on Zotenberg before moving to Regensburg.[81] He lived there for the rest of his life, residing near the court in quarters called the *Müllerische behausung*[82] and enjoying a congenial relationship with Bishop (later Cardinal) von Wartenberg.[83] After the latter's death in late 1661 there is little record, save for a handful of epicedia, regarding Hellwig's activities prior to his death thirteen years later.

Facts pertaining to his life during the 1650s are sparse and constitute a picture that is far from complete. A few intriguing odds and ends are available, however. For instance, in May 1651 Hellwig accompanied the enigmatic polymath Francis van Helmont, son of the renowned chemist Jan Baptist van Helmont, to Sulzbach, where van Helmont, who seems to have been residing of late in Nuremberg, was to be engaged as an adviser to Duke Christian August.[84] Just how Hellwig and van Helmont met is not known, but it is reasonable to speculate that their acquaintance was arranged through mutual friends and interests in Nuremberg. That circle probably included Christian August as well, for the duke frequented Nuremberg during 1650 on diplomatic missions on behalf of securing the confessional *Simultaneum* for Sulzbach. All three men had ties to the academic movement emanating from Matthias Bernegger in Strasbourg; that movement in turn was associated with neo-Platonic groupings ranging from Johann Andreae's *Unio Christiana* —

---

[80] The technical term used by Freher and Linden for Hellwig's office is *archiatrus*. Von Wartenberg (b. 1593) was one of the outstanding church administrators of the Counter Reformation period, remembered especially for his diplomacy as coadjutor on behalf of Catholic interests at the Westphalian peace negotiations, and for his leading role in diocesan reform of Regensburg. He was elevated to cardinal in April 1660. For a complete study, s. Schwaiger.

[81] As one of two "Testes vogati": StAN/ *Rep.*, 161.21, E^v. Johann, Maria, and Magdalena were involved in the transaction. Although the exact details of the transaction are unclear, it appears that Maria bought Johann's and Magdalena's interests in the house (*Rep.*, 163.91-92 and 168.166'. Maria alone sold the house in November 1654 (*Rep.*, 168.166-168).

[82] Bohmer, [E]1^v.

[83] *Prodromus*, A3^r.

[84] S. Jaitner, 301-302, who cites British Museum, London, Sloane MS, 530 fol. 9-10.

consisting mainly of Nurembergers, among them Pastor Johann Saubert, whom Hellwig admired — to that surrounding Johann Comenius, a friend of both Harsdörffer and Johann Michael Dilherr; for his part, Dilherr was a trusted adviser to the family of Duke Christian August and represented the Sulzbach Lutheran interests after 1650.

One must wonder what discussions Hellwig and van Helmont may have had about literature, whether, for instance, they spoke of the need for a translation of Boethius' *Consolatio*. We have noted in what low regard Knorr held Hellwig's translation. What is curious is that neither he nor van Helmont[85] mention Hellwig by name, though they can hardly have failed to know that he was the translator. Perhaps their restraint reflected personal regard for a friend.

A controversy with one Dr. Daniel Geyger[86] concerning the death of Cardinal von Wartenberg in December 1661 cast a cloud over Hellwig's life for much of 1662. We are relatively well informed about this episode since both men resorted to printed apologies of their respective positions. Dissatisfied with Chief Surgeon Hellwig's autopsy report,[87] Geyger circulated a letter (he later denied any malice, claiming to have written it only for the eyes of a friend) in which he contradicted the findings and offered his own diagnosis of the fatal illness. When the letter inevitably fell into Hellwig's hands,[88] he immediately prepared a defense. For the publication itself Hellwig collated three separate texts: a) the *Prodromus* proper; b) a printed copy of the original autopsy report;[89] c) a printed copy of Geyger's original

---

[85] Namely, in his introduction to the second edition of the Sulzbach translation: s. Helmont.

[86] Born in 1595 in Rosenheim (Bavaria), Geyger became a doctor of medicine in Passau in 1618. In 1629 he moved to Bratislava, Hungary, where he practiced medicine, apparently in the court of Cardinal Pasmann, until 1657. In that year he was invited to Regensburg where he practiced until his death in 1664 (Freher, 1394b-1395a). Hellwig describes him as a "vir primi senii, vultu austerus, garrulitate lepidus, actione morosus, alienis celeriter succensens, odio facile flagrans, Stoicum simulans, cervicosus, attamen eruditione non leviter tinctus, in sua professione satis clarus, ac in mechanicis exquisitissimus artifex" ("a man of distinguished age, austere in countenance, charmingly garrulous, morose in action, quicktempered towards others, inclined to erupt in hate, feigning stoicism, obstinate, though to be sure not lightly tinctured with learning, reasonably well known in his profession, and mechanically highly skilled." *Prodromus*, A3^r).

[87] Hellwig was assisted in the autopsy by one Dr. Preßl (Schwaiger, 86).

[88] On 18 January 1662 (*Prodromus*, A2^v).

[89] Relatio Medica, | **Von der Kranckheit und Absterben** | Jhrer Hoch=Fürſtl. Eminenz, | **Herrn Cardinals / Grafen von War=** | **tenberg / etc.** In *Prodromus*, D2^r-4^r.

letter.⁹⁰ In a letter to J. G. Volkamer in Nuremberg one month later (31 January 1662), in which he expresses sympathy with his old friend's physical ailments, Hellwig describes his frustration with Geyger. He goes on to announce that he has a defense ready for the printer and justifies its combative tone:⁹¹

> Nam quae non ferienda, ferenda sunt fortiter: Deus his etiam finem dabit. Neque ego ab omni parte beatus vivo, cum mihi ex Collegiis hic meis adversarius magnus D. Daniel Geyger assurgit, ex meri livoris et invidiae causa aemulus factus. Aut aemulatio malevolorum est virtuosa exercitatio proborum. Hic insultaverat in me clandestino, manuscriptum satyricum sub Germane stylo multis insinuvat, quo me ob morbum Cardinalis nostri acriter perstringit, et inscitiae et mortis inde reum me facit. Gratias ago Deo, in vanum quod laboraverit, ac omnium bonorum, imo Illustrium Haeredum ipsorum censuram sibi non gratam exinde incurrerit. Nihilominus ne famam meam neglexisse videar, animum sum[p]si, neque sine bonorum assensu et consolio, ut illum publice apologetico quodem confundam, quod brevi Latine elobaratum Noribergae prelo typographico submittere adlaboro. Non spero, quod a censore vestro morarer: velitatio etenim literaria est, nihil scurrilitatis, aut calumniosae denominationis habens contra Imperij statuta et bonas leges. Ut ut sit, alea jacta est: ludam cum antagonisti meo par et impar.⁹²

Geyger's *Responsum* similarly collates two disparate texts: a) the *Responsum* proper, composed in the same *velitatio literaria* genre as Hellwig's *Prodromus*,

---

⁹⁰ Bericht | über eine Relationem Medicam, Jhrer Hoch= | Fürſtl. *Eminenz*, Biſchofs und Cardinals von Warten= | berg Zuſtand und endliches Ableiben | betreffend. In *Prodromus*, D4ʳ-E2ᵛ.

⁹¹ The imprint bears no printer information. However, Hellwig indicates in the letter that he intended for the defense to be published in Nuremberg. As for the date of printing, it must be placed between February and April 1662, since Geyger's *Responsum* was ready for press by early May, according to his signed introduction.

⁹² "For things that cannot be repulsed must be bravely endured: God will finally put an end to such things. I myself am not content in all respects since a great adversary from among my colleagues here, Dr. Daniel Geyger, has attacked me, a man who has become my rival out of extreme spite and envy. But the rivalry of evil men is for good men an exercise in virtue. This Geyger mocked me in secret, circulating amongst a number of people a satyrical letter in German, in which he brazenly claimed that I had something to do with the Cardinal's illness, and accused me both of ignorance and the Cardinal's death. I thank God that he labored in vain and has incurred no gratitude, but rather the censure of all good men, and especially of the illustrious heirs themselves. Lest it seem that I have neglected my reputation, I have prepared, not without the agreement and advice of good men, to confound him publicly with a work in Latin in my own defense which I shall soon submit to a Nuremberg printer. I am sure that you will concur with me: this is a combative work, and yet containing nothing scurrilous or slanderous against the statutes and good laws of the land. Be that as it may, the die is cast: I shall engage my enemy however he see fit."

which refutes Hellwig point by point and enlarges on his own diagnosis of the cardinal's illness; b) a notarized copy of the suit against Hellwig following publication of the *Prodromus* which Geyger took as slanderous of his professional and personal reputations. No record has been located as to any further action in the matter, and Geyger passed away two years later.

On 24 May 1674 Hellwig was taken suddenly ill and for the next two weeks was attended by a Dr. D. Heigel.[93] Following a brief improvement between 31 May and 2 June Hellwig contracted a severe fever and thereafter failed rapidly. He died peacefully on 4 June.[94] Interment took place on 8 June in the cemetery of St. Peter's Church in Regensburg. In the handwritten burial register he is remembered as:

[...] der Edlvest und Hochgelehrte Herr Johann Helbig, Philosophiae et medicinae Doctor, und bei samt: Statt alhie Archiater und weitberümbter Practicus seel. seines alters 65 Jahr.[95]

Hellwig's papers were gathered by Volkamer who, in collaboration with Dr. Georg Hieronymus Welsch, began to organize them for publication.[96] When Welsch died in 1677, Volkamer persuaded the noted Augsburg physician, Dr. Lucas Schröck, to take on the project and see it through to completion. Volkamer himself provided the information for Schröck's brief biography of Hellwig.[97] The *Observationes Physico-Medicæ* which appeared three years later consist of over four hundred pages in the format: a) "Observatio" (a unique, perhaps sensational, case or physical abnormality never before adequately explained, e.g. a particular deformity; female beardedness; gluttonous appetite in the elderly; tobacco induced apoplexy); b) "Scholion Hellwigianum" (explanation, references to other cases and authorities); c) "Additamentum Schröckii" (editor's supplement).[98]

---

[93] Schröck—Volkamer, b2ᵛ. Whether this Dr. D. Heigel was related to Hellwig's former Pentagon colleague in Nuremberg, Dr. Heinrich Heigel (Schröck-Volkamer, b2ʳ) is not known.

[94] Freher, 1415a, says that his information comes directly from the funeral sermon for Hellwig (ed. MR has not been able to locate it, if it is in fact extant); cf. Schröck—Volkamer, b2ᵛ, who describe the final stages of Hellwig's illness. Among others, Herdegen, Goedeke, and Bosl incorrectly place Hellwig's death on 24 May. Cf. Omeis, 60.

[95] LkAR, *Kirchenbücher: Beerdigungen 1660-1690*, 450.

[96] Schröck, a4ᵛ. On Welsch, s. Schröck/ *Memoria*.

[97] "Ipse D. Hellwigius quis fuerit, ex vitæ historia, quam iterum benevolentiæ VOLCKAMERIANÆ debes, uberius jam cognosces [...]" (Schröck, b1ʳ).

[98] After the fortieth *Observatio* Schröck himself provides the *Scholion*.

II

Editorial Practice

THE CHAPTER that follows, A Descriptive Bibliography of the Works of Johann Hellwig, has three purposes: 1) to reconstruct an ideal copy for each work, while making note of all variants; 2) to describe the distinctive physical features of every copy, including binding, of a given title; 3) to comment on the work's significance and other qualities of interest. Each work is identified with a capital letter and number (e.g. B2.1) and described under eleven headings (with appropriate modifications for Occasional Verse, Manuscripts, Letters, and Other Publications):[99]

> Title: Transcription is given in quasi-facsimile form since the photographs that introduce the works are not always reliable indicators of every feature (e.g. red inking or original dimensions). In the question of letterpress, precision is aimed for; capitalizations, spellings, even misprints are precisely repeated, but noted by "*[sic]*." Similarly, antiqua and italics are reproduced approximately; Fraktur is represented by bold. Large and small capitals are distinguished only when the first letter of a word is large and the following small; otherwise, no attempt is made to reproduce the variety of font sizes that often appear on one title page since the photograph serves that end. Any editorial insertion (e.g. to note ornamental borders or dividing rule) is given in italicized square brackets. Simple line rules are introduced with the word "rule," or "double-rule"; multiple dimension rules with the word "ornamental rule"; larger figures with a descriptive word, such as "vignette." Each case is followed by measurements to the millimeter. End of lines are indicated by a single vertical stroke (|) . The sloping stroke, or virgule (/), of the original title has a space both before and after, as in most seventeenth-century texts. Diagraphs and ligatures are reproduced so far as mechanically possible: thus, æ, Æ, œ, Œ; but: antiqua shaft-s/t > "ſt"; antiqua abbreviation for etcetera > "etc.".

---

[99] To the degree that it is practical, editorial principles follow Fredson Bowers, *Principles of Bibliographical Description* (Princeton: Princeton University Press, 1949).

Collation: The formula provides information in the following order, with notes pertinent to Hellwig's works: Leaf: Hellwig's publications come in folio (2°), quarto (4°), and duodecimo (12°). Gatherings: π represents an unsigned gathering that is prefixed and uninferred; superscripted numbers indicate that all gatherings in a given unit have that same number of leaves; signings are always given in arabic numbers, regardless of original form; errors are corrected in parentheses and the letter "c"; $ is a notation for all gatherings, and the number that follows indicates up to what leaf they are signed; exceptions are listed following a hyphen. Finally, pagination or foliation is described, along with corrections; preliminary or additional pages are noted in square brackets.

Contents: The major sections of the book are identified by signature and compressed title or first sentence. The rigorous quasi-facsimile style of the title is eased: Fraktur is not reproduced; shaft-s > s; ñ is tacitly doubled. In the case of the "Sacrarium" an extensive rehearsal of contents is provided, given that the single manuscript is, practically speaking, inaccessible.

HT] Head-title, i.e. the abbreviated or altered title immediately preceding the beginning of the text proper. When no head-title is present, "[none]" is the indicator.

RT] The running-title on the headline. Alterations and errors are noted along with pertinent gathering signatures. Likewise, when no running-title exists, "[none]" indicates as much.

CW] Catchwords. The leaf on which the first catchword is to be found is indicated, with catchword. Errors are noted without quotation marks or interpunctuation. There are three types of error: the most common is an inaccurately printed catchword (spelling, font, etc.); the following word may be erroneously printed (i.e. catchword is correct form); a catchword may be missing. Corrections are given in square brackets.

Type: The description of typography begins with the commonest number of lines included on a page of text, inclusive of headline and direction line (signature/catchword); variants are observed. Dimensions noted are, first, those of the title itself on the title page (i.e. the block of text containable within a rectangle), then those of a page of text; both are measured in millimeters (perpendicular followed by horizontal). The note on type style indicates the basic style used throughout, followed by other varieties, including reduced or enlarged font size. Foreign language lettering is noted. Finally, the style of letters and numerals in the gathering signature is described, with variants.

Notes: Signing, illustrations, and ornamentation fall under this rubric. Signing conveys on which leaf it begins. Illustrations involve all pictorial matter, from clarifying graphics in pencil to copper engraved plates; each is briefly described — or, if there is a series of similar illustrations, such as coats of arms, the engravings are treated as a set. Included under ornamentation are head and end pieces, ornamental initials, and other ornaments of interest.

Commentary: This section is reserved for information or comment about the work not addressed in the General Introduction. When nothing else of particular interest remains to be remarked upon here, a note refers the reader to the pertinent sub-chapter of the General Introduction (e.g. "s. General Introduction: 'Translations'").

Bibliographical Data: As a rule, only standard resource works are adduced here (e.g. Jöcher, Goedeke, Dünnhaupt); secondary studies that mention the work are not included unless they contain bibliographies of particular relevance (e.g. Adler—Ernst). The reference works are listed in alphabetical order.

Copies: All known copies of Hellwig's works are listed here alphabetically by location city, American spelling. Each provides information about all or most (depending on availability) of the following categories: Sig.: = shelf number; B: = binding; C: = general physical condition of the book; P: = condition of paper; M/S: = markings and stamps; V: = variants to the ideal copy; S: = source, or provenance. When no information is available, the category is either omitted or the abbreviation [NR] ("not reported") is applied. The symbol "?" under Source indicates uncertain or undetermined.[100] Finally, the symbol [E] indicates that the copy has been examined by the editor (MR).

---

[100] A different set of questions is posed for occasional verse in section C *[q.v.]*.

Summary of normalizations

Except in the quasi-facsimile title and modified quasi-facsimile contents, normalizations have been silently applied as follows:

1. Capital J and I conform to modern usage.
2. Abbreviations have been realized:
    a) ẽ > en or em, as case may be; uñ > und; doubling line over n or m > nn or mm;
    b) d' > der; od' > oder;
    c) dz > das or daß;
    d) wz > was;
    e) Lat. abbreviation for etcetera > etc.
3. Umlauts: ° and inverted ᵉ are modernized as ä, ö, and ü.
4. Inverted n's and u's, d's and b's are corrected.
5. Shaft-s (also called: long-s) is transcribed as short "s".
6. q with accent > que (que with accent is mechanically unobtainable).
7. Fraktur > antiqua [except in A3, Contents, *q.v.*].
8. Americanized spellings of European place names are employed in the Descriptive Bibliography under the rubric "Copies" (thus: Cologne for Köln; Nuremberg for Nürnberg), and likewise for the list in the Acknowledgments and in the Index of Libraries. Bibliographical entries retain the original form (Köln, Nürnberg).
9. The two Fraktur forms of "d" and "r" cannot be distinguished.

Original forms are otherwise retained. The following cases deserve note:

1. Virgule (/) : a space precedes and follows.
2. Double-hyphen (=) in certain original compounds and when original line hyphenation occurs coincidentally with the edited text.
3. Lower case j and i.
4. Lower and upper case uU and vV.
5. Inconsistencies in capitalization.
6. Irregularities in spelling or form insofar as they are not erroneous.
7. Idiomatic form of foreign words.

A Descriptive Bibliography of the Works of Johann Hellwig

    A. Independent Works

    B. Translations

    C. Occasional Verse

    D. Manuscripts

    E. Letters

    F. Other Publications

ΑΛΦΑΒΗΤΟΝ ΙΑΤΡΙΚΟΝ
hoc est
BREVIS TOTIVS
MEDICINÆ HIPPOCRATICÆ IN
paucas Tabellas redactæ delineatio,
operâ

IOHANNIS HELLWIGII
NORIBERGENSIS.

Noribergæ typis & sumptibus Wolffgangi Endteri,
ANNO χρισσονίας

M DC XXXI.

Title page, *Alphabeton Iatrikon* (1631)
National Library of Medicine

A. Independent Works

A 1 ΑΛΦΑΒΗΤΟΝ ΙΑΤΡΙΚΟΝ
(1631)

Title:

[red] ΑΛΦΑΒΗΤΟΝ ΙΑΤΡΙΚΟΝ | hoc eſt | *[red]* BREVIS TOTIVS | MEDICINÆ HIPPOCRATICÆ IN | paucas Tabellas redactæ delineatio, | operâ | *[red]* IOHANNIS HELLWIGII | NORIBERGENSIS. | *[vignette: 72 x 103 mm.]* | *[red]* Noribergæ typis & ſumptibus Wolffgangi Endteri, | ANNO Χριστογονίας. | *[rule: 83 mm.]* | *[red]* M DC XXXI.

Collation: 2°: π², A-T², 40 leaves; [$1], pp. (pagination on internal sides of leaves only) [2] 1-30 27 (c 31) 28 (c 32) 33-38.

Contents: π1^r: t.p. π1^v: [bl.]. π2^r: Ded.: "VIRIS | MAGNIFICIS, NOBILISSIMIS ET | PRVDENTISSIMVS | DN. GEORGIO Volckhamer. | DN. ANDREÆ Im Hof." π2^v: Com. poem by Johann C. Rhumel to Hellwig: "Προσφωνησις | IANI CHVNRADI RHVMELI | MED. D. | ad Ornatissimum Dominum Iohannem Hellvvigium, Med. Studiosum | [...]." Ded. verse: "Votivâ Paries Tabulâ sacer indicat iste." [In each gathering, 1^r = chapter title; 1^v-2^r = double-page tables; 2^v = bl.]. A1^r: TABVLÆ PRIMÆ | PARS PRIMA, | Continens Artis Medicæ definitionem [...]; B1^r: TABVLÆ PRIMÆ | PARS SECVNDA, | Continens reliquam Physiologiæ partem [...]; C1^r: TABVLA SECVNDA | Continens Pathologiam seu doctrinam de rebus præ- | ter naturam [...]; D1^r: TABVLÆ TERTIÆ | PARS PRIMA, | Continens σημειωπκην seu doctrinam de signis [...]; E1^r: TABVLÆ TERTIÆ | PARS SECVNDA, | Continens reliquas signorum diagnosticorum partes [...]; F1^r: TABVLÆ TERTIÆ | PARS TERTIA, | Continens partem primam signorum prognostico- | rum [...]; G1^r: QVARTA, | Continens partem secundam signorum prognosti- | corum [...]; H1^r: TABVLÆ TERTIÆ | PARS QVINTA, | Continens partem tertiam ac vltimam signorum | prognosticorum [...]; I1^r: PRODROMVS | PRACTICÆ MEDICINÆ CONTINENS | vniversalem methodum medendi [...]; K1^r: TABVLÆ QVARTÆ | PARS PRIMA, | Continens υγιενην seu doctrinam de rebus non natura- | libus [...]; L1^r: TABVLÆ QVARTÆ | PARS

SECUNDA, | Continens reliquias υγιευης seu doctrinæ de rebus non na- | turalibus [...]; M1r: TABVLA QVINTA | Continens Diætam seu artem diætandi ægrotos [...]; N1r: TABVLÆ SEXTÆ | PARS PRIMA, | Continens Pharmaciam, & agit inprimis de indican- | tibus medicamenta [...]; O1r: TABVLÆ SECVNDÆ, | Continens differentias medicamentorum [...]; P1r: TABVLÆ SECVNDÆ | PARS TERTIA, | Continens medicamenta alterantia composita [...]; R1r: TABVLÆ SECUNDÆ | PARS QVINTA, | Continens artem componendi medicamenta [...]; S1r: TABVLÆ SEPTIMÆ | ET VLTIMÆ | PARS PRIMA, | Continens Chirurgiam [...]; T1r: TABVLÆ SEPTIMÆ | ET VLTIMÆ | PARS SECVNDA, | Continens reliquas recte administrandæ venæse- | ctionis [...]; T2v: "Errata Typographica sic sunt corrigenda:"

HT] [none]

RT] [none]

CW] (only on the two pp. of the preface) π2r ordo π2v TABVLA I

Type: 77-80 ll. per p., max. 87. Dimensions: title: 266 x 182 mm.; p. of text: 327 x 190/218 mm. (tables irregular). Style: ant. for chapter titles; ital. for explanations. Greek minuscules on t.p., passim. Gathering sig.: letters, ant.; nos. [none]. Family names in ded. Frak.

Notes:
Signing: begins A1.
Illustrations: [none].
Ornamentation: t.p.: triangular vignette, 72 x 103 mm. Orn. initials: "N" in ded.

Commentary: The work attempts to summarize in a comparatively brief series of tables the complex Hippocratic doctrine. Hellwig, who was only twenty-one when he wrote it, apologizes for his youth but says he was encouraged by certain men (i.e. his professors at Altdorf University) and hopes that it will prove useful to future physicians. For this work, which he dedicated to the Nuremberg city fathers, Hellwig was awarded the *Stipendium Aureum*. His older student friend at Altdorf, Johann Conrad Rhumel (1597-1661) — like Hellwig, he began medical practice in Nuremberg in 1634 — contributed a poem in which he applauded the work as a very useful reference guide: "Coi vox Senis est: Longa est ars rite medendi; | Artem sed longam, Tu facis esse brevem. | Nam brevis est Methodi typicæ structura; perenni | Felicem fructu mnemosynenque juvat."

Bibliographical data: Freher, col. 1414b; Herdegen, 243; Hirsch, 149; Jöcher, vol. 2, col. 1480; Kestner, 387; Linden, 601; Omeis, 60; Surgeon General, 1004; Waller, vol. 1, 197, no. 4291; Will/ *NGL*, 88; Zedler, vol. 12, col. 1328.

Copies:

1. Basel: Universitätsbibliothek. Sig.: Bot. 3876 Nr. 2. B: orig. parch., ca. 1635. C: exc. P: some foxing. M/S: hdwr. notes in text. S: Johann Reinhardt Widt, Strasbourg 1635 or 1636.

2. Bethesda: National Library of Medicine. Sig.: WZ250 .H477a 1631. S: hdwr. on t.p.: "Monasterij Wergodensis 1655".

3. Erlangen: Universitätsbibliothek. Sig.: 2° Trew C 521. B: orig. parch. C: exc. P: foxing. M/S: inside f.c., stamp of ownership, 270 x 215 mm. S: Trew-Sammlung. [E]

4. Freiburg: Universitätsbibliothek. Sig.: T 4695. B: reb. in boards. C: good. P: foxing. M/S: note on t.p.: "QF.A.1" (=St. Blasien). V: Gathering L bound before K. S: St. Blasien (Benedictine monastery ca. 1800).

5. Göttingen: Niedersächsische Staats- und Universitätsbibliothek. Sig.: 2 Med. Inst. 6/95. B: reb. in boards. C: slight damage, otherwise good. P: clean. S: ?

6. London: British Library. Sig.: 544.i.7 (2). B: reb. S: Sir Hans Sloane.

7. Mainz: Universitätsbibliothek (Medizinhistorisches Institut). Sig.: Gesmed 17 1631. B: orig. parch. C: bottom edges slightly shaved. P: foxing, some flaking. M/S (in f.m.): "18.6.63." S: Paris.

8. Munich: Universitätsbibliothek. Sig.: 2° Med. 322. B: orig. parch. C: fair. P: foxing. M/S (in f.m.): "Sum Alberti Menzelij, die XX. Junii A^o. MDCXXXI. Ex dono Perill. Dn. Werneri Comitis Tilly ex Urbis Ingolstadii"; hdwr. on t.p.: "Biblioth. acad. Ingolstad." S: [s. M/S].

9. Nuremberg: Germanisches National Museum. Sig.: NW 856e. B: reb. in orn. boards. C: fair. P: foxing, flaking. M/S: hdwr. on t.p.: "Hoffmann 1857". S: old holdings of GNM. [E]

10. Paris: Bibliothèque Nationale. Sig.: Fol. T^{27}. 12. B. orig. parch. C: exc. P: foxing. M/S: stamp on t.p.: "Bibliotheca regia". S: [s. M/S].

11. Uppsala: Universitetsbibliotek. Sig.: Waller 4291 fol. B: boards. C: fair. P: foxing. M/S: "Bibliotheca Walleriana". S: [s. M/S].

12. Zurich: Zentralbibliothek. Sig.: I.T.3. B: orig. parch. C: exc. P: foxing. M/S (in f.m.): hdwr.: "J R GYGER D. | A$^{\circ}$. 1640". S: ?

Die Nymphe NORIS
In
Zweyen Tagzeiten
vorgestellet;

Darbey mancherley schöne Gedichte/ und warhafte
Geschichte/ nebenst unterschiedlichen lustigen
Rätzeln/ Sinn- und Reimenbildern/
auch artigen Gebänden mit-
angebracht

D U R C H

einen Mitgenossen
der PegnitzSchäfer *c.*

Nürmberg.
Gedrukt und verlegt bey Jeremia Dümler.
Im Jahr 1650.

Title page, *Die Nymphe Noris* (1650)
Beinecke Rare Book & Manuscript Library

A 2   DIE NYMPHE NORIS
      (1650)

Title:

Die Nymphe *[om. caps]* **NORJS | JN | Zweyen Tagzeiten | vorgeſtellet; | DArbey mancherley ſchöne Gedichte / und warhafte | Geſchichte / nebenſt unterſchiedlichen luſtigen | Rätzeln / Sinn= und Reimenbildern / | auch artigen Gebänden mit= | angebracht | DURCH | einen Mitgenoſſen | der PegnitzSchäfer etc. | Nürmberg. | Gedrukt und verlegt bey Jeremia Dümler.** | *[rule: 61 mm.]* | **Jm Jahr 1650.**

Collation: 4°: A-N⁴ O1 N2 (c O2) O2-O4 P-2C⁴, 104 leaves plus 4 inserted plates; [$3 - A2], pp. [8] 1-193 192 (c 194) 193 (c 195) 196-197 [198-200].

Contents: A1ʳ: fp., verso [bl.] A2ʳ: t.p. A2ᵛ: "Vorrede | an den | Gunstgewogenen und Ehrliebenden | Leser." A4ᵛ: ded. poem to Nuremberg in Latin (title in Greek majuscules) "ΚΑΤΑΘΙÈΡΩΣΙΣ." [sic]. P. 1: [text begins: prose narrative with poems in various forms interspersed, in two parts]; title of Part I: "Der Nymphe NORJS | Erste Tagzeit." (Part I comprises pp. 1-102.) Pp. 7-8: two figure poems. Pp. 28-48: "Wappen der Adelichen Rathsfähigen Geschlechten." (twenty-eight coats of arms described, in quatrains). Pp. 57-61: "Wappen der Adelichen, doch unrathsfehigen Geschlechten." (eighteen families characterized by their coats of arms, in quatrains). Pp. 69-72: five dep. poems for Floridan [Sigmund Betulius], signed by individual members of P.Bl.O., under title "Die Pegnitz an den Floridan." Pp. 72-80: two com. poems by Floridan to P.Bl.O. Pp. 80-81: two floral poems. Pp. 83-91: ten figure poems. Pp. 92-95: ten riddle quatrains. P. 103: title of Pt. II: "Der Nymphe NORJS | Andere Tagzeit." (Part II comprises pp. 103-197). Pp. 110-111: two echo poems. Pp. 121-134: "wolverdiente und lobwürdige Personen des obersten Standes" (fifty notable men characterized by nicknames, in quatrains). Pp. 140-147: "Wappen der abgestorbenen Rathsfähigen Geschlechten" (twenty-six families characterized by their coats of arms, in quatrains). Pp. 162-166: eight single to seven-fold emblems. Pp. 167-170: verse epistle from Floridan to P.Bl.O., dated "T. 3 des Blumenmonats / | im Jahr 1647." Pp. 171-173: prose epistle from Floridan to P.Bl.O., dated "den 6. Herbstmonats / im | Jahre 1648." Pp. 183-186: twelve com. quatrains to men from the Kreß family history. P. [198]: farewell poem in Latin (title in Greek majuscules): "ΑΠΟΛΟΓΗΤΙΚΌΝ". Pp. [198-199]: "Gunstgewogner Leser." [= errata], verso [p. 200] bl.

HT] B1ʳ Der Nymphe NORJS | Erſte Tagzeit. O4ʳ Der Nymphe NORJS | Andere Tagzeit.

RT] (B-O3) Der Nymphe Noris Erste Tagzeit. ["Nymphen" for Nymphe on F2ʳ, G1ᵛ, J1ʳ, K2ʳ, N1ᵛ, O1ᵛ] (O4-2C3ʳ) Der Nymphe Noris Andere Tagzeit. ["Nymphen" for Nymphe on P3ᵛ, Q2ʳ; "Erste" erroneously for "Andere" on V3ʳ, Z3ʳ]

CW] begin on A2ᵛ kom= . Missing: N2ᵛ S2ʳ. Erroneous: A3ʳ [reduced font: heim=] K1ᵛ .Kl Es [Kl. Es] K3ʳ 2. Seyn [II. SEyn] M2ᵛ Helian [Helian(=)] [also: reduced font] M3ʳ Damit [Darmit] P2ʳ [reduced font: mit] P3ʳ M. Echo! [Mont. Echo!] Q4ʳ Die [die] 2A1ʳ dere [ders] 2B4ᵛ Du Nutz= [du nutz(=)]

Type: 34 ll. per p. [pp. with poems vary bet. 30-35 ll.] Dimensions: title: 118 x 115 mm.; p. of text: 117 x 119 mm. Style: Frak. Latin poems in ant.; Latin marginalia and notes in cursive on pp. 10, 11, 28, 48, 49, 50, 68, 82, 83, 95, 112, 115, 125, 126, 129, 130, 138, 150, 152, 165, 166, 174, 175, 178, 179, 180, 182. Greek majuscules in poem titles on A4ᵛ and p. [198]. Lemmata in reduced type. A2ᵛ-3ᵛ text in enlarged type and darkened. Gathering sig.: letters, Frak. capitals; nos., arabic.

Notes:
    Signing: begins A3.
    Illustrations [plates]: A1ʳ: copper engr. fp., 161 x 115 mm. (two winged figures in flight bearing the Nuremberg shields and a banner reading "NORJS," bucolic temple below with two shepherds and two nymphs in a field); foll. p. 28: twenty-eight coats of arms; foll. p. 56: eighteen coats of arms; foll. p. 140: twenty-six coats of arms; foll. p. 186: copper engr. of a triumphal arch, 161 x 113 mm.
    Ornamentation: Head vignettes: pp. 1, 103. End vignette: p. 102. Orn. initials: A2ᵛ "O"; O4ʳ "W". Other orns.: † : pp. 7, 8; grape cluster: pp. 7, 88.

Commentary: [s. General Introduction: "The Pegnesischer Blumenorden and *Die Nymphe Noris*"]

Bibliographical data: Adler—Ernst (Catalogue, 46-47, 75, 145, 152); *Auktionspreise*, vols. 11 (1960), 18 (1967), 20 (1969); Dünnhaupt, 331, no. 42 (also: 800, no. 56; 1027, no. 48); Ersch—Gruber, 254; Faber du Faur I, no. 556; Gervinus, 289; Goedeke, §58, 2; H-A-B, A 4803; Herdegen, 244; Heyse, no. 746; Jantz, no. 1325; Kosch, 863; Manheimer, 40, no. 191; Omeis, 60; Sammons, Pattern Poetry (8); Spahr, 13; Will/ *NGL*, 88.

Copies:

1. Bamberg: Staatsbibliothek. Sig.: Misc. q. 17/4. Sammelband: no. 4 of 15. B: orig. parch. on boards, with green silk ties (cut). C: good, some warping. P: foxing. M/S: [none]. S: ? [E]

2. Berkeley: Bancroft Library. Sig.: PT1737 .H44 .N9 BANCROFT. B: reb. (ca. 1820) in paper over boards. C: exc. P: light foxing. M/S: hdwr. on t.p.: "Friedrich Groeter Erlangen 1788". S: private library of Konrad Burdach [s. also M/S]. [E]

3-4. Berlin: Staatsbibliothek zu Berlin-Preußischer Kulturbesitz (2 copies):

   a. Sig.: Yu 4851 R. B: reb. (18th century) in parch., with title printed on f.c. C: good. P: foxing. M/S: [NR]. S: personal libraries of G. Volckert (18th century) and K. H. G. Meusebach (19th century).

   b. Sig.: Yu 4851ª R. B: reb. (19th century) in boards. C: good. P: foxing. M/S: [NR]. S: K. H. G. Meusebach.

5. Chicago: University of Chicago Library. Sig.: PT1737 .H42 N8 1650. B: reb. (ca. 1880-1920) in half morocco, marbled boards. C: fair (front board loose). P: light foxing. M/S: spine gilt-tooled, with stamp: "Hellwig Montano | *[rule: 5 mm.]* | NYMPHE NORIS | *[tooling]* | Nürnberg 1650". S: ? (acquired 1928/29).

6. Donaueschingen: Fürstliche Fürstenbergische Hofbibliothek. Sig.: I Fr 11b. B: reb. in boards. C: very fragile. P: foxing. M/S: [NR]. S: Joseph Freiherr von Lassberg. [E]

7. Erlangen: Universitätsbibliothek. Sig.: Ltg. AVII 299/2 (1975). Sammelband: no. 2 of 6. B: orig. boards. C: good. P: foxing. M/S:

hdwr. sig. on leaf before gathering A: "Von Hn. Cand. Erh. Cph. Bezzel verehrt." S: [s. M/S]. [E]

8. Göttingen: Niedersächsische Staats- und Universitätsbibliothek. Sig.: 8 Poet. Germ. II, 5751. B: reb. in boards. C: good. P: light browning. M/S: stamp on t.p.: "Ex Bibliotheca Acad. Georgiae Augustae". S: [s. M/S]. [E]

9-10. Heidelberg: Universitätsbibliothek (2 copies):

   a. Sig.: G 5669.

   b. Sig.: v. Waldberg 887.

11. Innsbruck: Universitätsbibliothek. Sig.: 203.681. B: reb. (19th century) in half parch. with marbled boards. C: exc. P: light browning. M/S: [NR]. V: two additional graphic inserts: a) bet. pp. 4/5: "Poëten Wäldlein gegen Nürnberg" (bottom left: "JGraff del."; bottom r.: "JKraus sc:"; b) bet. pp. 16/17: "Ælpianische Musen Lust" (bottom left: "P. Troschel. scul." S: Johann Schuler (acquired ca. 1900).

12. Leipzig: Universitätsbibliothek. Sig.: L. germ E 190. B: reb. in boards. C: fair. P: foxing. M/S: [NR]. S: ?

13. Lodz: Biblioteka Uniwersytecka. Sig.: But 1011770. B: orig. boards; portion of spine missing. C: good. M/S: a) hdwr. sig. on t.p.: "J. Niefert. 1800"; b) stamp on t.p.: "Göritz-Lübeck Stiftung. 1882"; c) stamp on plate 57 and p. 101: "[Stadt Bibliothek Berlin]". S: [s. M/S].

14. London: British Library. Sig.: 11517.e.13. B: parch.; stamped on f.c.: "CHKVKS", Kress coat of arms, and "1650". C: good. P: [NR]. M/S: [NR]. V: Additional engrs. interfoliated [no. indicates p. immediately preceding inserted leaf]: 6 (two): a) St. Johannis Friedhof [ref. p. 6], b) engr. port., Cornelius Marci [ref. p. 7]; 26: the two Nuremberg coats of arms; 28 (foll. plate 28): engr., city wall with lion's image; 30: "Nürmberger Burck" [ref. p. 30]; 48: Swedish encampment, 1632 [ref. p. 48: Wallenstein's camp]; 106: engr. port., Jobst Christoff Kreß [ref. p. 106]; 126: engr. port., Christoff Kreß, †1535 [ref. p. 127]; 130 (two): a) engr. port., Johann Rieter, [ref. p. 130], b) engr. port., Hieronimus Kreß, †1596 [ref. p. 131]; 132 (six): engr. port., a) Christoff Führer [ref. p. 132], b) engr. port., Georg Volkamer [ref. p. 132], c) engr.

port., Andreas ImHoff, †1637 [ref. p. 133], d) engr. port., Johann Friderich Löffelholtz [ref. p. 133], e) engr. port., Sigmund Gabriel Holtzschuher [ref. p. 133], f) engr. port., Johann Jacob Tetzel [ref. p. 133]; 134: engr. port., Lucas Friderich Beheim [ref. p. 134]. Stubs foll. p. 184 suggest that further illustration leaves were originally present. Attached at end: four quarto leaves, printed in three cols., with the title: "Verzeichnis aller Jahr- und Viehmärckt im gantzen Reich". S: Christoph Kreß von Kressenstein (s. B).

15. Lüneburg: Ratsbücherei. Sig.: DL 71. B: combination of older and newer parch. covers; on spine above: "1667"; below, same number upside down. C: [NR]. P: light foxing. M/S: [NR]. S: ?

16. Madison: University of Wisconsin, Memorial Library. Sig.: (Rare Book Dept.) X47XP H365. B: reb. in modern library binding of buckram. C: fair. P: fair. M/S: a) hdwr. on t.p.: "[Hellwig, Johann]"; stamp on t.p.: Oettingen-Wallerstein seal. S: ? [E]

17. Munich: Bayerische Staatsbibliothek. Sig.: Res. 4° P.o.germ. 153. B: reb. in boards. C: good. P: light foxing, sides trimmed. M/S: stamp on t.p.: "Bibliotheca Regia Monacensis". S: ? [E]

18. New Haven: Beinecke Rare Book and Manuscript Library. Sig.: Zg 17 .H38 .650. B: orig. white parch.; on spine: "Nymphe | Noris | von | Montano". C: exc., spine somewhat rubbed. P: light foxing. M/S: a) inside f.c.: bookplate of Curt and Emma von Faber du Faur; b) hdwr. on leaf inserted before first gathering: "13.V.49"; c) on same leaf, owner's sig. S: Curt von Faber du Faur. [E]

19-22. Nuremberg: Germanisches National Museum (4 copies):

   a. Sig.: G 7877ra. B: reb. (20th century) in parch.; on spine above, short title with date of publication; below: "Guido von Volkamer". C: exc. P: clean. M/S: a) inside f.c., Volkamer bookplate; b) on leaf inserted before first gathering, recto: 1.] p. refs. to Volkamer family in *Noris*: 47, 123, 132; 2.] private library no. 3433, purchase price, DM 12, purchase date, August 1911. S: Norica Coll. of Guido von Volkamer. [E]

   b. Sig.: G. 7877^r. Sammelband: no. 2 of 6. B: reb. in red-tinted boards with two green silk ties (broken); f.c., above, Kress coat of arms stamped in gold, with "IWKVKS"; below: "1650".

C: good. P: foxing. M/S: inside f.c.: engr. port. from 1655, Johann Wilhelm Kress at 66 years of age, with family arms and subscript noting his offices as Geheimer Rat, Losunger, Schultheiß. V: Five leaves inserted before first gathering: a) leaf 1^r, hdwr. above: "Dieses Büchlein / weil es dieser Zeit nicht wol mehr zu bekommen ist / soll hinfüro bey meiner lieben Posteritet / wegen der Kreßischen Vorschickung Neunhof / zur Bedächtnus Verbleiben"; b) 1^{r-v}: table of contents; leaf 2^r-3^v: [bl.]; leaf 4^r: index of illustrations in *Noris* that pertain to Kress family; leaf 4^v-5^v: [bl.]. Additional engrs. interfoliated (no. indicates p. immediately preceding inserted leaf): 4 (two): a) [double-p.] Armbrust-Schiessen on Hallerwiese, 29 July — 28 August 1650, b) fireworks celebration hosted by Duke D'Amalfi at St. Johannis Schießplatz, 14 July 1650; 6 (two): a) St. Johannis Friedhof [ref. p. 6], b) engr. port., Cornelius Marci [ref. p. 7]; 24: "Deß Heil. Röm. Reichs Stadt Nürmberg"; 26: the two Nuremberg coats of arms; 28 (foll. plate 28): engr., city wall with lion's image; 30: "Nürmberger Burck" [ref. p. 30]; 34: Schöner Brunn am Markt [ref. p. 35]; 42: Fleischbrücke [ref. p. 43]; 44: new Rathaus [ref. p. 44]; 46: procession of Emperor Matthias into Nuremberg, 1612 [ref. p. 46]; 48: Swedish encampment, 1632 [ref. p. 48: Wallenstein's camp]; 64: Schoppershof [ref. p. 65]; 106 (three): a) engr. port., Jobst Christoff Kreß [ref. p. 106], b) Gleißhammer [ref. p. 107], c) banquet and fireworks at Gleißhammer, 4 June 1650; 128 (two): a) engr. port., Hieronymus Baumgartner [ref. p. 128], b) engr. port., Andreas ImHof d. Ä., †1579 [ref. p. 129]; 130 (two): a) engr. port., Johann Rieter [ref. p. 130], b) engr. port., Hieronymus Kreß, †1596 [ref. p. 131]; 132 (six): engr. port., a) Christoff Führer [ref. p. 132], b) Georg Volkamer [ref. p. 132], c) engr. port., Andreas ImHof, †1637 [ref. p. 133], d) engr. port., Johann Friderich Löffelholtz [ref. p. 133], e) engr. port., Sigmund Gabriel Holtzschuher [ref. p. 133], f) engr. port., Johann Jacob Tetzel [ref. p. 133]; 134: engr. port., Lucas Friderich Beheim [ref. p. 134]; 182: Kraftshof 1641 [ref. p. 182]; 184 (four): a) engr. port., Antoni Kreß, †1513 [ref. p. 185], b) Neunhof 1633, c) engr. port., Caspar Kreß [ref. p. 185], d) Retzelsdorf 1620; also, stubs of leaves visible after 184. S: Johann Wilhelm Kreß von Kressenstein. [E]

c. Sig.: P.Bl.O. 1236^a. B: orig. white parch. C: fragile (loose binding). P: heavy foxing, edges scraped. M/S: a) inside f.c., unidentified coat of arms [L. Hesekiel?] with two fields (r., single rose; left, moon and stars in one of five compartments); b) on inserted leaf before first gathering, recto, seal of P.Bl.O.; c) above recto: "Ludovici Hesekiel"; d) stamp on t.p.: "Ex Bibliotheca Regia Berolinensi". V: final leaf missing. S: [s. M/S]. [E]

d. Sig.: P.Bl.O. 4. Sammelband: no. 14 of 19. B: handsome restoration in manuscript leaf (black and red Latin text) parch. On spine, hdwr.: "Joh. Claj GedichtSachen samt der Noris und andren getruckten Schäfereyen." C: good, spine slightly damaged. P: light foxing. M/S: inside f.c.: a) bookplate of P.Bl.O.; b) bookplate of former owner, Stadtbibliothek; c) hdwr. on fp. [Japanese waxed paper] of *Noris*: "Ex donatione Autoris [approx.] 1ὁ χ1ἡμν. Sigism. Bet."; d) ink underlinings and nota-tions throughout in the hand of Sigmund von Birken. V: On plate foll. p. 140 names have been added by hand in alphabetical order; only the foll. are legible to editor (Birken's spellings retained): Bamberger; Ehinger; Eschnloher; Hegner; Katterbeck; Kestel; Koburger; Meichsner; Münzmeister; Neumärker; Pilgram von Eib; Rehlinger; Schützer; von Stein; Steinbürger; Stern; Weigel; Wolff; Zollner. S: Bibliothek des Pegnesischen Blumenordens. [E]

23. Princeton: University Library. Sig.: 3455 .944 .368. B: reb. (20th century) in linen. C: fair (covers soiled). P: foxed, waterstained, end leaves soiled. M/S: hdwr. on t.p.: "Johann Helwig". S: ? [E]

24-25. Strasbourg: Bibliothèque Nationale et Universitaire (2 copies):

a. Sig.: Cd 139 180. B: orig. boards; printed on f.c.: "CHKVKS", with Kress arms, "1657". C: good. P: clean, light foxing. M/S: [NR]. V: Additional engrs. of Kress family interfoliated (no. indicates p. preceding inserted leaf): 106: engr. port., Jobst Christoff Kreß [ref. p. 106]; 126: engr. port., Christoff Kreß, †1535 [ref. p. 127]; 130 (two): a) engr. port., Johann Rieter [ref. p. 130], b) engr. port., Hieronymus Kreß, †1596 [ref. p. 131]; 132: engr. port., Georg Volkamer [ref. p. 132]; 184 (five): a) engr. port., Hupold Kreß [ref. p. 184], b) engr. port., Conrad Kreß [ref. p. 184], c) engr. port., Antoni Kreß, †1513 [ref. p. 185], d) engr. port., Caspar Kreß [ref. p. 185], e) Neunhof 1630 and Retzelstorf 1620. S: a) Freiherr von Waltzahn, Weimar; b) Christoph Kress.

b. Sig.: Cd 144 484. B: [NR]. C: poor. P: fragile, heavy foxing. M/S: [NR]. S: Hugo Barbeck, Nuremberg.

26. Vienna: Universitätsbibliothek. Sig.: I 115 505 A. B: reb. (19th century) in half-parch. C: fair. P: foxing. M/S: on t.p.: a): "L. Deissinger"; b) "a. Walish 24/IV 82 = 3 fl./gbd" [i.e. bought by Walish at auction, 24 April 1882, for 2 fl.]. S: [s. M/S].

27. Wolfenbüttel: Herzog August Bibliothek. Sig.: 116.3 Quod. (2). Sammelband: no. 2 of 4. B: orig. white pigskin on boards, with green silk ties. On spine, hdwr. contents. C: exc. P: light foxing, flaking. M/S: [none]. S: Duke August of Braunschweig-Lüneburg (acquired ca. 1660-1665). [E]

28-30. Wroclaw: Biblioteka Uniwersytecka (3 copies):

a. Sig.: 395288. B: reb. in boards (19th century). C: good. P: clean. M/S (in f.m.): a) stamp: "STADT BIBLIOTHEK i. BRESLAU M. MAGD."; b) earlier sig: 4 N 235^m. S: former Maria Magdalena Bibliothek, Breslau.

b. Sig.: 480484. B: reb. in boards (19th century). C: Part II destroyed. P: clean. M/S: stamp on t.p.: "BIBLIOTHECA MILICHIANA GORLICENSIS". S: former Milichsche Gymnasialbibliothek, Görlitz.

c. Sig.: 494030. B: reb. in boards (19th century). C: Part II destroyed. P: clean. M/S: a) hdwr. on f.c.: "Geschenk des Herrn Prof. Dr. Aug. Kahlert"; b) stamp on fp.: "SCHLES. VATERLANDISCHE GESELLISCH."; c) stamps: fp., recto and verso, and t.p.): "Bibliothek des Schles. Gesellsch. für Vaterl. Kultur aufbewahrt in der K. u. Univ. Bibl. Breslau." S: [s. M/S].

31. Würzburg: Universitätsbibliothek. Sig.: Horn 745. B: orig. boards, covered with manuscript leaf (black and red Latin text) parch. C: good. P: light foxing. M/S: inside f.c.: a) hdwr. sig.: "Paul Harsdörfer"; b) hdwr.: "Helwig, J."; hdwr.: "Horn 745". S: a) Paul Harsdörfer; b) acquired at auction, 1857, from private coll. of Dr. Franz Philipp Horn (1781-1856), Oberpflegamtsdirektor. [E]

32. [unaccounted for] University Park: Pennsylvania State University Library. [s. *NUC* 1973-77, p. 136]

33. [war loss] Berlin: Stadtbibliothek. Sig.: GL 1881.

JOHANNIS HELLVVIGII,
PHIL. MEDICI,
PRODROMUS
APOLOGETICUS
SUPER RELATIONE MEDICA,
de Eminentiſſimi ac Illuſtriſſimi
Cardinalis de Wartenberg
morbo & obitu,
ad
DANIELEM GEYGERUM,
Philoſoph. Medic. Chirurgum.

Title page, *Prodromus Apologeticus* (1662)
Fürst Thurn und Taxis Zentralarchiv, Hofbibliothek

A 3   PRODROMUS APOLOGETICUS
      (1662)

Title:

JOHANNIS HELLVVIGII, | PHIL. MEDICI, | PRODROMUS | APOLOGETICUS | SUPER RELATIONE MEDICA, | de Eminentiſſimi ac Illuſtriſſimi | Cardinalis de Wartenberg | morbo & obitu, | ad | DANIELEM GEYGERUM, | Philoſoph. Medic. Chirurgum.

Collation: 4°: A-D⁴ E², 18 leaves; [$3 - E2], unpaginated.

Contents: [A1ʳ]: t.p. [A1ᵛ]: [bl.]. A2ʳ: [text begins] "Clarissime Domine Doctor, | & Collega." D1ᵛ: announces attachment of orig. autopsy report: "Benevole Lector!" D2ʳ: orig. autopsy report: Relatio Medica, | **Von der Kranckheit und Absterben** | **Jhrer Hoch=Fürstl.** *Eminenz,* | **Herrn Cardinals / Grafen von War=** | **tenberg / etc.** D4ʳ: printed copy of Daniel Geyger's letter: Bericht | **über eine** Relationem Medicam, **Jhrer Hoch=** | **Fürstl.** *Eminenz,* **Bischofs und Cardinals von Warten=** | **berg Zustand und endliches Ableiben** | **betreffend.**

HT] [none]

RT] [none]

CW] begin on A2ʳ: ctas, . Erroneous: C3ʳ Aulam [Aula] C3ᵛ [reduced font: lute] C4ʳ addu- [ducunt] [also: reduced font]

Type:
   A-D1: 34 ll. per p. Dimensions: title: 81 x 97 mm.; p. of text, incl. lemmata: 160 x 115 mm. Style: ant.; ital. for quotations and emphasis; Frak. for German lemma on C3ʳ. Gathering sig.: letters, ant.; nos., roman. Variants: nos. italicized on B3; letter italicized on C1.
   D2-E2: 35 ll. per p. incl. CW. Dimensions: p. of text: 161 x 97 mm. (no lemmata). Style: Frak.; ant. ital. for Latin titles, names, and medical terminology. Gathering sig.: letters, Frak.; nos., roman.

Notes:
Signing: begins A2.
Illustrations: [none].
Ornamentation: Head vignettes: A2^r; D2^r. Orn. initial: D2^r "D".

Commentary: This work was occasioned by Daniel Geyger's attack on the conclusions of Hellwig's autopsy of Cardinal von Wartenberg. Thanks to the *Prodromus* we have printed copies of both Hellwig's autopsy report as well as Geyger's initial letter, so that the entire episode can be followed step-by-step: a) Geyger's letter, written mid- to late-December 1661; b) Hellwig's discovery of the clandestinely circulated letter, 18 January 1662; c) Hellwig's defense (*Prodromus*) ready by the date of his letter to Volkamer, 31 January 1662, and published shortly thereafter; d) Geyger's suit against Hellwig for defamation of character; e) his *Responsum*, ready by Spring 1662. Hellwig's letter to Volkamer shows that he was seeking a Nuremberg publisher.

Bibliographical data: Dieterichs, DC L. 25 (19); Geyger/ *Resp.*, passim.

Copies:

1. Berlin: Staatsbibliothek zu Berlin-Preussischer Kulturbesitz. Sig.: Kq 10 899. B: reb. in boards. C: exc. P: light foxing. M/S: stamp on t.p.: "Königl. Bibliothek Berlin". S: [s. M/S].

2. Edinburgh: National Library of Scotland. Sig.: DC L. 25 (19). Sammelband: no. 19. B: unbound, with narrow piece of mottled paper glued around spine. C: fair. P: foxing. M/S: [none]. S: Coll. of Georg Septimus Dieterichs, Regensburg; purchased at auction in 1820 by Library of the Faculty of Advocates (forerunner of National Library of Scotland). [E]

3. Eichstätt: Katholische Universität, Universitätsbibliothek. Sig.: 824: K 302. Sammelband: no. [NR]. C: fair. P: heavy foxing. M/S: "Bibliotheca Aulica Eystettensis". S: [s. M/S].

4. Regensburg: Fürst Thurn und Taxis, Zentralarchiv, Hofbibliothek. Sig.: MD. Pathol. N. ad 617. Sammelband: no. 5 of 7. Hdwr. on spine, contents of vol. B: orig. pig skin. C: exc. P: foxing. M/S: [none]. S: (acquired late 18th century). [E]

5. Vienna: Universitätsbibliothek. Sig.: I 203 450 A. B: reb. (19th century) in boards. C: good. P: light foxing. M/S: a) hdwr. on t.p.: "214/ XVI E"; b) "[Domus] probat. Soc. Iesu ad S. Annam Viennae 1701"; c) stamp on t.p.: "BIBLIOTH. VNIVERSIT. VINDOBONENSIS". S: [s. M/S].

JOHANNIS HELLWIGII,
Philosophiæ & Medicinæ Doctoris,
Physici quondam Ratisbonensis excellentissimi,

OBSERVATIONES PHYSICO-MEDICÆ,

posthumæ,
in lucem editæ,
Scholiisque adauctæ
à

LUCA SCHRÖCKIO, LUC. fil. Medic. Doctore, Reipubl. August. Physico,
& Academico Curioso.

AUGUSTÆ VINDELICORUM,
Apud THEOPHILUM GOEBELIUM,
LITERIS KOPPMAYERIANIS,
A. S. R. M. DC. LXXX.

Title page, *Observationes Physico-Medicæ* (1680)
National Library of Medicine

A 4   OBSERVATIONES PHYSICO-MEDICAE
      (posthumous: 1680)

Title:

JOHANNIS HELLWIGII, | Philoſophiæ & Medicinæ Doctoris, | Phyſici quondam Ratisbonenſis excellentisſimi, | OBSERVATIO- | NES | PHYSICO- | MEDICÆ, | poſthumæ, | in lucem editæ, | Scholiisque adauctæ | à | LUCA SCHRÖCKIO, LUC. fil. Me- | dic. Doctore, Reipubl. Auguſt. Phyſico, | & Academico Curioſo. | *[orn. rule: 4 x 105 mm.]* | *AUGUSTÆ VINDELICORUM,* | APUD THEOPHILUM GOEBELIUM, | LITERIS KOPPMAYERIANIS, | *A. S. R.* M. DC. LXXX.

Collation: 4°: a-a2 a2 (c a3) a4 b² A-H⁴ I-3I², 220 leaves; [$3 - a3, b2, 3H3, 3I2], pp. [12] 1-422 [14].

Contents: a1ʳ: fp.; a1ᵛ: [bl.]. a2ʳ: t.p. a2ᵛ: [bl.]. a3ʳ: ded. by Lucas Schröck: "PERILLUSTRI | Liberæ Sacr. Rom. Imp. Civitatis | Ratisbonensis | SENATUI, | [...]." a4ᵛ: "LECTORI BENEVOLO | *SALUTEM!*" b1ᵛ: "VITA HELLWIGIANA." b2ᵛ: memorial poem by Johann Jacob Kerscher for Johann Hellwig: "EPIGRMMA" *[sic]*. A1ʳ: [text begins] "OBSERVATIO I. | Infans acephalus. | [...] | *SCHOLION HELLWIGIANUM.*" A1ᵛ: *"ADDITAMENTUM SCHRÖCKII."* [This chapter format holds through OBSERVATIO XL; thereafter the scholia are by Schröck.] 3G4ʳ: "Index I. Observationum." 3H3ʳ: "Index II. rerum notabilium."

HT] [none]

RT] [none]

CW] begin on a2ʳ: tius . Missing: A3ʳ 3G4ᵛ

Type: 31 ll. per p. (22 ll. in the ded.). Dimensions: title: 158 x 123 mm.; p. of text: 159 x 113 mm. Style: ant.; ital. for quotations and indices, each "Scholion" and "Additamentum," and for the medical case description immediately under each "Observatio." Arabic script, p. 195; Greek minuscules, p. 192, passim. German proper names, Frak., except where

Latinized. Gathering sig.: letters, ant. capitals (except gatherings a-b2: ant. lower case); nos., arabic.

Notes:
  Signing: begins a2.
  Illustrations: 1) a1^r: fp., 169 x 129 mm. (Hellwig's bust in a round, with reliquary between Noris the nymph and a muse; below middle: Hellwig's shield; below left: "J. Z. Rauler delin."; below r.: "Melchior Hafner sc."; 2) bet. pp. 44/45: illustration to Observatio XVI: "Homo monstrosus," 164 x 126 mm.; below r.: "M. Haffner sculp."; 3) bet. pp. 310/311: illust. to Observationes CX, CXX, CXXI, 164 x 130 mm.; below r.: "M. Haffner sc."
  Ornamentation: Head vignettes: a3^r; a4^r; b1^v; A1^r; 3G4^r; 3H3^r. End vignettes: b1^r; b2^v; 3G3^v; 3I2^v (triangular). Orn. initials: a3^r "G"; a4^v "E"; b1^v "I"; b2^v "M"; A1^r "A". Other: A1^r and resp. first pp. of indices have small floral orn. at top.

Commentary: [s. General Introduction: "Later Life and Medical Writings"]

Bibliographical data: Georgi, 234; Herdegen, 244; Hirsch, 149; Jöcher, vol. 2, col. 1480; Kestner, 387; Linden, 601; Will/ *NGL*, 88.

Copies:

1. Amberg: Staatliche Provinzialbibliothek. Sig.: Med. 299. B: orig. parch. on boards. C: good (spine slightly damaged). P: foxing. M/S: [NR]. S: Zisterzienserkloster Waldsassen (Oberpfalz/ Bayern)

2-3. Augsburg: Staats- und Stadtbibliothek (2 copies):

   a. Sig.: 4° Med 502. B: orig. parch. C: exc. P: clean. M/S: [NR]. S: Lucas-Schröck-Bibliothek.

   b. Sig.: 4° Med 1341/Adl. B: orig. parch. C: fair (spine slightly damaged). P: clean. M/S: [NR]. S: Augustiner-Chorherrenstift St. Georg Augsburg.

4. Basel: Universitätsbibliothek. Sig.: Lh VII 18. B: orig. parch. C: fair (spine defective). P: flaking. M/S: [NR]. S: ?

5. Bethesda: National Library of Medicine. Sig.: WZ250 .H477o 1680. S: ? [E: microfilm]

Descriptive Bibliography 47

6. Darmstadt: Hessische Landes- und Hochschulbibliothek. Sig.: S 1768. B: orig. boards; hdwr. on spine, name of author and title; older and current catalogue nos. C: good. P: clean. M/S: a) inside f.c.: "B G Mücke"; b) stamp on a1^v: "Grosherzoglich Hessische Hofbibliothek". S: a) Benjamin Gottfried Mücke (b. 1745, physician); b) Sammlung Baldinger.

7. Dresden: Sächsische Landesbibliothek. Sig.: Path. gen. 383. B: boards; on spine, encased title with hdwr.: "Hellwig, Observationes phys. med." C: fragile (binding only partially intact; gathering A is loose). P: foxing. M/S: two stamps on t.p.: a) above: "J. B."; b) middle: arms of Electoral Saxony. S: Churfürstliche Bibliothek.

8. Edinburgh: University Library. Sig.: G*23 .73. B: reb. (18th century) in leather. C: fair (binding loose). On spine, stamp of Edinburgh University Library. P: light foxing. M/S: hdwr. on t.p.: a) "Ex Libris Bibliothecæ Edinensis"; b) "B. H. d. ig". S: [s. M/S].

9. Erlangen: Universitätsbibliothek. Sig.: Trew X 823. B: orig. leather; on spine, gilded ornamentation. C: exc. P: foxing. M/S: a) inside f.c., bookplate: "SIMVLARE NESCIT" and having a dog with neck collar bearing initials "C. I. T." [= Christoph Jacob Trew]; b) hdwr. on fp.: "sum Job. Petri Prükelij D. Physis. Ratisponae Academici Curiosi." S: Sammlung Trew. [E]

10. Firenze: Biblioteca Nazionale Centrale. Sig.: [NR]. B: parch. C: good. P: foxing. M/S: [NR]. S: Targioni Tozzetti.

11. Glasgow: University Library. Sig.: Ck. 2. 22. B: reb. in leather on millboard. C: exc. P: light foxing. M/S: [NR]. S: Dr. William Hunter, 1718-1783 (bequeathed 1783 to library).

12. Gotha: Forschungsbibliothek. Sig.: Med. 4° 32/1 (2). Sammelband: no. 2. B: orig. parch. on boards. Gilded on f.c.: "FHZS 1681". C: exc. P: clean. M/S (in f.m.): "Bibliotheca ducalis Gothana". S: a) [s. M/S]; b) Friedrich Herzog zu Sachsen.

13. Göttingen: Niedersächsische Staats- und Universitätsbibliothek. Sig.: 8 Med. Prax. 3852/75. B: reb. in parch.; hdwr. on spine: [title]. C: fair. P: clean. M/S: [NR]. S: ?

14. Greifswald: Ernst-Moritz-Arndt-Universitätsbibliothek. Sig.: Vf 35. Sammelband: no. [NR]. B: reb. on thin wood with colored paper and parch. spine. C: damaged. P: foxing. M/S: [NR]. S: medical library of Christian Stephan Scheffel, Professor of Medicine, Greifswald, †1760 (acquired 1760, accession no. 5200).

15. Krakow: Uniwersytet Jagielloński, Biblioteka Jagiellońska. Sig.: Med. 6005. B: orig. leather; spine gilded and tooled: "OBSERVATIONES PECHLINI HELWIGII". C: exc. P: light foxing. M/S: hdwr. inside f.c.: "darował [= given by] Ferdynand Kojsiewicz. 1851." S: [s. M/S]. Bound with J. N. Pechlin: *Observationum physico-medicarum lib. tres*. Hamburg: ex Off. Schultziana, 1691.

16. Leipzig: Universitätsbibliothek. Sig.: Allg. Path. 400. B: reb. in boards. C: fair. P: foxing. M/S: a) "Ex libris: C. E. Kapp"; b) [pasted over a)]: "J. W. Schlegel". S: [s. M/S].

17. London: British Library. Sig.: 1165.e.5. B: reb.

18. Marburg: Universitätsbibliothek. Sig.: XI aB 115 an XI aB 123. Sammelband: no. [NR]. B: orig. parch.; hdwr. on spine, names of resp. authors. C: exc. P: clean. M/S: a) stamp on t.p., verso: "Bibliotheca Marburgensis"; b) hdwr.: "[illegible], Dr. med. in Friedberg/ Hessen (1707)." S: a) Georg Philipp Michaelis (1712-1783), Prof. of Medicine, Marburg; b) Pastor Grunhagen, Höchst/ Nidda (fl. 1700); [s. also M/S, b)].

19-20. Munich: Bayerische Staatsbibliothek (2 copies):

   a. Sig.: Ex 4° Med. g. 108$\underline{m}$ [presently inaccessible].

   b. Sig.: Ex 4° Med. g. 108$\underline{n}$. B: orig. orn. pig skin on boards. C: good (ties broken). P: clean. M/S: [NR]. S: ?

21. Oslo: Universitetsbiblioteket, Abteilung: "Altes Buch." Sig.: catalogued under "Johannis Hellwig".

22. Oxford: Bodleian Library. Sig.: 4° H9 (1) Med. (Old Library Reading Rooms).

23. Oxford: Queen's College Library.

24. Padua: Museo Civico, Biblioteca. Sig.: G. 4086. B: orig. boards; hdwr. on spine, author, title, and "192". C: good. P: foxing. M/S: [NR]. S: ?

25. Paris: Bibliothèque Nationale. Sig.: 4° Td5. 52. B: orig. parch. C: good. P: foxing. M/S: [NR]. S: ?

26. Philadelphia: The Library Company. Sig.: Log 525.Q. B: reb. (18th century) in speckled calf skin; rebacked (late 19th century). C: good. P: foxing. M/S: [NR]. S: presumably Dr. William Logan of Bristol, England († 1758).

27. Philadelphia: Thomas Jefferson University (Jefferson Medical College). Sig.: 610.8 H36.

28. Prague: Národní v Praze. Sig.: 18 H 196. B: reb. in leather on boards; hdwr. on spine, author, title, impress. C: exc. P: foxing. M/S: [none]. S: ?

29. Regensburg: Staatliche Bibliothek. Sig.: Med. 497. B: orig. patent leather; on f.c., embossed supralibros of city of Regensburg: eagle above coat of arms with keys of Peter; on spine, gold tooling. C: fragile. P: foxing, esp. at edges. M/S: [NR]. S: ?

30. Rome: Biblioteca Apostolica Vaticana. Sig.: Racc. Gen. Medicina IV. 1253.

31. St. Petersburg: [former] Biblioteka Akademii Nauk CCCP.

32. Salzburg: Universitätsbibliothek. Sig.: 62.247 I. B: orig. parch.; on spine and on f.c., arms supralibros of Archbishop Max Gandolf, and "1668". C: fair (staining on spine, silk ties broken). P: foxing. M/S: stamp on t.p.: "K. K. Studien Bibliothek Salzburg." S: erstwhile Erzbischöfliche Hofbibliothek, private coll. of Cardinal Archbishop Max Gandolf von Kuenburg (1668-1687); [s. also M/S].

33. Schwerin: Mecklenburgische Landesbibliothek. Sig.: HST V 630. B: orig. parch.; hdwr. on spine: [title]. C: fair. P: foxing. M/S: on t.p., stamp of the Hennemannsche Stiftung. S: Großherzögliche Regierungsbibliothek (acquired 1846 from private coll. of Wilhelm Hennemann, former Hofarztes Geheimrat).

34. Strasbourg: Bibliothèque Nationale et Universitaire, Medizinische Abteilung. Sig.: J 102 834. B: orig. parch. C: fragile (salvaged from fire of 1944). P: heavy foxing. M/S: stamp on t.p., verso: "LANDESBIBLIOTHEK STRASSBURG". S: ?

35. Tübingen: Universitätsbibliothek. Sig.: Jd 26. 4°. B: orig. parch. C: good. P: clean. M/S: [NR]. S: Hofbibliothek Ellwangen.

36. Uppsala: Universitetsbibliotek. Sig.: Obr 44:52. B: orig. parch. C: fair. P: foxing. M/S: [NR]. S: private coll. of Zacharias Johansson Strandberg (1712-1792).

37. Vienna: Österreichische Nationalbibliothek. Sig.: +69.D.67. B: orig. parch. C: good. P: clean. M/S: [NR]. S: ?

38. Vienna: Universitätsbibliothek. Sig.: I 37 256 A. Sammelband: no. 3 of 3. B: reb. in parch. with white leather spine; on spine, above: "A. S."; below: "1775". C: good. P: foxing. M/S: a) inside f.c., bookplate with arms: "EX BIBLIOTHECA MONASTERII SEITENSTETTENSIS"; b) on facing leaf, recto, bookplate: "Geschenk des Benedictiner-Stiftes Seitenstetten vom 26. September 1888." S: Benedictiner-Stift Seitenstetten.

39. Winterthur: Stadtbibliothek. Sig.: D.106. B: orig. half-parch. with gold impress on f.c.: "Hellwigii Observat Phys: Med." C: exc. P: foxing. M/S: hdwr. on t.p.: "Ex libris Joh. Henr. Kronaueri Mdcis. 1764." S: [s. M/S].

40. Wroclaw: Biblioteka Uniwersytecka. Sig.: 393899. B: orig. parch. (17th/18th century). C: exc. P: clean. M/S: stamp in f.m.: "Ex Bibl. ad aed. Mar. Magdal." S: former Maria Magdalena Bibliothek, Breslau.

41. Zurich: Zentralbibliothek. Sig.: IB 89. B: orig. leather. C: exc. P: foxing. M/S: [NR]. S: ?

42. [unaccounted for] Frankfurt a. M.: Senkenbergische Bibliothek.

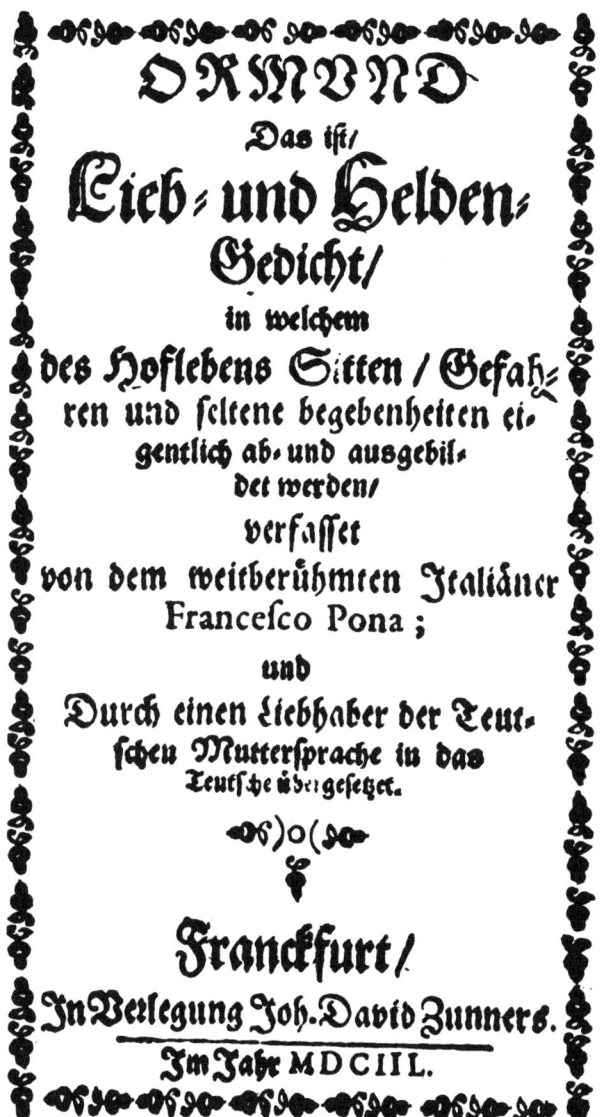

Title page, *Ormund* (1648)
Herzog August Bibliothek

B. Translations

B 1 ORMUND
B 1.1 First printing, 1648

Title:

[inside an orn. frame] **ORMUND | Das iſt / | Lieb= und Helden= | Gedicht / | in welchem | des Hoflebens Sitten / Gefäh= | ren und ſeltene begebenheiten ei= | gentlich ab= und ausgebil= | det werden / | verfaſſet | von dem weitberühmten Jtaliäner | Franceſco Pona; | und | Durch einen Liebhaber der Teut= | ſchen Mutterſprache in das | Teutſche übergeſetzet. | *[triangular orn.: 9 x 15 mm.]* | Franckfurt / | Jn Verlegung Joh. David Zunners. | *[rule: 40 mm.]* | Jm Jahr MD CIIL.**

Collation: 12°: (*)¹² (*)(*)1-(*)(*)6 (**)7 [c (*)(*)7] (*)(*)8-(*)(*)10 A-L¹² M⁴ [N¹], 167 leaves; [$7 - (*)6], pp. [44] 1-119 220 (c 120) 121-197 196 (c 198) 199-215 214 (c 216) 217-236 337 (c 237) 238-289 [1].

Contents: (*)1ʳ: fp. (*)1ᵛ: [bl.]. (*)2ʳ: t.p. (*)2ᵛ: [bl.]. (*)3ʳ: ded.: "Dem Durchleuchtigen / Hochgebor= | nen Fürsten und Herrn / | Herrn ANTONIO | HULDERICHO / | Hertzogen zu Braunschweig und | Lüneburg / etc. seinem gnädigen | Fürsten und Herrn." (*)6ʳ: engr. port. of Anton Ulrich, with ded. poem by Hellwig. (*)6ᵛ: ded. poem: "Ad Effigiem Serenißimi Principis | ANTONI HULDERICI | Brunswic. atque Lunæburg. | Ducis etc. | Epigramma," signed by G. P. Harsdörffer. (*)7ʳ: "Auf | Des Urhebers dieses Gedichtes | Bildniß," followed by two com. poems, in Latin and German, by Hellwig. (*)7ᵛ: "Vorrede. | Freundlicher / wohlgeneigter | Leser." (*)11ʳ: "Der günstige Leser lasse sich | ferners erinnern:". (*)12ʳ: seven com. poems to Hellwig, under the title: "Ehrengedichte | Zu ausfertigung des Teutschen | Ormunds." (*)(*)10ʳ⁻ᵛ: [bl.]. A1ʳ: [text begins] "ORMUNDUS | Erstes Buch." B6ʳ: "Das zweite Buch." D4ʳ: "Das dritte Buch." F9ᵛ: "Das vierte Buch." H6ᵛ: "Das fünfte Buch." K6ᵛ: "Das sechste Buch." M2ᵛ: "Das sibende Buch."

HT] ORMUNDUS | [Erstes Buch, *etc.*]

RT] pp. 2-289 verso: "ORMUNDUS"; recto: [resp.] "ERSTES." "ZWEYTES." "DRITTES." "VIERTES." "FUNFTES." "SECHSTES." "SIBENDES BUCH."

CW] begin on (*)3ʳ mü= . Missing: E3ᵛ E5ᵛ J12ʳ K2ᵛ L12ʳ. Erroneous: (*)(*)7ᵛ Wer [VI. WEr] (*)(*)8ᵛ Als [VII. | I. | ALs] D12ᵛ zucht [Zucht]

Type: 31 ll. per p. Dimensions: title, incl. frame: 112 x 61 mm.; p. of text: 108 x 53 mm. Style: Frak.; ant. and ant. ital. for Latin texts. Gathering sig.: letters, Frak. capitals; nos., roman.

Notes:
  Signing: begins (*)3.
  Illustrations (numbered 1-16 on resp. engr.): 1) fp.: Ritter Ormund crowned by Fama; 2) bet. (*)6/7: engr. port. of Francesco Pona; 3) bet. (*)12/(*)(*)1: man with net and masks; 4) bet. A5/6: tournament of Prince Osimir against bridal suitors; 5) bet. B4/5: Prince Osimir's tomb, with Prince and his mourners; 6) bet. B10/11: Giliander attempts by night to serenade Ormund's wife and is seized by guards; 7) bet. C7/8: ship of Ormund and wife wrecked in a storm; 8) bet. D8/9: Queen Dorispina abducted in woods by two agents of king; 9) bet. E1/2: Thesimir bathes in a spring in woods; 10) bet. E11/12: sheriff discovers French Queen Erminda following assassination attempt in woods; 11) bet. G4/5: Ulalius abducts spouse on street; 12) bet. G7/8: ship captain and nobleman walk along shore where they meet Lindoris, disguised as a fisherwoman; 13) bet. J5/6: Sileus, son of Moor King, together with hunting party, watch shipwreck of Luind and wife; 14) bet. K12/L1: in fleeing, Rodoant and Ormund come upon a wild man in woods; 15) bet. L7/8: young man forces wife to eat flesh of her dead lover; servant holds torch, body parts lie on ground; 16) bet. M6/7: Giliander meets Lisaura secretely in temple of Scottish camp, while priest overhears. Other: (*)6ʳ: engr. port. of Anton Ulrich, Duke of Braunschweig-Lüneburg.
  Ornamentation: Head vignettes: (*)3ʳ; (*)6ᵛ; (*)7ʳ; (*)7ᵛ; (*)11ʳ; (*)12ᵛ; (*)(*)4ʳ; (*)(*)7ʳ; (*)(*)8ʳ; (*)(*)9ʳ; A1ʳ; B6ʳ; D4ʳ; F9ᵛ; H6ᵛ; K6ᵛ; M2ᵛ. End vignettes: (*)(*)9ᵛ; B5ᵛ; D3ᵛ; F9ʳ; M2ʳ. Orn. initials: (*)3ʳ "W"; (*)7ᵛ "W"; (*)10ʳ "D"; (*)11ʳ "D"; A1ʳ "E"; B6ʳ "N"; D4ʳ "D"; F9ᵛ "E"; H6ᵛ "A"; K6ᵛ "G".

Commentary: Although only eight copies are reported, the work seems to have been widely known in the seventeenth century. Next to *Die Nymphe Noris*, this is the most frequently cited work by Hellwig in literary histories — although most do not know the second printing (1666) — and accounts for his primary reputation as a translator.

Bibliographical data: Adler—Ernst (Catalogue, 165); Dünnhaupt, 327, no. 22 (also: 796, no. 45; 1025, no. 37); Ersch—Gruber, 254; Faber du Faur I, no. 555; Graesse, vol. 3, 237a; H-A-B, A 166; Jantz, no. 1326; Kosch, 863; Maltzahn, 358, no. 1907; Manheimer, 40, no. 192; Schottel, 1183.

Copies:

1. Bamberg: Staatsbibliothek. Sig.: L. it. d.25. B: orig. parch.; hdwr. on spine: [title]. C: exc. (green silk ties cut). P: light foxing. M/S: hdwr. on t.p.: "Sum Ex lib: Johan: Neydecker IVD 1648." V: p. 238-298 (+3); N2^r: "Verzeichnuß der Kupffer= | stükklein / wohin dieselbe | einzuhefften."; engr. no. 9 missing. S: [s. M/S]. Bound with Johann Hütter: *Ludus Latrunculorum*, 1647. [E]

2. London: British Library. Sig.: 12450.a.5. B: reb.

3. Munich: Bayerische Staatsbibliothek. Sig.: P.o. it. 842. B: orig. parch. C: fair (soiled, torn). P: clean. M/S: [NR]. S: ?

4. New Haven: Beinecke Rare Book and Manuscript Library. Sig.: Zg17. H38. 648. B: orig. parch.; paper over spine; hdwr. on f.c.: [title]. C: warped, dirty. P: foxing. M/S: bookplate of Curt and Emma von Faber du Faur. V: RT] K8^r Vierdtes Buch (c Funftes Buch). S: Curt von Faber du Faur. [E]

5. Vienna: Österreichische Nationalbibliothek. Sig.: 93. 436-A. B: orig. parch. C: exc. P: clean. M/S: [NR]. V: f.m. 41 pp. S: old MS catalogue no.: "HS: Kauf: 1898 / Gilhofer."

6. Wolfenbüttel: Herzog August Bibliothek. Sig.: Lk 678$\underline{^a}$. B: orig. orn. parch. on boards. C: exc. (some shaving). P: light foxing; fore-edges gilded. M/S: a) hdwr. on fp.: "FAHZBUL"; b) numerous hdwr. corrections in ink of printing errors throughout. S: Ferdinand Albrecht Herzog zu Braunschweig und Lüneburg, 1636-1687. [E]

7. Zwickau: Ratsschulbibliothek. Sig.: '28.11.41/1'.

8. [war loss]. Munich: Stiftsbibliothek Abtei St. Bonifaz. Sig.: 8° P.o. ital. 310.

ORMVND

Das ist/
Lieb- und Helden-Gedicht/

In welchem deß
Hof-Lebens
Sitten/ Gefährligkeit und unvermuhtliche Begebenheiten eigentlich abgebildet und verfasset

von
FRANCISCO PONA,
dem weitberühmten Italiäner/
Durch einen Liebhaber der Hochteutschen Sprache übersetzet/
Zum Andernmahl gedruckt

—)o(—

Franckfurt/
Verlegts Joh. David Zunner/
Truckts Egidius Vogel.
M DC LXVI.

Title page, *Ormund* (1666)
Herzog August Bibliothek

B 1   ORMUND
B 1.2   Second printing, 1666

Title:

ORMUND | Das ist / | Lieb= und Helden= | Gedicht / | Jn welchem deß | Hof=Lebens | Sitten / Gefährlichkeit und | unvermuhtliche Begebenhei= ten eigentlich abgebildet | und verfaſſet | von | FRANCISCO PONA, dem weitberühmten Jtaliäner / | Durch einen Liebhaber der Hoch= teutſchen Sprache überſetzet / | Zum Andernmahl gedruckt | *[orn.: 4 x 14 mm.]* | Franckfurt / | Verlegts Joh. David Zunner / | Truckts Egidius Vogel. | *[rule: 30 mm.]* | M DC LXVI.

Collation: 12°: (*)¹² (*)(*)¹⁰ A-L¹², 154 leaves; [$7 - (*)7, (*)(*)6, (*)(*)7], pp. [44] 1-264.

Contents: (*)1ʳ: fp. (*)1ᵛ: [bl.]. (*)2ʳ: [bl.]. (*)2ᵛ: t.p. (*)3ʳ: ded.: "Dem Durchleuchtigen / Hochgebor= | nen Fürsten und Herrn / Herrn | ANTONIO | HULDERICHO / | Hertzogen zu Braunschweig | und Lüneburg / etc. seinem gnä= | digen Fürsten und | Herrn." (*)7ᵛ: engr. port. of Duke Anton Ulrich, with ded. poem by Hellwig. (*)8ʳ: ded. poem: "Ad Effigiem Serenissimi | Principis | ANTONI HULDERICI | Brunswic. atque Lunæburg | Ducis etc. | Epigramma," signed by G. P. Harsdörffer. (*)8ᵛ: "Auf | Deß Urhebers dieses Gedichtes | Bildniß," followed by two com. poems, in Latin and German, by Hellwig. (*)9ʳ: "Vorrede. | Freundlicher wolgeneigter | Leser." (*)12ᵛ: "Der günstige Leser lasse | sich ferners erinnern:". (*)(*)2ʳ: seven com. poems to Hellwig, under the title: "Ehren= Gedichte | Zu Außfertigung deß Teutschen | Ormunds." A1ʳ: [text begins] "Ormundus | Erstes Buch." B4ʳ: "Das zweyte Buch." C11ᵛ: "Das dritte Buch." F2ᵛ: "Das vierte Buch." G10ʳ: "Das fünfte Buch." J8ᵛ: "Das sechste Buch." L3ʳ: "Das siebende Buch."

HT] Ormundus | [Erstes Buch, *etc.*]

RT] pp. 2-263 verso: "Ormundus"; recto: [resp.] "Erstes." "Das Zweyte." "Das dritte." "Das vierte." "Das fünfte." "Das sechste." "Das siebende Buch."

CW] begin on (*)3ʳ: gese= . Erroneous: (*)8ʳ Auff [Auf] (*)11ʳ er= [Er] (*)(*)9ʳ Wer [VI. Wer] (*)(*)10ᵛ OR [Or] B11ᵛ Auff [Auf] E3ʳ dieweil [Dieweil] E10ᵛ Mal [Mahl] F12ᵛ gestalt [ihrer] K5ᵛ Name a [Namen]

Type: 33 ll. per p. Dimensions: title: 109 x 52 mm.; p. of text: 114 x 53 mm. Style: Frak. Gathering sig.: letters, Frak. capitals; nos., roman.

Notes:
    Signing: begins (*)3.
    Illustrations: 1) (*)1ʳ: fp. (Ritter Ormund crowned by Fama); 2) (*)7ᵛ: engr. port. of Anton Ulrich, Duke of Braunschweig-Lüneburg.
    Ornamentation: Head vignettes: (*)3ʳ; (*)8ʳ; (*)9ʳ; (*)12ᵛ; (*)(*)2ʳ; (*)(*)3ᵛ; A1ʳ; B4ʳ; C11ᵛ; F2ᵛ; G10ʳ; J8ᵛ; L3ʳ. End vignettes: (*)(*)1ᵛ; (*)(*)10ᵛ; C11ʳ; F2ʳ; G9ᵛ; J8ʳ. Other: small orns. middle on headline: (*)3ᵛ-6ʳ.

Commentary: The 1666 reprinting by the original publisher, Zunner (Frankfurt a.M.), bears a slightly altered title and displays orthographic and other variants, as well as gilded fore-edges. All sixteen orig. plates, together with the copper engraved portrait of Pona, have been removed without comment. This does not add up to a new edition, however, for Hellwig's translation itself remains intact.

Bibliographical data: Goedeke, §183, 58, no. 1; §192, 13; Graesse, vol. 3, 237a [year erroneous: 1606]; H-A-B, B 602.

Copies:

1. Berlin: Universitätsbibliothek. Sig.: 11: an: Vz 7505. B: orig. parch.; impress on f.c.: "CESVK 1666". C: good (warping on spine). P: foxing. M/S: [NR]. S: Jacob and Wilhelm Grimm.

2. Wolfenbüttel: Herzog August Bibliothek. Sig.: Lk 679. B: orig. paper on boards; spine covered with parch. C: fragile (spine torn at top). P: foxing. M/S: bookplate inside f.c.: "EX BIBLIOTHECA DUCIS BRUNSVICENSIS ET LUNEBURGENSIS" with arms. S: Herzog Ludwig Rudolf von Braunschweig-Lüneburg, 1671-1735. [E]

3. Wroclaw: Biblioteka Uniwersytecka. Sig.: 541256. B: reb. (19th century) on boards. C: exc. P: clean. M/S (in f.m.): a) hdwr.: "Guttmann Berlin 1835 Jun."; b) stamp: "V. REHDIGER. STADT BIBLIOTHEK i. BRESLAU" with old sig.: 8 nE 3890. S: [s. M/S]

H. Wilibalds Pirkheimers
Beschreibung
des Flekkens Neuhofes/
aus dem Latein in das Teutsche
übergesetzet /
benebenst mit gebührlichen Anmerkungen und etlichen
Poetischen Gedanken vermehret.

Gedrukt im Jahr 1648.

Title page, *Neunhof* (1648)
Germanisches National Museum

B 2   NEUNHOF

B 2.1   First printing, 1648

Title:

H. Wilibalds Pirkheimers | Beſchreibung | des Flekkens Neuhofes *[sic]* / | aus dem Latein in das Teutſche | übergeſetzet / | benebenſt mit gebührlichen Anmerkungen und etlichen | Poetiſchen Gedanken vermehret. | *[rule: 72 mm.]*. | Gedrukt im Jahr 1648.

Collation: 4°: A-B⁴, 8 leaves; [$3], unpaginated.

Contents: A1r: t.p. A1ᵛ: [bl.]. A2ʳ: ded.: "Denen Woledlen / Gestrengen Vesten | Ferdinand Jenischen / | Georg Seyfried Kolern / | meinen insonders hochgeehrten Herren / und | *respectivè* lieben Schwägern / auch eins theils Gevatteren / | und dann | der Woledlen und Vielehrentugendreichen Frauen / | Maria Sabina Jenischen / | geborner Kolerin / meiner insonders hochgeehrten Frau | Gevatterin und Schwägerin / | wie auch | der Woledlen und Vielehrentugendreichen Jungfrau / | Anna Philipina / | geborner Kolerin / meiner insonders hochgeehrten | Jungfer Baasen." A3ʳ: [text begins] "Kurzer Auszug | Eines Lateinischen Schreibens Herrn Wilibald | Pirkheimers an einen guten Freund / den schönen Flekken | Neuhof betreffend / denen Inhabern zum Theil desselben | zu Ehren ins Teutsch übergesetzt." B2ʳ: "Anmerkungen". B3ᵛ: eight poems on individual Neuhof attractions, under the title: "Poetische Gedanken".

HT] Kurzer Auszug | Eines Lateinischen Schreibens Herrn Wilibald | Pirkheimers an einen guten Freund / den schönen Flekken | Neuhof betreffend / denen Inhabern zum Theil desselben | zu Ehren ins Teutsch übergesetzt.

RT] [none]

CW] begin on A2ʳ Oft= . Erroneous: A2ᵛ

Type: 36 ll. per p. ("Anmerkungen," 40 ll.). Dimensions: title: 59 x 118 mm.; p. of text: 168 x 121 mm. Gathering sig.: letters, Frak.; nos., roman.

Notes:
> Signing: begins A2.
> Illustrations: [none]
> Ornamentation: Head vignettes: A2^r; A3^r; B3^v.

Commentary: An editorial note to the 1758 reprinting of Hellwig's translation would suggest that he worked from the Goldast edition: "Dieses Schreiben Herrn Wilibald Pirckheimers [...] ist in Melchior. Goldasti edirten Operibus Bilibaldi Pirckheimeri, welche zu Frankfurt 1610. in Fol. gedruckt worden, in denen Epistolis p. 232. 233. 234. zu finden." Hellwig omits the final part of the original as well as a passage in the middle.

Bibliographical data: Herdegen, 243; Will/ *BNW*, series I, vol. 2, 322, no. 1483; Will/ *NGL*, 88.

Copies:

1-2. Nuremberg: Germanisches Nationalmuseum (2 copies):

> a. Sig.: G 7664. Sammelband [same as 7877^r above under A2, 19-22, b)]: no. 1 of 6. M/S: on t.p.: a) above, hdwr. sig.; b) crossed out: "28,635"; c) on r.: "= 4876"; d) below: stamp of imperial eagle. V: a) on t.p., verso, engr. port., Paulus Coler; b) foll. B1: double-p. map of Neunhof. S: Caroline Rhau. [E]
>
> b. Sig.: P.Bl.O. 4. Sammelband [same as A2, 19-22, d)]: no. 19 of 19. S: Bibliothek des Pegnesischen Blumenordens. [E]

Herrn Wilibald Pirckheimers
Beschreibung
des
Mark-Fleckens
Neunhof,

in Lateinischer und Teutscher Sprach,

mit denen

nöthigsten Anmerkungen.

Gedruckt im Jahr Christi 1758.

Title page, *Neunhof* (1758)
Germanisches National Museum

B 2   NEUNHOF
B 2.2   Second printing, 1758

Title:

Herrn Wilibald Pirckheimers | Beſchreibung | des | Mark=Fleckens | Neunhof, | in Lateiniſcher und Teutſcher Sprach, | mit denen | nöthigſten Anmerkungen. | *[double rule: 119 over 113 mm.]* | **Gedruckt im Jahr Chriſti 1758.**

Collation: 4°: A-B⁴ C², 10 leaves; [$3], pp. [3] 4-20.

Contents: A1ʳ: t.p. A1ᵛ: printer's remark: "Dieses Schreiben Herrn Wilibald Pirckheimers [...] ist in Melchior. Goldasti edirten Operibus Bilibaldi Pirckheimeri [...]." A2ʳ: [text begins] "Nobili & clarissimo Viro D. Bernhar- | do Adelmann de Adelmannsfelden, | &c. Bilibaldus Pirckheimer | S. P. D."

HT] [none]

RT] [none]

CW] begin on A2ʳ: left col.: [ant.] re; r. col.: [Frak.] bun=

Type: 34 ll. per p. Text in double cols.: Latin left, German r.; lettered fns. in reduced font. Dimensions: title: 123 x 120 mm.; p. of text: 163 x 114 mm. Style: ant. for Latin text and names; Frak. for German text, printer's remark, and fns. Gathering sig.: letters, Frak. capitals; nos., roman.

Notes:
  Signing: begins A2.
  Illustrations: [none]
  Ornamentation: Head vignettes: A2ʳ. End vignettes: C2ᵛ. Orn. initials: A2ʳ (beginning of German text) "H". Other: small orns., middle on headline: pp. 4-20.

Commentary: This reprinting in new format (no place, no publisher given) is not a new edition, since Hellwig's translation remains essentially unchanged. Alterations are limited to modernization of orthography and punctuation; division of some paragraphs; occasional idiomatic alterations: e.g. "ob zuvielfältigen Geschäfften" > "wegen vielfältiger Geschäften." Mayer (1828), vii-viii, observes: "Als diese Uebersetzung [i.e. 1648] selten wurde, erschien sie wieder [i.e. 1758] [...]. Die Anmerkungen sind aus der vorigen Ausgabe theils beibehalten, theils vermehrt, oder davon weggelassen. Die poetischen Gedanken fehlen ganz. Dediziert ist sie Niemanden. Der lateinische Text steht zur Seite; in der ersten Ausgabe fehlt er ganz. Die Uebersetzung ist die Dr. Hellwigs, welcher den Schluß und eine Stelle in der Mitte wegließ, wo auch bei der letzten Ausgabe der lateinische Text fehlt."

Bibliographical data: Will/ *BNW*, series I, vol. 2, 322, no. 1484.

Copies:

1-2. Erlangen: Universitätsbibliothek (2 copies):

    a. Sig.: 4° Hist. 619^{ex}/16. B: orig. boards. C: exc. P: foxing. M/S: a) inside f.c., bookmark indicating gift to library from Elias von Steinmeyer, with accession no.: 10926; b) A1^v: library bookmark of the old Königliche Universität Erlangen. S: [s. M/S]. [E]

    b. Sig.: K. B. (2595). B: reb. in heavy paper. C: exc. P: foxing. M/S: a) hdwr. inside f.c.: "Herrn Universitätsprofessor Dr. Theodor Kolde zu freundlicher Erinnerung. Ansbach 27. April 1906. Frhr. v. Weihern"; b) below, stamp of the old Königliche Bibliothek Erlangen, with accession no.: 72419. S: [s. M/S]. [E]

3. Nuremberg: Germanisches Nationalmuseum. Sig.: G7673. B: heavy paper. C: good. P: clean. M/S: on t.p., bookmark of Frhr. v. Aufseß. S: [s. M/S]. [E]

Severini Boethii
Christlich vernünftiges
Bedenken,

Wie man sich bey vordringendem Gewalt und Wohlergehen der Gottlosen/auch unrechtmässigem Leiden und Ubelgehen der Frommen zu trösten habe/

In fünf Bücher verfasset/

Dem Liebhaber der Teutschen Sprache zu Nutzen aus dem Latein übergesetzt; benebenst richtiger Beschreibung des Boëthii Lebenslaufes.

Nürnberg/
Gedruckt bey Christoff Gerhard/
In Verlegung Johann Taubers.
1 6 6 0.

Title page, *Christlich Vernünftiges Bedenken* (1660)
Herzog August Bibliothek

B 3   CHRISTLICH VERNÜNFTIGES BEDENKEN
       (1660)

Title:

SEVERINI BOETHII | Chriſtlich vernünftiges | Bedenken / | Wie man ſich bey vordrin= | gendem Gewalt und Wohler= | gehen der Gottloſen / auch unrecht= | mäſſigem Leiden und Ubelgehen | der Frommen zu trö= | ſten habe / | Jn fünf Bucher verfaſſet / | Dem Liebhaber der | Teutſchen Sprache zu Nu= | tzen aus dem Latein übergeſetzt; | benebenſt richtiger | Beſchreibung des Boëthii | Lebenslaufes. | *[orn.: 5 x 14 mm.]* | Nürnberg / | Gedruckt bey Chriſtoff Gerhard / | Jn Verlegung Johann Taubers. | 1660.

Collation: 12°:)(¹² A¹² B1-B5 B7 (c B6) B7-B12 C-F¹² G1-G2 G4 (c G3) G4-G12 H-L¹² M⁶; 152 leaves; [$6 - A7, D6, E6, F6, M4, M5, M6; + B7]; pp. [24] 1-276.

Contents:)(1ʳ: fp.)(1ᵛ: [bl.].)(2ʳ: t.p.)(2ᵛ: [bl.].)(3ʳ: ded.: "Den Edlen / Ehrnvesten / Fürsich= | tigen / Hoch= und Wohlweisen | Herren / H. Paul Memminger / [...] | H. Johann Jacob Koch / [...] | Wie auch | Den Edlen und Vesten | H. Ferdinand Jenisch / | H. Wolfgang Achatz | Gutbrod / [...] | Meinen sonders großgünstigen und | hochgeehrten Herren *respectivè* | Gevattern und Schwägern.")(3ᵛ: "Zuschrift.")(10ᵛ: com. poem to Hellwig by C. L. Dietherr: "Auf des [...] Kunst= und Geistvollen Herrn Uberse= | *[tz]*ers anmuhtiges / ewiggrünendes | Lobbeginnen." A1ʳ: "Von dem Lebens=Lauf des | Urhebers dieses Buchs." A7ʳ: [text begins]: "Des | ANIC. MANL. TORQ. | SEVERINUS BOETHIUS, | Vom Trost | aus der Vernunft=Lehre | Erstes Buch." C1ᵛ: "Das Ander Buch." E1ᵛ: "Das Dritte Buch." H1ʳ: "Das Vierdte Buch." K7ʳ: "Das fünfte Buch." M6ʳ: "Nachricht | an den günstigen Leser."

HT] Des | ANIC. MANL. TORQ. | SEVERINUS BOETHIUS, | Vom Trost | aus der Vernunft=Lehre | [Erstes Buch, *etc.*].

RT] [underlined]:)(4ʳ-10ʳ, recto and verso: "Zuschrift." A1ʳ-7ʳ (pp. 2-13), verso: "Lebens= Lauf des Urhebers"; recto: "dieses Buchs." A7ᵛ-M5ʳ, verso: "SEVERINI BOETHII"; recto: *[resp.]* "Erstes", "Anders", "Drittes", "Vierdtes", "Fünftes Buch." Erroneous: K8ʳ: "Vierdtes Buch." (c "Fünftes Buch.").

CW] begin on)(3ʳ: Zuschrift. . Missing: B2ᵛ C12ᵛ. Erroneous: A5ʳ Mœonia [*Mœoniâ*] B2ʳ weder / [weder]

Type: 28 ll. per p. Dimensions: title: 116 x 56 mm.; p. of text: 116 x 56 mm. Style: Frak.; ant. for Latin texts and names. Latin quotations in ital. Gathering sig.: letters, Frak. capitals; nos., roman.

Notes:
Signing: begins)(4.
Illustrations:)(1ʳ: fp. (Boethius in prison visited by Philosophia, with muses in background and book title above; below r.: "P. Troschell font."
Ornamentation: Head vignettes:)(3ᵛ;)(10ᵛ; A1ʳ; A7ʳ; C1ᵛ; E1ᵛ; H1ʳ; K7ʳ. End vignettes:)(12ᵛ; A6ᵛ; G12ᵛ; K6ᵛ; M5ᵛ. Orn. initials:)(3ᵛ "E";)(10ᵛ "W"; A1ʳ "A"; A7ʳ "D"; C1ʳ "N"; E1ᵛ "D"; H1ʳ "J"; K7ʳ "A". Other: t.p. bet. title and place of publication (s. Title);)(4ʳ-10ʳ: "Zuschrift" set within two small orns.;)(11ʳ-12ᵛ: two small orns. in place of RT; M4ᵛ-5ᵛ: p. nos. (instead of RT) set within two small orns.

Commentary: [s. General Introduction: "Translations"]

Bibliographical data: Ersch—Gruber, 254; Faber du Faur I, no. 557; Goedeke, §58, 3; H-A-B, B B601; Kosch, 863; Will—Nopitsch, pt. 6, 58.

Copies:

1. Coburg: Landesbibliothek. Sig.: Sche 208:1. B: orig. parch. C: exc. (ties cut). P: light foxing. M/S: inside f.c.: "I.C.V.S.G.Z." S: Johann Conrad von Scheres, a.k.a. Zieritz (1641-1704). Bound with Justus Sieber, *De salute christiana*, Dresden 1659.

2. Einsiedeln: Stiftsbibliothek. Sig.: Ll 2812. B: orig. parch. C: exc. P: light foxing. M/S: hdwr. on t.p.: "Monrij Einsidlensis 1699". S: since 1699 in Stiftsbibliothek Einsiedeln. [Monrius was monastery's librarian; he was P. Mauritius von Fleckenstein, a Benedictine monk from Einsiedeln, b. 1659; librarian 1685 to ca. 1704].

3. Göttingen: Niedersächsische Staats- und Universitätsbibliothek. Sig.: 8 Auct. Lat. V, 7466. B: reb. in parch.; tooling on spine. C: fair. P: light foxing. M/S: [NR]. S: ?

4. Leipzig: Universitätsbibliothek. Sig.: BST 12° 33. B: reb. in boards. C: fair. P: foxing. M/S: [NR]. S: Deutsche Gesellschaft Leipzig.

5. Munich: Bayerische Staatsbibliothek. Sig.: A. lat. b 79. B: orig. parch. C: fair. P: foxing. M/S: [NR]. S: ?

6. New Haven: Beinecke Rare Book and Manuscript Library. Sig.: Zg17 .H38 .660. B: orig. parch. (spine slightly cracked); on spine, hdwr. titles and residue of old label. C: exc. P: clean. M/S: a) hdwr. inside f.c.: [title]; b) Oettingen-Wallerstein stamp on t.p. S: Faber du Faur; [s. also M/S]. Bound with J. B. Schupp, *Der Geplagte Hiob*. [E]

7. Wolfenbüttel: Herzog August Bibliothek. Sig.: Lh 114. B: orig. leather on boards, with silk ties and gilded fore-edges. C: exc. P: clean. M/S: [none]. S: monastery "Zur Ehre Gottes" in Salzdahlum (bequeathed to H-A-B 1857). [E]

8. Wroclaw: Biblioteka Uniwersytecka. Sig.: 381158. B: reb. (18th or 19th century) in half-leather and boards. C: exc. P: clean. M/S: a) four hdwr. notes: 1.] "Sum ex Libris Gotfridi Stolle Lyg. Siles. Phil. st. A. 1693"; 2.] "B: v. Bältingslawia"; 3.] "Johann David, Raschke, XVIII Jht."; 4.] "Johann Ephraim Scheibel Vrat. 1810 J."; b) stamp: "Bibl. Bernhard. Vratisl." S: former Stadtbibliothek Breslau (sig.: 8 V 294); [s. also M/S].

9. Zurich: Zentralbibliothek. Sig.: Ch 303. B: orig. parch. and boards. C: good. P: foxing. M/S: [NR]. S: ?

10. Zwickau: Ratsschulbibliothek. Sig.: '28.7.19/1'.

C. Occasional Verse

C1. Independent Poems	72
C2. Attributions	86
C3. Verse Inserts	87

Abbreviations: themes and types

    alt = alternating
    aph = aphorism
    art = artifact
    avi = aviary
    buc = bucolic
    coa = coat of arms
    con = congratulatory
    deb = debate
    ded = dedicatory
    dep = departure
    dev = devotional
    did = didactic
    ech = echo
    edi = edifice
    emb = emblematic
    eph = epitaph
    epi = epicedium
    ept = epithalamium
    flo = floral
    gar = garden
    gen = genealogical
    gth = genethliacon
    his = historical
    hun = hunting
    let = letter(s)
    mem = memorial
    mot = motto

myt = myth
nat = nature
ono = onomatopoeic
pan = panegyrical
pra = prayer
rid = riddle
uto = utopian

Abbreviations: bibliographical

attr. = attributed
comp. = companion piece
eul. = eulogy
q.v. = *quod vide*: which see
sig. = signed

Note: The bibliography of occasional verse employs a cumulative ordering system that accounts simultaneously for the number of poems within each of the three parts (independent poems, C1.; attributions, C2.; verse inserts, C3.) as well as the total number of poems (these being noted after a slash (/). There are fifty-seven independent poems (C1.1 through C1.57); ten attributions (C2.1/58 through C2.10/67); and 218 verse inserts (C3.1/68 through C3.218/285). Each entry begins with the first line or semantic unit of the poem. There follow: a) abbreviation of poem's thematic type; b) addressee, with brief identification; c) form of Hellwig's signature; d) eulogist or conferrer. A new paragraph gives a truncated version of the title of collection in which poem is found. Bibliographical data, as well as page or leaf reference and language of poem, are provided in square brackets. For full bibliographical information, short-titles are keyed to Bibliographical Resources.

Etsi quis claudit, velut hæc pia fœmina clausit,
In terris meliùs claudere nemọ potest.
    Feci teslandi affectus & debiti honoris
Ergaq; Præclarum Agnatum patris inſtar amandum
          Sebastianus Kobius
            Hilperh. Franc.

S Iſte Tuas lacrumas, Tua nam dulciſſima Conjux
    Percipit in templo gaudia pura poli.
Vixit: ſed fragilem vitam, jam vivit in ævum,
    Linque modò, factum eſt ſic ſtatuente DEO.
Quiſquis ex exemplo hoc vitam bene vivere diſce,
    Reſpice! Res hominum, quàm facilè urna premat.
           Pij affectus ergò F. Georg. Sig. Fürst.

V Ita quid est hominum? Flos eſt, qui tempore verno
    Pulchrè habet, at vento concutiente perit.
Eſt eadem navis multis expoſta procellis,
    Quam varij erroris millè pericla premunt,
Dùm mundi pelagus cunctarum turbine rerum
    Æſtuat, & denſis volviturusq; malis.
Fœlix ò nimium, cui recto tendere clavo
    Et curſu placido littus arare datur.
Ergò igitur Vir Clare tuo moderare dolori,
    Siquoq; FLos perijt Conjugis ille tuæ.
Quid? perijt non, non. Sed tranſitione beatâ
    Elyſijs campis perpeté honore viret.
Et jam nunc poſtu postor tot discrimina gaudet,
    Curarumq; expers nullâ pericla timet.
Namq; piorum animæ Cœleſti ſede morantur,
    Exulat hinc omnis, poſt laboratq; dolor.

Hæc

Hæc reputans, lachrymas abſterge & lumina ſicca:
    Namq; redire negat, eos jubet ILLA ſequi.
          Teſtandi affectus ergò ſteriliſ venâ f.
            Johannes Helvvigius Noricus.

M ORS HELENAM RAPVIT: ſic qui non cœlica doctus
    Scita ſit, ingeminet: Sancto nos nomine Chriſti
Gaudentes aliter, KOBI: DEVS ABSTVLIT ILLAM.
Nec non & fœtum materno viſcere clauſum.
Optimus ille Pater, quondam cum venerit hora,
Judicij magni, vita revocabit ad auras
Illos, qui recubant durâ ſub mole ſepulchri;
    Idem conſortem thalami, & tot pignora dulce
Reſtituet tibi, vosque omnes cæli axe locabit.
Fœlicem fauſtumquè diem, qui talia nobis
Cernere permittet: Fiet, puto, tempore primo.
           Ηʹ ſiandα συμπαθείας faciéb.
           Tobias Vnderholtzer Norib.

F Erreus ille quidem, ferro vel durior ipſo
    Sit, quem non tua ſors aſperrima tangat & angat.
Quando tibi moritur Conjux digniſſima vitâ,
    Virgo, delicium Muſæ gentisq; amorq;
KOBI, delicium Muſæ gentis amorq;
    Heu mihi! poſt ſenos infauſto ſidere partus,
Nunc ipſo perijt tandem cum pignore Mater,
    Inq; ſuâ prolem non-natam condidit alvo.
Hoc tibi cordolium KOBI eſt, hoc luctus acerbus.
    Attamen hunc tantum minuatq; levetq; dolorem
Unum velle DEI, qui, quod dedit, abſtulit idem.
    Sit nomen Domini benedictum. Scilicet obṛ
Ille etiam reddes multo cum fœnore vitæ.

Et Ma-

"Vita quid est hominum?"
epicedium for Elena Kob (1629)
Universitätsbibliothek, Erlangen

C1.   Independent Poems

1629

C1.1 "VIta quid est hominum?" Epi, Altdorf, for Elena Kob née Bärnbeck (wife of Johann Kob, professor of philosophy, Altdorf University); sig.: Johannes Helwigius Noricus; eul.: Georg König.

> In: **LeichSermon | Bey der Chriſtlichen und | Volckreichen Begräbnuß / der Erbarn und | Vieltugendreichen Frawen ELENA [...]**. Altdorf: Balthasar Scherffen. F3^v-4^r. 18 ll., Lat. [Trew: Thl. XIX, 83/28]. [E]

1638

C1.2 "SAucius ad costas heu!" Ept, Nuremberg, for Johann Kob (professor of law, Altdorf University) and Maria Müllich née Trammel; sig.: Johannes Helwigius Phil. & Med. D.

> In: *Ευφημιαι* | *Viro Clariβimo,* | Dn. JOHANNI KOBIO, | [...]. *Ob secundas Nuptias* | *Cum* | *Lectiβimâ omniumque virtutum genere ſplen-* | *didiſſimâ feminâ* | MARIA MÜLLICHIA [...]. Nürnberg: Jeremia Dümler. No. VII. A4^v. 16 ll., Lat. [StBN: Gen K. 50,1 (2 copies)]. [E]

1640

C1.3 "LŒFLHOLTZI vitæ dum rumpunt." Epi, Nuremberg, for Johann Friderich Löffelholtz, b. 1587 (Nuremberg *Septemvir* and rector); sig.: Iohannes Hellwigius Phil. & Med. Doctor; eul.: Nicolaus Rittershausen.

In: Laudatio Funebris | *Magnifico, Ampliβimo, Nobiliβimo &* | *Prudentiβimo* | *Viro Domino* | JOHANNI-FRIDE- | RICO LÖFFELHOLTZIO à | Colberg [...]. Altdorf: [n.p.]. No. XII. 12 ll., Lat. [= Cato: O2ᵛ. Koch: No. 3535; Trew: Thl (XIX,1); GNM: Merkel D 2039]. [E]

C1.4 "O Todt! ô grimmer Todt!" Epi [comp. to "LOEFLHOLTZI vitæ dum rumpunt", *q.v.*]. O2ᵛ-3ʳ. 14 ll., Ger. [E]

1643

C1.5 "GLeichwie der Blumen Pracht." Epi, Nuremberg, for Christoph Jacob Pömer (son of Albrecht Pömer); sig.: Johannes Hellwigius, Phil. & Med. Doctor; eul.: Cornelius Marci.

In: Emblema Idumæi, | Oder | Hiobs Sinn=Bild / | Von der auffgehenden und Abfallenden | Menschen=Blum: [...]. | Bey trawriger Leichbegängnus | Deß Edlen und Veſten / | Chriſtoph=Jacob | Pömers [...]. [Nürnberg: n.p.]. No. II. F1ʳ. 14 ll., Ger. [Trew: Altd. Anh. 11/b 28]. [E]

1644

C1.6 "HUc quis gregales accelerans." Ept, Nuremberg, for Carl Erasmus Tetzel (son of Johann Jacob Tetzel) and Anna Felicitas née Haller (daughter of Johann Albert Haller); sig.: Johannes Hellwigius, D.

In: *MELIMELA GAMICA* | In raros Honores & feſtivas Nuptiarum ſolennitates [...]. Nürnberg: Endter. A3ᵛ-4ʳ. 28 ll., Lat. [Trew: Sch. L. 208 ᵇ/3]. [E]

C1.7 "MIrandos Neonymphe geris quos." Ept [comp. to "HUc quis gregales accelerans," *q.v.*], for Hieronymus Wilhelm Schlüsselfelder (Hellwig's brother-in-law; son of Carl Schlüsselfelder) and Maria Salome née Tetzel (daughter of Johann Jacob Tetzel). A4ʳ⁻ᵛ. 20 ll., [Ger.]/Lat./Ger. [E]

C1.8 "DEmum sollicitus dies peractus." Ept, Nuremberg, for Michael Ruprecht Besler (Nuremberg physician, member of Collegium Medicum) and Catharina Barbara née Rosa (daughter of Johann Rosa); sig.: Johannes Hellwigius, Phil. & Medic. Doct.

> In: ROSETVM NVPTIA- | LE CONCINNATITIUM, | IN HONOREM | SPONSI, | *Viri Clariſſimi, Excellentiſſimi & Experientiſſimi,* | Dn. MICH. RUP. BESLERI, | [...] ac SPONSÆ, | *Rectiſſimæ & Florentiſſimæ Virginis,* | CATHARINÆ BARBARÆ [...]. Nürnberg: Wolfgang Endter. No. XVIII. B4ᵛ-C1ʳ. 16 ll., Lat. [Trew-Sched.: 1011*]. [E]

C1.9 "TRaurigkeit weiche nun völlig." Ept [comp. to "DEmum sollicitus dies peractus," *q.v.*]. C1ʳ⁻ᵛ. 30 ll., Ger. [E]

C1.10 "SIste gradum properas quamvis." Epi, Nuremberg, for Johann Gravius (poet laureat and rector of St. Egidien Gymnasium, Nuremberg); sig.: Johannes Helwigius D.; eul.: Johann Gundermann.

> In: **Lob und Lohn** | **der Knechte Gottes** [...]. | **Bey der Volckreichen Leich=Verſamblung** | **Deß Erbarn / Achtbarn** | **und Wolgelehrten Herrn Johannis Graven** [...]. [n.p.: n.p.]. D3ᵛ. 8 ll., Lat. [LkAN: Nbg St. Joh. 55/7; GNM: Merkel 2037; Trew: Thl IX, 68/31 (alt:40]. [E]

1646

C1.11 "NArcissis, violis, tulipis, ne." Epi, Nuremberg, for Johann Jacob Tetzel (Nuremberg *Septemvir*, former president of Collegium Medicum); sig.: Johannes Hellvvigius, D.).

> In: THRENODIÆ | *Beatis Manibus* | VIRI | *MAGNIFICI, NOBILISSIMI,* | *maximè Strenui atque Prudentiſſimi,* | DN. JOHANNIS IACOBI | TETZELII, | à **Kirchenſittenbach** [...]. Nürnberg: Endter. No. XIX. C3ʳ⁻ᵛ. 18 ll., Lat. [Leipzig: Vit. N 2290; LkAN: Nbg St. Joh. 55/13]. [E]

C1.12 "SInget Klag= und Traurenlieder!" Epi [comp. to "NArcissis, violis, tulipis, ne," *q.v.*]. C3ᵛ-D1ʳ. 80 ll., Ger. [E]

C1.13 "ALterius quicunque lubens // derodit." Ded, Nuremberg, to the reader; sig.: Johannes Hellvvigius, D.

In: Georg Philipp Harsdörffer: Specimen Philologiæ Germanicæ. Nürnberg: Wolfgang Endter. No. IV.)()()()(7^{r-v}. 6 ll., Lat. [Faber du Faur: I, no. 503]. [E]

C1.14 "COrporis haud nævos sic." Epi, Nuremberg, for Wolfgang Stöberlin (elder member of Nuremberg's College of Pharmacists); sig.: Johann Hellwig der Artzney Doctor.

In: THRENODIÆ | Beatis Manibus | VIRI | Integerrimi & Peritiſſimi | DN. WOLFGANGI STÖBERLINI [...]. Nürnberg: Sartorius. No. IX. B1^r. 4 ll., Lat. [StBN: Gen. S. 206,3]. [E]

C1.15 "NImmer so der Kräuterkrafft." Epi [comp. to "COrporis haud nævos sic," *q.v.*]. B1^r. 4 ll., Ger. [E]

C1.16 "STadt / Rath / Kirch / Schul." Epi [comp. to "COrporis haud nævos sic," *q.v.*]. B1^r. 4 ll., Ger. [E]

C1.17 "UT quæ horto prætexta." Ept, Nuremberg, for Johann Leonard Fürer and Anna Elisabeth née Schlüsselfelder (daughter of Wilibald Schlüsselfelder); sig.: Johannes Hellvvigius, D.

In: VOTA SECUNDA, | *Secundis Nuptiis* | VIRI | *Genere, Virtute & Eruditione Nobi-* | *lisſimi,* | JOANNIS LEONARDI | FURERI ab Haimendorff, | *Sponſi;* | Ut & | *Nobilisſimæ Florentisſimæque Virginis,* | ANNÆ ELISABETHÆ [...]. Nürnberg: Wolfgang Endter. No. IV. A3^r. 4 ll., Lat. [StBN (2 copies): Gen. F. 57, 124 and 128]. [E]

C1.18 "DEn Garten nicht allein aus Zier." Ept [comp. to "UT quæ horto prætexta," *q.v.*]. A3^r. 4 ll., Ger. [E]

C1.19 "SIc Pegnesiacas modulatus Pastor." Ded, Nuremberg, to the Nuremberg Stadtrat.

In: *Noris*, A4^v. 10 ll., Lat. [E]

C1.20 "SEyn dann künftig unser Auen." Dep, Nuremberg, for Sigmund Betulius; sig.: J. H. In: "Die Pegnitz an den Floridan," no. II.

In: *Noris*, p. 70, 9 ll., Ger. [E]. Reproduced 1669 in: SvB/ *Guelfis*, 127, with editorial changes, as: "Sind dann künftig unsre Auen," 12 ll.; reproduced in Birken's *Biographia* (rpt. in Jöns—Laufhütte, 37), with additional variants, 12 ll. [E]

1647

C1.21 "NOn benè, qui benè." Pan, Nuremberg, for Ernst Christoph Homburg (poet, 1605-1681); sig.: Johann Hellwig/D.

In: Ernst Christoph Homburg: **J. Cats Selbſtſtreit / | das iſt / | Kräfftige Bewegung deß Fleiſches | wider den Geiſt.** Nürnberg: Wolfgang Endter. No. II. A7^r. 6 ll., Lat. [Faber du Faur: II, no. 258a]. [E]

C1.22 "HIer spielt die Liebe nicht." Pan [comp. to "Non benè, qui benè," *q.v.*]. A7^v-8^r. 12 ll., Ger. [E]

C1.23 "NOn hunc sævities morbi." Epi, Nuremberg, for Johann Saubert, b. 1592 (pastor of Nuremberg's St. Sebald's Church; sig.: Johann Hellwig/D.; eul.: Michael Weber.

In: ΘPHNΩΔIAI | *in* | Beatiſſimum quidem, ſed toti CHRISTI Eccle- | ſiæ obitum luctuoſiſſimum | *VIRI* | *Plurimum Reverendi, Excellentiſſ. Clariſſimi* | DN. JOHANNIS | SAUBERTI [...]. Appended to: **Chriſtliche Trawr= und Leich= | predigt /** | [...] **Bey der Volckreichen / Trawrigen | Leichbeſtattung | Deß Geiſtreichen und werthen Manns /** | **Herrn** | JOHANNIS SAUBERTI [...]. Nürnberg: Wolfgang Endter. No. XXV. C1^r. 8 ll., Lat. [Leipzig: Vit. N 2038; Stolberg: IV/1, no. 19673; Trew: T 642/2]. [E]

C1.24 "KRank seyn mich nicht bekränkt." Epi [comp. to "Non hunc sævities morbi," *q.v.*]. C1^v-2^r. 52 ll., Ger. [E]

1648

C1.25 "EDle Herren / Edle Frau / Edle Jungfer." Ded, Nuremberg, for Ferdinand Jenisch, Georg Seyfried Koler, Maria Sabina Jenisch née Koler, and Anna Philipina née Koler; sig.: J. H. D. beygenannt Montano.

In: *Neunhof*, A2^{r-v}. 36 ll., Ger. [E]

C1.26 "SI quid Nobilitas, Pietas." Epi, Nuremberg, for Johann Jodoc Schmidmajer (Nuremberg *Ratsherr*); sig.: Johann Hellwig/D.; eul.: Johann Paul Felwinger.

In: POST FUNERA | VIRTUS | Nobiliſſimi atque Præſtrenui | DN. JOHANNIS JODOCI **Schmid**= | **majers** [...]. Nürnberg: Jeremia Dümler. No. VII. F2^v. 10 ll., Lat. [Trew: Thl. XIX, 74/3, bzw. 91/2ª; GNM: Merkel 2039; LkAN: Nbg St. Joh. 55/17]. [E]

C1.27 "Wann rett der Adelstand." Epi [comp. to "SI quid Nobilitas, Pietas," *q.v.*]. F2^v. 8 ll., Ger. [E]

C1.28 "ACh Fried! was Friedgeschrey?" Epi, Nuremberg, for Paul Jenisch, b. 1602 (evangelical pastor in Augsburg); sig.: Johann Hellwig der Artzney Doctor und Physicus ordinarius in Nürnberg; eul.: Philipp Weber.

In: **Der Gerechten** | **Sichere Rühe / und rühige Sicherheit /** | **nach trauriger Chriſtlichen Leichbegängnuß** | **Deß** | **Weiland Ehrwürdigen /** | **und Wolgelehrten Herrn** M. PAVLI | **Jenischen** [...] | **seel.** | **Gedächtnuß.** Augsburg: Johann Schönigk. No. XX. G1^{r-v}. 64 ll., Ger. [Stolberg: II, no. 13332; Trew: Thl. XIX, 91/9]. [E]

C1.29 "COnjugium jugum & est blandum." Ept, Nuremberg, for Wilhelm Imhof (son of Wilhelm Imhof) and Maria Helena née Pömer (daughter of Albert Pömer); sig.: Johannes Hellwigius D.

In: ARA NUPTIALIS, | *Nobilißimo ac Splendidißimo* | DN. GUILIELMO IM HOFIO, | [...] NEC NON | *Nobiliſſimæ pariter & Florentiſſimæ Virgini,* | MARIÆ HELENÆ [...]. Nürnberg: Jeremia Dümler. No. IX. A3^v. 4 ll., Lat. [StBN: Gen. I 1,97]. [E]

C1.30 "Der Ehestand scheinet." Ept [comp. to "COnjugium jugum & est blandum," *q.v.*]. A3ᵛ. 4 ll., Ger. [E]

C1.31 "In GNATO fulget GENITORIS." Ded, Nuremberg, to Duke Anton Ulrich of Braunschweig-Lüneburg, b. 1633; sig.: J. H. D.

In: *Ormund*, (*) 6ʳ. 4 ll., Lat. [E]

C1.32 "Non glyptes faciem poterat." Pan, Nuremberg, for Francesco Pona (author of *L'Ormondo*, 1635); sig.: I. H. D.

In: *Ormund*, (*) 7ʳ. 4 ll., Lat. [E]

C1.33 "ES kan deß Künstlers Kunst." Pan [comp. to "Non glyptes faciem poterat," *q.v.*]. (*) 7ʳ. 4 ll., Ger. [E]

1649

C1.34 "LAus est sub Patriæ molli." Epi, Nuremberg, for Lukas Friedrich Behaim, 1587-1648 (Nuremberg *Septemvir*); sig.: Johannes Hellwigius, D; eul.: Wilhelm Ludwell.

In: *LAUDATIO FUNEBRIS* | VIRI | *Magnifici, Nobiliſſimi, Ampliſſimi, longèque* | *Prudentißimi* | Dn. LUCÆ FRIDERICI | **BEHAIM** [...]. Nürnberg: Wolfgang Endter. No. VII. Pp. 38-39. 10 ll., Lat. [GNM: Merkel D 2039]. [E]

C1.35 "WOl dem / den ruhig deckt." Epi [comp. to "LAus est sub Patriæ molli," *q.v.*]. P. 39. 12 ll., Ger. [E]

In tumulum.

HOrarum Vir cunctarum pietate secundus
nulli, Nœslerus, conditur hoc tumulo.
Rarus & insignis Medicus, faciliscq; Poëta:
& gravis Orator, Philosophumcq; decus.
Præceptori & Fautori de me optimè merito ponebam ingens
Johannes Fabricius, Norimbergæ
ad D. Mariæ Pastor.

Qui puer antè fuit, juvenis plenuscq; vigore,
Adhc senectutem carpere capit iter:
Quin varias hominum relevavit corpora morbis,
In stygioscq; stitit gurgite mortis aquas.
Mors tamen obrepsit nullo medicamine abacta,
Injecitcq; suas intremefacta manus.
Sed quid? an Elysias mors hunc non duxit ad oras,
Læta ubi perpetuô gaudia fonte fluunt.

Mœstus pos.
Georgius König, D. & P. P.

MArchia quem genuit, decoravit & Iala Tellus
Lauru, Doctorem Norica Musa colit,
Nunc lugent Proceres, planctu comitantur & ægri;
Defuncti tumulum viscera præda manent.
Assidethic busto Medicina, illicq; lacessunt
Se mœrore Sophi, squalida Suada jacet.
Tum Charites cineres simul & Polymathesis ornant
Floribus Elysiis, Famacq; dictat epos:
NOESSLERI exuvias quamvis tegit urna GEORGI,
Ast se semajor Spiritus Astra petit.
Dn. Præceptoris, Hospitis & Affinis quon-
dam suspiis cineribus ευχαιμονως ξ
Δυτηρώς apposuit & scripsit Ratisbonæ
Johannes Hellwigius, Phil. & Med. D.
p. t. Reverendiss. & Illustr. Principi & E-
piscopo Ratisb. à consiliis medicis.

FAta salutiferis tardans aliena medelis
Fato NOESLERUS cessit & ipse levi.
Igneus ingenii vigor, aurea verba magistri
Pulpita Phœbigenum destituére gravis.
Attamen ille sui meliori parte superstes
Numinis ætheria sedebeatus agit.
Joannes Rhodius
Patavii

NOESSLERI ad tumulum, cum MUSIS plorat APOLLO,
& lacrymis CHARITUM lumina mœsta madent.
Cur? Quia MUSARUM, CHARITUMcq; & APOLLINIS, isthoc
in Cultore suo, corruit hospitium.
Sed quid opus nobis, geniles ponere voces?
Quassa ACADEMIÆ nota columna ruit.
Servet EAM DEUS, & tueantur amentcq; PATRONI:
Artium ut emineat tam celebrata domus!
Lugens tantis Viris, & Amici since-
rissimi mortem Lmcq; F.
Norimbergæ
Joh. Michaël Dilherrus,
Pastor ad S. Sebaldi
& Prof. P.

HEu lachrymosa dies, nigroscq; notanda lapillo!
quâ Nœsler sævâ morte peremptus obit!
Ingenio magnus, doctrinâ & arte celebris;
Alter Aristoteles, alter & Hippocrates:
Pharmaca qui quondam languentibus apta parasti,
Ipse tibi moriens nulla parare potes

E 2   Hora-

1650

C1.36 "MArchia quem genuit, decoravit." Epi, Regensburg, for Georg Nößler, b. 1591 (professor of medicine and Hellwig's "Tischwirt" at Altdorf University); sig.: Johannes Hellwigius, Phil. & Med. D. p.t. Reverendiss. & Illustr. Principi & Episcopo Ratisb. a consiliis medicis; eul.: Georg König.

In: **Leich=Sermon | Bey der anſehlichen und Volckreichen / doch Trau= | rigen begräbnüß | Deß | Weyland Edlē / Ehrn= | veſten und Hochgelärten Herrn Georg | Nößlers** [...]. Altdorf: Georg Hagen. E2^r. 10 ll., Lat. [Stolberg: III, no. 17261; Trew: 1059*]. [E]

C1.37 "QUod cœco baculus, Prætori." Con, Regensburg, to Justus Hieronymus Kestel, on becoming a doctor of law; sig.: Johannes Hellwigius D.; bestowed by Johann Kob, Dean of Faculty of Law, Altdorf University.

In: CARMINA GRATULATORIA | IN HONOREM ET GRATIAM | *NOBILIS ET AMPLISSIMI* | VIRI | DN. JUSTI HIERONYMI KESTELII | NORIBERGENSIS, INCLYTÆ REIP. | RATISBONENSIS PRÆTORIS [...]. Altdorf: Georg Hagen. No. IIX. A4^r. 6 ll., Lat. [Trew: Altd. Anh. 9/35]. [E]

C1.38 "HIs Patriæ cecinit MONTANUS." Dep, Regensburg, on his departure from Nuremberg; [unsigned].

In: *Noris*, 2C3^v [p. 198]. 8 ll., Lat. [E]

1654

C1.39 "PRæfica! quæ sese vox." Epi, Regensburg, for Johann Christoph Schlüsselfelder, b. 1613 (Nuremberg *Ratsherr*); sig.: Johannes Hellwig, Phil. & Med. Doctor, ac Reverendissimo Episcopo Ratisponensi p.t. a consiliis medicis; eul.: Johann Michael Dilherr.

In: Sichere | Seelen=Verwahrung | eines glaubigen Chriſten / | [...] bei | trauriger und Volckreicher | Leichbeſtattung | Des | Edlen / Ehrnveſten / Fürſichtigen und Wohlweiſen | Herrn Johann Chriſtoph | Schlüſſelfelders [...]. Nürnberg: Wolfgang Endter d. Ä. No. V. C4ʳ⁻ᵛ. 16 ll. + emblem, Lat. [Leipzig: Vit. N 2082; Stolberg: IV/1, no. 20153]. [E]

1655

C1.40 "ICh weiß nicht wie mir ist." Epi, Regensburg, for Anna Rosina Heberlein née Geissenhausser, b. 1632 (wife of Johann Paul Heberlein, corector of Regensburg Gymnasium); sig.: Johann Hellwig D.; eul.: Matthaeus Schmoll.

In: [...] Zu letzten Chriſtlichen Ehren / | Als ein | Gedächtnuß und Grabmahl / | Der EhrenTugendreichen Frawen | ANNÆ ROSINÆ [...]. Regensburg: Christoff Fischer. No. II. D1ᵛ-2ᵛ. 56 ll., Ger. [Stolberg: II, no. 10037]. [E]

C1.41 "COrpore cum socio si Spiritus." Epi, Regensburg, for Christoff Sigmund Donauer, b. 1593 (Regensburg evangelical pastor); sig.: Johannes Hellvvig D.; eul.: Christoff Adam Rüden.

In: EPICEDIA, | Beatiſsimæ Memoriæ, | PERQUAM | *Reverendi, Excellentiſſimi, Clariſſimique* | DN. CHRISTOPHORI | SIGISMUNDI DONAVERI [...]. In: [...] **Bey anſehnlicher und ſehr Volckreicher | Begräbnuß | Des weiland WolEhrwürdigen / GroßAchtbarn | und Hochgelährten Herrn | Chriſtoff Sigmund | Donauers** [...]. Regensburg: Christoff Fischer. No. IV. H1ʳ⁻ᵛ. 24 ll., Lat. [Stolberg: I, no. 7429]. [E]

1656

C1.42 "REgis cum officium est." Epi, Regensburg, for Georg König (professor of theology and former rector of Altdorf University); sig.: Johannes Hellwig, Phil. & Med. Doctor; eul.: Johann Conrad Dürr.

In: VIRTUTES ET MERITA | VIRI | *Perquàm Reverendi,* *Amplißimi atque Excellentißimi* | *DN.* GEORGII KÖNIG [...]. Nürnberg: Wolfgang d. J. and Johann Endter. No. XXXV. E4ᵛ. 8 ll., Lat. [Trew: Ltg. II, 118ª/5]. [E]

C1.43 "IS DEUS AGRICOLÆ qui." Ept, Regensburg, for Hieronymus Agricola (Regensburg jurist) and Catharina Barbara née Donauer (daughter of Christoph Sigismund Donauer); sig.: Johannes Hellvvig D.

In: ΕΥΦΗΜΙΑΙ, | Nobili, Ampliſs. & Conſultiſs. VIRO, | DN. HIERONYMO AGRI- | COLÆ [...] | Cum | [...] | CATHARINA BARBARA [...]. Regensburg: Christoff Fischer. No. V. A3ʳ. 8 ll., Lat. [Trew: Altd. Anh. 9/71]. [E]

1658

C1.44 "NOridos in gemitus Pastores." Epi, Regensburg, for Georg Philipp Harsdörffer, b. 1607 (poet, polymath, and Nuremberg *Ratsherr*); sig.: Johannes Hellwigius, Phil. & Med. Doctor; eul.: Johann Michael Dilherr.

In: **Der Menſchen Stand** | **in GOTTES Hand.** | [...] | **Bei** | **Volckreicher und Trübſeeliger Leichbegängnis** | **Deß** | **Wohl=Edlen / Geſtrengen / Fürſichtigen und** | **Hochweiſen Herrn** | **Georg Philipp Hars=** | **dörffers** [...]. Nürnberg: Wolffgang Endter d. J. E2ʳ. 12 ll., Lat. [Stolberg: II, no. 11413; Trew: 4 Thl. XIX, 92]. [E]

1660

C1.45 "FLebilis heu! tenor est Fati." Epi, Regensburg, for Peter Portner, b. 1580 (elder Regensburg *Ratsherr*); sig.: Johannes Hellvvig D.; eul.: Erasmus Gruber.

In: **Chriſtliche Betrachtung der heilſamen** | **Sterbe=Kunſt** [...]. | **Bey Chriſtlicher / Anſehenlicher / und überauß Volckreicher** | **Begräbnuß /** | **Des WolEdlen / Geſtrengen / Fürſichtigen /** | **und** | **Hochweiſen Herren** | **PETRI Portnern** [...]. Regensburg: Christoff Fischer. No. VII. F3ᵛ-4ʳ. 26 ll., Lat. [Stolberg: III, no. 18109]. [E]

1661

C1.46 "PAcem alij celebrent multo." Epi, Regensburg, for Simon Göring, b. 1584 (Creussen *Altbürgermeister*); sig.: Johannes Hellwig, Phil. & Med. D. ac p.t. Eminentissimo & Illustrissimo Cardinali Wartenberg a Consiliis medicis; eul.: Johann Leonhard Rinder.

In: חֲ]] | BEATEMORIENTIUM | ΧΑΡΑΝΙΚΙΟΦΩΝΗΣΙΣ. | Das ißt / | | Vierfacher Freud= und Siegesruff | Des Hocherleuchten Apoßtels Pauli [...] | Und im Leben und Sterben wol vermercket / | Von dem | Edlen / Ehrnveßten / Fürßichtigen und | Wolweißen | H. Simon Göring [...]. Bayreuth: Johann Gebhardt. No. V. G1ʳ. 16 ll., Lat. [Stolberg: II, no. 10644; Trew: Thl. XIX, 201/284]. [E]

C1.47 "PLaudite Pastores; sertum de flore." Pan, Regensburg, for Georg Philipp Harsdörffer (author of tr.); sig. Ioh. Hellwig, D.

In: **Der schönen** | **DIANA** | **Dritter Theil /** | **Jn fünff Büchern be=** | **griffen.** In: **DIANA,** | **Von** | **H. J. De Monte-Major** [...]. Parts 1-2 tr. by Johann Ludwig Freiherr von Kueffstein. Part 3 tr. by Georg Philipp Harsdörffer [orig. by C. Gil Polo]. Nürnberg: Michael Endter. No. I. M1ʳ. 8 ll., Lat. [Faber du Faur: I, no. 513]. [E]

1669

C1.48 "SI Pietas, animi integritas." Epi, Regensburg, for Anna Maria Schorer née See, b. 1637 (wife of Rupprecht Schorer, Regensburg *Ratsherr*); sig.: Johannes Hellwig D.; eul.: Christoph Sigmund Donauer.

In: SPIRITUALIS FIDEI CLYPEUS | **Geißtlicher** | **Glaubens=** **Schild:** | [...] **Bey der traurigen und ßehr Volckreichē** **Leichbeßtattung** | **Der Weyland** | **Edlen / viel Ehr und** **Tugendreichen** | **FRAUEN** | ANNÆ MARIÆ | **Schorerin /** **gebornen Seein** [...]. Regensburg: Christoff Fischer. Nr. VIII. F1ᵛ. 16 ll., Lat. [Leipzig: Fam. nob. et civ. 1029 ᵈ/16; Stolberg: IV/1, no. 20490]. [E]

C1.49 "INsignes planctus insignia pectora." Epi, Regensburg, for Johann Michael Dilherr, b. 1604 (Nuremberg pastor of St. Sebald's Church); sig.: Johannes Hellvvig, Phil. & Med. Doctor; eul.: Adolf Saubert.

In: **Tauben=Raſt der Chriſten=Seelen / | In deß Lebens=Felſes Hölen.**[...] **| Bej anſehlich=volkreicher/doch höchſtbetrauerlicher | Leichbegängnis / | Deß | WolEhrwürdig= und Hochgelehrten Herrn | Johann Michael Dilherrn** [...]. Nürnberg: Johann und Wolfgang Endter. No. IV. Pp. 7-8. 22 ll., Lat. [Darmstadt: 331 (8); H-A-B: Wa 1243; SB-PK: Ee 700-696; Trew: T 948 b]. [E]

C1.50 "MArmore quid latitat?" Epi, Regensburg, for Anna Maria Winckler née Stetten, b. 1640 (wife of Benedict Winckler von Döliz); sig.: Johannes Hellwig, Phil. & Med. Doctor, Collegii Medici Norimbergensis, ejusdemque Facultatis in Repubi. Ratisp. Senior; eul.: Georg Paul Jenisch.

In: **Vil=geplagtes | aber auch | GOtt=gelaſſenes Hiob-Hertz |** [...]. **Bey Volckreicher und wehmütiger Leich=Beſtattung | Der weiland | Wol=Edlen / VilEhr= und Tugendreichen | Frauen | ANNA MARIA** [...]. Augsburg: Jacob Koppmayer. d1ʳᵛ. 18 ll., Lat. [Stolberg: IV/1, no. 21501]. [E]

C1.51 "ACh wie thöricht!" Epi [comp. to "MArmore quid latitat?" *q.v.*]. d1ᵛ-2ʳ. 32 ll., Ger. [E]

1670

C1.52 "HAtte Treu / und Redlichkeit." Epi, Regensburg, for Bartholomaeus Fräntzel, b. 1605 (Regensburg *Ratsherr*); sig.: Johann Hellwig D.; eul.: Johann Georg Lang.

In: **Heilige Walfarth | Frommer Chriſten über drey unumbgängliche | Angſt-Berge |** [...]. **| Bey Chriſtlicher Volckreicher Leichbeſtattung | Des Weilandt | Edlen / Veſten / Fürſichtigen und Wolweiſen | HERRN | Bartholome Fräntzeln** [...]. Regensburg: Christoff Fischer. No. VIII. E4ʳ. 12 ll., Ger. [Laubach: Lud K 6.51; Stolberg: I, no. 9057]. [E]

C1.53 "Cum LUX, CRUX, SORS, MORS." Epi, Regensburg, for Isabella Jacobe Syroth née Schiltel, b. 1617 (wife of Emmeran Syroth, Regensburg *Ratsherr*); sig.: Johannes Helwigius Phil. & Medic. Doctor, & facultatis suæ Senior; eul.: Johann Georg Lang.

> In: Epicedia | *Nobilißimæ Dominæ,* | DN. ISABELLÆ IACOBES [...]. In: PIORUM | *GRAVAMEN & LEVAMEN.* | Das iſt: | [...] | **Bey Hochanſehnlicher und Volckreicher | Leichbeſtattung | Der Weiland | WohlEdlen / Hoch und viel Ehrentugendreichen | FRAUEN | Iſabella Jacobe Syrothin** [...]. Regensburg: Christoff Fischer, 1671. No. VI. [F1ᵛ] 16 ll., Lat. [Laubach: Lud K 6.71; Stolberg: IV/2, no. 24582]. [E]

1674

C1.54 "QUI vitam multis potuit servare." Epi, Regensburg, for Johann Lehner, b. 1623 (Regensburg physician); sig.: Johannes Helwig, Phil. & Medicinæ Doctor; eul.: Christoph Sigmund Donauer.

> In: PIORUM | CERTAMINA ET PRŒMIA: | [...]. | **Bey der traurigen und ſehr Volckreichen | Leich=Beſtattung | Des Weyland | Edlen / Veſten und Hochgelehrten | HERRN | Johann Lehners** [...]. Regensburg: Paul Dalnsteiner. No. III. A2ᵛ. 10 ll., Lat. [Stolberg: II, no. 14949]. [E]

[Incomplete or unconfirmed]

C1.55 "Egregium molitur opus dum." Pan, for Georg Queck, 1596-1632 (Nuremberg physician and former rector of Altdorf University); sig.: Johannes Hellwig Phil. et Med. Doctor.

> In: Port. coll., Nuremberg. Artist: Johann Pfann. 6 ll., Lat.

C1.56 "Cuor forte rompe la cattiua forte." Nuremberg; sig.: à Johanne Hellwigio Phil. et Med. Doctore, et ibidem Patriæ Reipub. Physico ordinario. In: [autograph, 6 October 1636]. 5 ll., Lat. [BaySb].

C1.57 Ept, Nuremberg, for Johann Sext (fellow P.Bl.O. poet and typographer-corrector for Endter publishers) and Susanna née Grünwald (daughter of Johann Grünwald).

In: SUCCLAMATIONES VOTIVÆ, | VIRO | Præ ſtantis ſimo atque Eruditis ſimo, | DN. JOHANNI SEXTO: | [...] | Ac | VIRGINI | Lectis ſimæ & Pudicis ſimæ, | SUSANNÆ [...]. [n.p.: n.p.]. A3ᵛ. [in Nuremberg].

C2. Attributions

C2.1/58 "Freylich es will sich gebühren." Ept, Nuremberg, for Johann Röder und Maria Rosina née Schmid; attr. to: Montano / der Hägende. In: **Lu ſtgedicht | Zu hochzeitlichem Ehrenbegängniß | Herrn D. | Johann Röders / | und | Jungfer | Maria Roſina Schmidin / | auf | der ſiebenröhrigen Schilffpfeiffen | Pans | wolmeinend | geſpielet | von den Pegnitzhirten.** Nürnberg: Wolfgang Endter. A1ᵛ. No. I. 7 ll., Ger. [Faber du Faur: I, no. 516, (2 copies)]. [E]

C2.2/59 "Der Nelken Purpurkleid." Flo, on his *Ordensblume*; attr. to: Montano - die Feldnäglein. In: SvB/ *Fortsetzung*, pp. 65-66. 8 ll., Ger. [E]

C2.3/60 "DIch / such ich lieber Lust [...]." Rid, completion of "lost" poem written by Strephon, "Die Ein——samkeit"; attr. to Montano. In: SvB/ *Fortsetzung*, pp. 75-76. 44 half-ll., Ger. [E]

C2.4/61 "M. | Der Stumme stummt und mummt." Ono, on the letter "M"; attr. to Montano. In: SvB/ *Fortsetzung*, p. 78. 4 ll., Ger. [E]

C2.5/62 "MAn hat mit Recht." Pan [with Georg Philipp Harsdörffer], on the Golden Age; attr. to: Montano. In: SvB/ *Fortsetzung*, pp. 79-80. 21 ll., Ger. [E]

C2.6/63 "IHr Blätter / Wetterspiel." Pan, to "Laub und Gras"; attr. to: Montano. In: SvB/ *Fortsetzung*, p. 83. 14 ll., Ger. [E]

C2.7/64 "In der Luft." Pan, for Klajus [Johann Klaj]; attr. to: Montano. In: SvB/ *Fortsetzung*, p. 96. 6 ll., Ger. [E]

C2.8/65 "Vor Anbegin der Welt." Rid, on shadows ("Schatten"); attr. to: Montano. In: SvB/ *Fortsetzung*, pp. 99-100. 8 ll., Ger. [E]

C2.9/66 "Feldnelken wachsen viel." Ept; attr. to: Montano der Blumreich. In: SvB/ *Kriegs*, p. 209. 6 ll., Ger. [E]

C2.10/67 "Freylich sind wir Roß und Mäuler!" Pan, for Joachim and Magdalena Pipenburg; attr. to: Montano. In: SvB/ *Winters*, pp. 149-150. 12 ll., Ger. [E]

C3. Verse Inserts
(All locations Nuremberg and all verses in German and 4 ll., unless otherwise indicated. Only those attributed — either by name of by context — to Hellwig are included.)

1645

C3.1/68 "MUntre Bäume dieser Auen." Pan, for Georg Philipp Harsdörffer. In: "Lobgedicht," pp. 46-47. 12 ll. [E]

C3.2/69 "Wo Tugend der Jugend beliebet." Pan, for Georg Philipp Harsdörffer. In: "Lobgedicht," p. 51. [E]

1646
[All verse inserts from Book I of *Die Nymphe Noris* are organized under 1646, by the end of which year Book I was largely complete. For Book II, s. 1650.]

C3.3/70 "Es hat der Vater Herbst." Pan, for Georg Philipp Harsdörffer. In: "Hirtengedichte," p. 36. [E]

C3.4/71 "Strephon erfreut." Pan, for Georg Philipp Harsdörffer. In: "Hirtengedichte," p. 39. 12 ll. [E]

C3.5/72 "Löbliche Sinne mit Lusten." Pan, for Georg Philipp Harsdörffer. In: "Hirtengedichte," p. 41. 12 ll. + emblem. [E]

C3.6/73 "Wie der Wespenfaule Brut." Pan, for Georg Philipp Harsdörffer. In: "Hirtengedichte," p. 42. [E]

C3.7/74 "ES war die Schattendek." Nat, on the sunrise. In: *Noris*, p. 1. 12 ll. [E]

C3.8/75 "DEin Lob / ô Gott." Pra (contrafacture), morning devotion. In: *Noris*, pp. 3-4. 28 ll. [E]

C3.9/76 "Es klatschet und platschet." Hun/ono, on the Schießplatz near St. Johannis Friedhof. In: *Noris*, pp. 5-6. [E]

C3.10/77 "Obwol mich die Dapferkeit." Mem, for Johann Jacob Tetzel [cf. C1.11-12]. In: *Noris*, p. 7. [E]

C3.11/78 "Schertz: Schmertz! | nichts besteht / alls vergeht." Mem (figure poem), for Cornelius Marci, † 1646 (Protestant minister, Nuremberg). In: *Noris*, p. 7. 17 ll. [E]

C3.12/79 "Hier | beacht: | Heut an mir." Mem (figure poem), for "H. H." [Helena Hellwig], 1619-1645 (sister of Johann Hellwig). In: *Noris*, p. 8. 13 ll. [E]

C3.13/80 "ES hat die HimmelsGnad." Deb [with Johann Georg Volkamer], on the comparative values of the lives of shepherd and courtier. In: *Noris*, pp. 12-15. 32 ll. (of 64). [E]

C3.14/81 "DAs freye Luftkind hier." Avi/alt [with Johann Georg Volkamer], on the bird traps near Ziegelstein. In: *Noris*, pp. 19-21. 12 ll. (of 24). [E]

C3.15/82 "Es klappern / und plappern." Avi/ono/alt [with Johann Georg Volkamer], on sounds associated with birds. In: *Noris*, pp. 21-22. 24 ll. (of 48). [E]

C3.16/83 "Neronsburg heisst und ist der Francken Cron." Pan, to city of Nuremberg. In: *Noris*, p. 24. 12 ll. [E]

C3.17/84 "DEr Nymphen NORIS Macht." Mot, above entrance to Temple of Noris. In: *Noris*, p. 27. [E]

C3.18/85 "DEr Vogel und die Blum bezieren." Coa, Baumgartner. In: WARG, p. 28. [E]

C3.19/86 "DAs Glük den Helden lehrt." His, Roman occupation of Nuremberg area, ca. 10 B.C. In: HQ, p. 29. [E]

C3.20/87 "WIe ein Bach schnell." Coa, Böheim. In: WARG, p. 29. [E]

C3.21/88 "DUrch hohe KaisersGunst." His, origin of 912. In: HQ, p. 29. [E]

C3.22/89 "WAs ist des Menschen Thun?" Coa, Dörrer. In: WARG, p. 30. [E]

C3.23/90 "REdligkeit und frischer Muth." His, destruction of 1105. In: HQ, p. 30. [E]

C3.24/91 "Ein Seegschnitt machet oft." Coa, Ebner. In: WARG, p. 30. [E]

C3.25/92 "Vor Alters meine Hut." His, imperial transfer of the castle, 1313 and 1347. In: HQ, p. 30. [E]

C3.26/93 "DEr Lilie Silberglantz bezeugt." Coa, Führer. In: WARG, p. 31. [E]

C3.27/94 "WIe ein zerstümlets Glied." His, reconstruction of 1140. In: HQ, p. 31. [E]

C3.28/95 "DEr Mensch nicht sonder Sorg'." Coa, Groland. In: WARG, p. 31. [E]

C3.29/96 "EIns Degen Andacht." Edi, St. Lorenz Church, 1274. In: HQ, p. 32. [E]

C3.30/97 "ZUm Schutz der jungen Zucht." Coa, Grundherr. In: WARG, p. 32. [E]

C3.31/98 "DApferkeit die Jugend zieret." His, imperial tournament, 1198. In: HQ, p. 32. [E]

C3.32/99 "WAs soll das Richtscheid wol?" Coa, Haller. In: WARG, p. 33. [E]

C3.33/100 "GRoß ist gute Werk' erweisen." Edi, Heilig Geist Spital, 1339. In: HQ, p. 33. [E]

C3.34/101 "DEs HERREN Namen." Coa, Harsdörffer. In: WARG, p. 33. [E]

C3.35/102 "DAß hier auch dieses Orts." His, accident at wedding of Emperor Rudolf, 1284. In: HQ, p. 34. [E]

C3.36/103 "WEr viel weiß / viel Schue zureisst." Coa, Holtzschuer. In: WARG, p. 34. [E]

C3.37/104 "AUs des Kaisers milden Schatze." Edi, Frauenkirche, 1355. In: HQ, p. 34. [E]

C3.38/105 "WEr zu Wasser und zu Land." Coa, Im Hof. In: WARG, p. 35. [E]

C3.39/106 "SO war die guldne Bull." His, Golden Bull, 1356. In: HQ, p. 35. [E]

C3.40/107 "GLeichwie ein runder Zirk." Coa, Koler. In: WARG, p. 35. [E]

C3.41/108 "WIe meine Quelle rinnt zum Nutz." Art, Schöner Brunn, 1362. In: HQ, p. 35. [E]

C3.42/109 "DAs Schwert hier blinket hell." Coa, Kress. In: WARG, p. 36. [E]

C3.43/110 "WAs Gnadengunst das Reich." His, transfer of imperial relics, 1424. In: HQ, p. 36. [E]

C3.44/111 "WIe ein Lamm ist sonder Schuld." Coa, Löffelholtz. In: WARG, p. 37. [E]

C3.45/112 "MEines Stiefters Andacht mich." Art, Im Hof altar, 1496. In: HQ, p. 37. [E]

C3.46/113 "ZUr Aufnam dieses Lands." His, sale of Burggrafenburg, 1427. In: HQ, p. 37. [E]

C3.47/114 "WAs des Menschen Hand vermöge." Art, Tomb of St. Sebald, 1519. In: HQ, p. 39. [E]

C3.48/115 "WIe der weiche Fisch wolsteht." Coa, Muffel. In: WARG, p. 39. [E]

C3.49/116 "KUhnheit / die aus Frevel kommt." His, First Margrave War, 1450. In: HQ, p. 39. [E]

C3.50/117 "FReyer Sinn und Adel liebet." His, jousting tournament between Margrave Albrecht and Nuremberg patrician families, 1454. In: HQ, p. 40. [E]

C3.51/118 "WIe der dreygesetzten Blum." Coa, Nützel. In: WARG, p. 40. [E]

C3.52/119 "WAs MenschenHände thun." Edi, Stadtbibliothek, [n.d.]. In: HQ, p. 41. [E]

C3.53/120 "GOld die Ehr' / und Schwartz das Leiden." Coa, Pfintzing. In: WARG, p. 41. [E]

C3.54/121 "WIe ein Balk den Bau erhält." Coa, Pömer. In: WARG, p. 41. [E]

C3.55/122 "MEinen Platz der Mars besitzet." Edi, construction of new portal for Zeughaus, 1588. In: HQ, p. 41. [E]

C3.56/123 "WIe das schöne Frauenbild." Coa, Riether. In: WARG, p. 42. [E]

C3.57/124 "DEn Geitz / den Eigennutz." His, evacuation of Jews, 1499. In: HQ, p. 42. [E]

C3.58/125 "DEr dreyer Schlüssel Zier." Coa, Schlüsselfelder. In: WARG, p. 43. [E]

C3.59/126 "MEnschenGeist wil alles zwingen." Edi, reconstruction of Fleischbrücke, 1597. In: HQ, p. 43. [E]

C3.60/127 "WIe beeder Fakkel Liecht." Coa, Schürstab. In: WARG, p. 43. [E]

C3.61/128 "SChnell die weltlich' Ehr." His, introduction of Reformation, 1525. In: HQ, p. 44. [E]

C3.62/129 "KEin ringes Spiel / schau!" Coa, Stark. In: WARG, p. 44. [E]

C3.63/130 "KLugheit und Gerechtigkeit." Edi, renovation of Rathaus, 1616. In: HQ, p. 44. [E]

C3.64/131 "DEr Lilie Silberfarb und Ruch." Coa, Stromer. In: WARG, p. 45. [E]

C3.65/132 "EIn freyer Held wolt' hier." His, Second Margrave War, 1552. In: HQ, p. 45. [E]

C3.66/133 "WO mit Witz die Dapferkeit." Coa, Tetzel. In: WARG, p. 45. [E]

C3.67/134 "HIer zu sondern Ruhm und Nutz." Edi, Roßmühle, 1620. In: HQ, p. 46. [E]

C3.68/135 "DAs Glük / das schwankend Glük." Coa, Toppler. In: WARG, p. 46. [E]

C3.69/136 "OBrigkeit / die Gott gesetzet." His, triumphal entry of Emperor Matthias, 1612. In: HQ, p. 46. [E]

C3.70/137 "DEr Mohr zwar Glük verspricht." Coa, Tucher. In: WARG, p. 47. [E]

C3.71/138 "KUrtzweil / die mit Maß geschicht." Edi, opening of Nuremberg theater, 1628. In: HQ, p. 47. [E]

C3.72/139 "DIe Tugend vest besteht." Coa, Volkamer. In: WARG, p. 47. [E]

C3.73/140 "SChikt uns Gott ein Leiden zu." His, Wallenstein's siege, 1632. In: HQ, p. 48. [E]

C3.74/141 "WAs soll der Lilie Weiß'." Coa, Welser. In: WARG, p. 48. [E]

C3.75/142 "WEr diesen Wunderbau beschaut." Mot, above exit, Temple of Noris. In: *Noris*, p. 51. 8 ll. [E]

C3.76/143 "Ohne Falsch und Heucheley." Mot, on altar of Temple of Noris. In: *Noris*, p. 52. 2 ll. [E]

C3.77/144 "WEr der Sonnen Glantz beachtet." Pan/myt (ode) [with Johann Georg Volkamer], to Noris the nymph. In: *Noris*, pp. 55-56. 38 ll. [E]

C3.78/145 "WIe der Mond verwandlet sich." Coa, Cämmerer. In: WAUG, p. 57. [E]

C3.79/146 "ES wird durch die Natur." Coa, Dietherr. In: WAUG, p. 57. [E]

C3.80/147 "KUnst und guter Sinnverstand." Coa, Gugel. In: WAUG, p. 58. [E]

C3.81/148 "ALs ein Blitz der Pfeil hinfleuchet." Coa, Heiden (Hagelsheimer). In: WAUG, p. 58. [E]

C3.82/149 "WEm Gott Gutt und Ehr bescheret." Coa, Kötzler. In: WAUG, p. 58. [E]

C3.83/150 "DApferkeit und KlugheitRuhm." Coa, Oertel. In: WAUG, p. 58. [E]

C3.84/151 "HIer trägt der edle Löw." Coa, Oelhafen. In: WAUG, p. 59. [E]

C3.85/152 "ES mahnet dieses Thier." Coa, Pucher. In: WAUG, p. 59. [E]

C3.86/153 "NIemand sich auf hohe Gunst." Coa, Roggenbach. In: WAUG, p. 59. [E]

C3.87/154 "DIe äussre schöne Gstalt." Coa, Schedel. In: WAUG, p. 59. [E]

C3.88/155 "EIn Mann soll seyn behertzt." Coa, Scheurl. In: WAUG, p. 60. [E]

C3.89/156 "WIe sich dieser edle Vogel." Coa, Schlaudersbach. In: WAUG, p. 60. [E]

C3.90/157 "HAlte rein im HertzenSchrein." Coa, Schleicher. In: WAUG, p. 60. [E]

C3.91/158 "WIe die Rosen lieblich blüen." Coa, Schmidmair. In: WAUG, p. 60. [E]

C3.92/159 "NIchts so herrlich hier bestehet." Coa, Stokhamer. In: WAUG, p. 61. [E]

C3.93/160 "MIt sonderm Wolstand." Coa, Von Thill. In: WAUG, p. 61. [E]

C3.94/161 "SO muß gewechslet seyn." Coa, Voyt. In: WAUG, p. 61. [E]

C3.95/162 "EIn Ruhm ist nidres Orts." Coa, Waldstromer. In: WAUG, p. 61. [E]

C3.96/163 "Und unsre Lieder hier." Pan, to the German language. In: *Noris*, p. 67. 2 ll. (appended to "Der Teutschen Teutscher Sprach" of Strephon and Klajus). [E]

C3.97/164 "Des Menschen Sinn zwar viel erdenkt." Aph, translation of "Homo proponit, deus disponit." In: *Noris*, p. 68. 2 ll. [E]

C3.98/165 "O | so | leb' | und schweb'" [pattern poem: tower]. Pan, on the coat of arms of Georg Philipp Harsdörffer. In: set of figure poems, no. II. In: *Noris*, p. 84. 27 ll. [E]

C3.99/166 "Auf! singet und springt!" [pattern poem: shawm]. Pan, for Sigmund Betulius. In: set of figure poems, no. VII. In: *Noris*, p. 88. 17 ll. [E]

C3.100/167 "EIn Maul / und doch kein Maul." Rid, about a pig. In: set of riddles, no. VII. In: *Noris*, p. 94. [E]

C3.101/168 "DEn Wolff ich stetigs irr'." Rid, about a lamb. In: set of riddles, no. VIII. In: *Noris*, p. 94. [E]

C3.102/169 "WAnn die Sonn zur Ruhe rennt." Dep [with Johann Georg Volkamer, Georg Philipp Harsdörffer, Johann Klaj, Friedrich Lochner, Johann Sechst, Christoph Arnold], end of day. In: *Noris*, pp. 98-99. 6 ll. (one strophe of seven-strophe poem). [E]

C3.103/170 "O höchster Gott!" Dep/pra (contrafacture), end of day. In: *Noris*, pp. 100-102. 32 ll. [E]

1647

C3.104/171 "Die Weide gerne wächst." Pan, for Georg Philipp Harsdörffer. In: "Schauplatz," pp. 17-19. 28 ll. [E]

C3.105/172 "Gleichwie die Element in ihrem Streit." Pan, for allegorical figure Vollkommenheit. In: "Schauplatz," p. 22. [E]

C3.106/173 "Das / was der Spielend jetzt." Pan, for Georg Philipp Harsdörffer. In: "Schauplatz," p. 23. [E]

1648

C3.107/174 "der Tod / | der blosse Tod" [pattern poem: "Egyptische flammenseule"]. Epi, for Queen Erminda. In: *Ormund*, p. 116. 8 ll., Ger. [E]

C3.108/175 "Ich weiland vest, bevest." Pan, to the Burgstallung at Neunhof. In: "Poet. Gedanken," no. 1. B3^v. [E]

C3.109/176 "Zerfliessender Spiegel / Crystalline Helle." Pan, to the fountain at Neunhof. In: "Poet. Gedanken," no. 2. B3ᵛ-4ʳ. [E]

C3.110/177 "Nicht eben dieses Orts." Pan, to the church at Neunhof. In: "Poet. Gedanken," no. 3. B4ʳ. [E]

C3.111/178 "Stoltzer Baum." Pan, to the linden tree below the church at Neunhof. In: "Poet. Gedanken," no. 4. B4ʳ. 8 ll. [E]

C3.112/179 "Was ist doch / saget mir / der Wirth." Pan, to the public house at Neunhof. In: "Poet. Gedanken," no. 5. B4ʳ. [E]

C3.113/180 "Diese Höle / diese Gruft." Pan, to the hermit's cave at Neunhof. In: "Poet. Gedanken," no. 6. B4ᵛ. 8 ll. [E]

C3.114/181 "Die Dapfrekeit / die Lieb zur Tugend." Pan, on the Koler coat of arms, Neunhof. In: "Poet. Gedanken," no. 7. B4ᵛ. 14 ll. [E]

C3.115/182 "Schwartz im gelb' / und gelb im schwartz." Pan, on the Jenisch coat of arms, Neunhof. In: "Poet. Gedanken," no. 8. B4ᵛ. [E]

1650
[All verse inserts from Book II of *Die Nymphe Noris* are organized under 1650, date of publication; for Book I, s. 1646.]

C3.116/183 "WAchet auf / ihr meine Sinne!" Dev (contrafacture), morning thoughts. In: *Noris*, pp. 103-105. 48 ll. [E]

C3.117/184 "HIer ist nichts dann Lust und Freude." Gar [with Johann Georg Volkamer], on the Jobst Christoff Kress estate. In: *Noris*, p. 107. [E]

C3.118/185 "O Menschenkind betracht." Did [with Johann Georg Volkamer], on the pond at Jacob Im Hof's Gleißhammer. In: *Noris*, p. 108. 8 ll. [E]

C3.119/186 "Echo! Deine Wohnungsöde." Ech, to the echo at Gleißhammer. In: *Noris*, p. 110. 28 ll. [E]

C3.120/187 "WIe ein rauer Ostwind." Did, on the death of a child. In: *Noris*, p. 114. 6 ll. [E]

C3.121/188 "ANdacht lieben / seiner Haab." Eph, Conrad Groß, †1356, "der Freygebige." In: WLP, p. 121. [E]

C3.122/189 "WIewol mein Will gewest." Eph, Barthold Tucher, †1379, "der Bedachtsame." In: WLP, p. 122. [E]

C3.123/190 "WAs ich gemeiner Stadt." Eph, Ulrich Stromer d. J., †1385, "der Vorsichtige." In: WLP, p. 122. [E]

C3.124/191 "GEmeiner Stadt das best." Eph, Ulrich Stromer, †1387, "der Getreue." In: WLP, p. 122. [E]

C3.125/192 "WAs nutzen kan der Forst." Eph, Peter Stromer, 1387, "der Nutzliche." In: WLP, p. 122. [E]

C3.126/193 "DEr Vätter Lebensart weiland." Eph, Marquard Mendel, †1388, "der Andächtige." In: WLP, p. 123. [E]

C3.127/194 "WAs zu Lieb dem Vatterland." Eph, Sebald Pfintzing, †1431, "der Dienstliche." In: WLP, p. 123. [E]

C3.128/195 "OBwol das Vatterland." Eph, Berthold Volkamer, †1452, "der Ernsthafte." In: WLP, p. 123. [E]

C3.129/196 "SOlte sehen Kindeskinder." Eph, Conrad Baumgartner, †1464, "der Glükseelige." In: WLP, p. 123. [E]

C3.130/197 "WAs mein Verstand vermocht." Eph, Ruprecht Haller, †1489, "der Begnadete." In: WLP, p. 124. [E]

C3.131/198 "VIeler Potentaten Land." Eph, Gabriel Muffel, †1498, "der Gezierte." In: WLP, p. 124. [E]

C3.132/199 "NIcht mindre Klugheit." Eph, Ulrich Grundherr, †1500, "der Anordnende." In: WLP, p. 124. [E]

C3.133/200 "BUrgund mich hat geehrt." Eph, Wilhelm Haller, †1504, "der Verständige." In: WLP, p. 124. [E]

C3.134/201 "DEr Himmel / Erd und Meer." Eph, Martin Böhaim, †1506, "der Gepreisseste." In: WLP, p. 125. [E]

Descriptive Bibliography 97

C3.135/202 "KOenigs Ladislaus Gnad." Eph, Johann Harsdörffer, †1511, "der Bemühete." In: WLP, p. 125. [E]

C3.136/203 "WAs ich dem Vatterland gedient." Eph, Leonhard Groland, †1521, "der Fleissige." In: WLP, p. 125. [E]

C3.137/204 "WAs Feindschafft und Gefahr." Eph, Wilhelm Dörrer, †1524, "der Unverschuldte." In: WLP, p. 125. [E]

C3.138/205 "NIcht Menschen / HimmelsGab." Eph, Antoni Tucher, †1524, "der Weisse." In: WLP, p. 126. [E]

C3.139/206 "DEr Fürst aus Preussenland." Eph, Caspar Nützel, †1529, "der Angeneme." In: WLP, p. 126. [E]

C3.140/207 "WAs Rom und Griechenland." Eph, Wilibald Pirckheimer, †1530, "der Gelehrte." In: WLP, p. 126. [E]

C3.141/208 "DIe Pfaltz / schau!" Eph, Andreas Tucher, †1531, "der Sieghaffte." In: WLP, p. 126. [E]

C3.142/209 "WEr Kunst und Wissenschafft liebt." Eph, Hieronymus Ebner, †1532, "der Löbliche." In: WLP, p. 127. [E]

C3.143/210 "DIe Tugend nicht besitzt." Eph, Martin Geuder, †1532, "der Tapfere." In: WLP, p. 127. [E]

C3.144/211 "OBwol der Kaiser mir." Eph, Christoff Kreß, †1535, "der Demühtige." In: WLP, p. 127. [E]

C3.145/212 "WEr eyfert / eyfre recht." Eph, Christoff Koler, †1536, "der Eyferige." In: WLP, p. 127. [E]

C3.146/213 "MEinen unverdrossnen Fleiß." Eph, Wilhelm Schlüsselfelder, †1549, "der Unverdrossene." In: WLP, p. 128. [E]

C3.147/214 "WIe mein getreuer Dienst." Eph, Hieronymus Holtzschuher, †1551, "der Geliebte." In: WLP, p. 128. [E]

C3.148/215 "WAs Reichthum nicht vermag." Eph, Sebastian Groß, †1558, "der Ansehliche." In: WLP, p. 128. [E]

C3.149/216 "GEdult die ist und noht." Eph, Hieronymus Baumgartner, †1565, "der Gedultige." In: WLP, p. 128. [E]

C3.150/217 "DAs reinest' Element." Eph, Johannes Stark, †1572, "der Sinnreiche." In: WLP, p. 129. [E]

C3.151/218 "ES ist ein feiner Ruhm." Eph, Jobst Tetzel, †1575, "der Daurende." In: WLP, p. 129. [E]

C3.152/219 "WAs mehrers Schuldigkeit vermag." Eph, Andreas Im Hof, †1579, "der Giltige." In: WLP, p. 129. [E]

C3.153/220 "EIn Wort zu seiner Zeit." Eph, Philipp Geuder, †1581, "der Beredsame." In: WLP, p. 129. [E]

C3.154/221 "IM Welsch= Teutsch= Niederland." Eph, Johann Rieter, †1584, "der Edele." In: WLP, p. 130. [E]

C3.155/222 "WEr was dem Vatterland zu Lieb." Eph, Jacob Füterer, †1586, "der Rüstige." In: WLP, p. 130. [E]

C3.156/223 "ICh trug zu freyer Kunst." Eph, Sebald Welser, †1589, "der Dankbare." In: WLP, p. 130. [E]

C3.157/224 "MIt Maß man halte Hauß." Eph, Wilibald Schlüsselfelder, †1589, "der Häußliche." In: WLP, p. 130. [E]

C3.158/225 "DEr Musen schrofer Steig." Eph, Bartholm Pömer, †1590, "der Fähige." In: WLP, p. 131. [E]

C3.159/226 "EHrfahrnheit und Verstand." Eph, Hieronymus Kreß, †1596, "der Gesuchte." In: WLP, p. 131. [E]

C3.160/227 "WEr Schätze samlen wil." Eph, Andreas Im Hof, †1597, "der Milde." In: WLP, p. 131. [E]

C3.161/228 "DIe kluge Wachsamkeit." Eph, Hieronymus Baumgartner, †1602, "der Wachsame." In: WLP, p. 131. [E]

C3.162/229 "EGypten / Palestin / Italien." Eph, Christoff Führer, †1610, "der Versuchte." In: WLP, p. 132. [E]

C3.163/230 "OBschon im Alter mich." Eph, Paulus Harsdörffer, †1613, "der Inbrünstige." In: WLP, p. 132. [E]

C3.164/231 "WIe manchen Staat und Land." Eph, Christoff Löffelholtz, †1619, "der Vielwissende." In: WLP, p. 132. [E]

C3.165/232 "IN mir die Sanftmuht selbst." Eph, Georg Volkamer, †1633, "der Sanfftmüthige." In: WLP, p. 132. [E]

C3.166/233 "FRomkeit / der Weißheit Quell." Eph, Andreas Im Hof, †1637, "der Fromme." In: WLP, p. 133. [E]

C3.167/234 "ALtdorf mir zu danken hat." Eph, Johann Friderich Löffelholtz, †1640, "der Pflantzende." In: WLP, p. 133. [E]

C3.168/235 "WAs Unheil falsches Schrott." Eph, Sigmund Gabriel Holtzschuer, †1642, "der Verhütende." In: WLP, p. 133. [E]

C3.169/236 "MEin kluger Sinnverstand." Eph, Johannes Jacob Tetzel, †1646, "der Kluge." In: WLP, p. 133. [E]

C3.170/237 "NAch meinem Tod bedenkt." Eph, Lucas Friderich Böheim, †1648, "der Aufrichtige." In: WLP, p. 134. [E]

C3.171/238 "SO / so / so / Nachsinnen üben." Buc, on public virtues. In: *Noris*, pp. 135-136. 32 ll. [E]

C3.172/239 "SOlte Noht und Unglük." Coa, Ammon. In: WAb, p. 140. [E]

C3.173/240 "INS Feuer / ja zum Tod getrost." Coa, Brunsterer. In: WAb, p. 141. [E]

C3.174/241 "GEdult hier überwind." Coa, Eyßvogel. In: WAb, p. 141. [E]

C3.175/242 "NIcht im finstern Jammerthal." Coa, Faltzner. In: WAb, p. 141. [E]

C3.176/243 "WIe in dem roten Feld." Coa, Flechsdörffer. In: WAb, p. 141. [E]

C3.177/244 "WEr sich der Weißheit Zucht." Coa, Füterer. In: WAb, p. 142. [E]

C3.178/245 "IM Schweiß des Angesichts." Coa, Grabner. In: WAb, p. 142. [E]

C3.179/246 "SOnder Anstoß leichtlich." Coa, Graser. In: WAb, p. 142. [E]

C3.180/247 "WEr mit Creutz und Trübsal." Coa, Gross. In: WAb, p. 142. [E]

C3.181/248 "OB weiland Haiden wir." Coa, Hayden. In: WAb, p. 143. [E]

C3.182/249 "WIe auf der hohen Wartt'." Coa, Hirschvogel. In: WAb, p. 143. [E]

C3.183/250 "WEh dem / der menschlich." Coa, Krauter. In: WAb, p. 143. [E]

C3.184/251 "BEy Ernst und bey Schimpf." Coa, Langmann. In: WAb, p. 143. [E]

C3.185/252 "WEr hier in dieser Welt begehret." Coa, Mendel. In: WAb, p. 144. [E]

C3.186/253 "ES grunt der hohe Ruhm." Coa, Ortlieb. In: WAb, p. 144. [E]

C3.187/254 "DIe Birke war zu Rom." Coa, Pirkheimer. In: WAb, p. 144. [E]

C3.188/255 "WEm durch Verstand sein Thun." Coa, Puck. In: WAb, p. 144. [E]

C3.189/256 "DEr Knoblauch beygestekkt." Coa, Sachs. In: WAb, p. 145. [E]

C3.190/257 "KLugheit und Aufrichtigkeit nutzet." Coa, Schmuggenhof. In: WAb, p. 145. [E]

C3.191/258 "DIe Hoffnung / Lieb und Glaub'." Coa, Schopper. In: WAb, p. 145. [E]

C3.192/259 "DRey S in sich vereint." Coa, Seubold. In: WAb, p. 145. [E]

C3.193/260 "SO / so sich seltzam kartt." Coa, Teuffel. In: WAb, p. 146. [E]

C3.194/261 "WEr in der Ehre baut." Coa, Vorchtel. In: WAb, p. 146. [E]

C3.195/262 "GLeich wie ein junger Stier." Coa, Wagner. In: WAb, p. 146. [E]

C3.196/263 "OEfters bey den Siegespalmen." Coa, Zenner. In: WAb, p. 146. [E]

C3.197/264 "DEr hat das beste Glük." Coa, Zingel. In: WAb, p. 147. [E]

C3.198/265 "OBwol hier derer Stamm." Mot, above door leading into the "Wappen der abgestorbenen Rathsfähigen Geschlechten." In: *Noris*, p. 147. [E]

C3.199/266 "LEtten schlagen / Ziegel streichen." Mot/did, above door of brick plant. In: *Noris*, p. 157. [E]

C3.200/267 "DIe Lieb erscheinet seyn." Emb (subscriptio), about the plant bittersweet. In: *Noris*, p. 161. [E]

C3.201/268 "TRau wol riet weg das Pferd." Emb (subscriptio), five-fold pictures of a piece of cloth. In: *Noris*, p. 164. 10 ll. [E]

C3.202/269 ["DIeser Pierinnen Stadt"]. Pan [with Johann Georg Volkamer, Georg Philipp Harsdörffer, Johann Klaj, Friedrich Lochner, Johann Sechst, Christoph Arnold], on Altdorf University. In: *Noris*, pp. 176-177. 5½ ll. (of 42). [E]

C3.203/270 "DEr Marcomanner Fürst Hostwitz." Gen, the first Kreß, ca. 885. In: Kreß, p. 183. [E]

C3.204/271 "IN dieser Landsart hier." Gen, Friderich Kreß, fl. 1291. In: Kreß, p. 183. [E]

C3.205/272 "WAs kluger Sinnverstand vermag." Gen, Otto Kreß, † ca. 1339. In: Kreß, p. 184. [E]

C3.206/273 "WEr Gott vor Augen stellt." Gen, Friderich Kreß, † ca. 1406. In: Kreß, p. 184. [E]

C3.207/274 "DAs arme Jungfervolk." Gen, Hupold Kreß, fl. 1427. In: Kreß, p. 184. [E]

C3.208/275 "WEr gutes Wandels sich." Gen, Conrad Kreß, †1430. In: Kreß, p. 184. [E]

C3.209/276 "ES hat gemeiniglich." Gen, Sebald Kreß, †1477. In: Kreß, pp. 184-185. [E]

C3.210/277 "DEn tapfern Rittersmuht." Gen, Hanns Kreß, †1500. In: Kreß, p. 185. [E]

C3.211/278 "WIe meinen treuen Raht." Gen, Antoni Kreß, †1513. In: Kreß, p. 185. [E]

C3.212/279 "WAs bey verlobtem Par." Gen, Caspar Kreß, †1521. In: Kreß, p. 185. [E]

C3.213/280 "DEr Schwaben Bund mich." Gen, Christoff Kreß, †1537. In: Kreß, p. 185. [E]

C3.214/281 "DEr Franken Craiß." Gen, Hieronymus Kreß, †1596. In: Kreß, p. 186. [E]

C3.215/282 "Bey guldner Friedenszeit." Emb, motto over Amalthea. In: *Noris*, p. 187. 2 ll. [E]

C3.216/283 "Wer noch im Hass entbrannt." Emb, motto over Bellona. In: *Noris*, p. 187. 2 ll. [E]

C3.217/284 ["DU guldnes Himmelskind!"] Uto [with Johann Georg Volkamer, Georg Philipp Harsdörffer, Johann Klaj, Friedrich Lochner, Johann Sechst, Christoph Arnold], on the coming Child of Peace. In: *Noris*, pp. 192-193. (unspecified, of 28 ll.). [E]

C3.218/285 "ANfangs aus blossem Nichts." Dev, end of day. In: *Noris*, pp. 195-197. 40 ll. [E]

*SACRARIUM
BONAE MEMORIAE
NORIBERGENSIUM
consecratum
à
Johañe Hellwigio.
Phil. et Medic. Doctore.*

Title page, "Sacrarium Bonæ Memoriæ Noribergensium"
Österreichische Nationalbibliothek

D. Manuscripts

D 1 SACRARIUM BONAE MEMORIAE NORIBERGENSIUM
(late 1640s assumed)

Title:

SACRARIUM | BONÆ MEMORIÆ | NORIBERGENSIVM | conſecratum | à | Johañe Hellwigio | Phil. et Medic. Doctore.

Collation: 12°: π^1 A-E^{12} F^9, 71 foliated leaves: [1] 1-11 [+11a] 12-58 [+58a] 59-67 [1]; [$1], unpaginated.

Contents: π1^r: [bl.]. π1^v: [bl.]. A1^r: t.p. A1^v: [bl.]. A2^r: "LECTORI BENEVOLO | Æviternitatem et sortem | beatam." A3^v: "SACRARIUM | bonæ memoriæ | NORIMBERGENSIUM *[sic]* | consecratum. | *[rule: 150 mm.]* | MONUMENTA | quæ in Æde Divo sebaldo sacrata | inveniuntur." A7^r: "MONUMENTA | QUÆ IN ÆDE DIVO LAURENTIO SACRA- | ta inveniuntur." A11^r: "MONUMENTUM | IN SACELLO D. ANNÆ VEL VULGO | cunctis animabus sacro in | vicinia Templi Laurentini." A11^v: [bl.]. A12^r: [bl.]. A12^v: [bl.]. B1^r: "MONUMENTA | QUÆ IN CŒNOBIO ÆGIDIANO OR= | dinis S. Benedicti." B3^r: "MONUMENTA | QUÆ IN CŒNOBIO AUGUSTINIANORUM." B4^r: "MONUMENTA | QUÆ IN CŒNOBIO DOMINICANORUM | sive Prædicatorum." B6^r: "MONUMENTA, | QUÆ IN CŒNOBIO FRANCISCANORUM." B6^v: "MONUMENTA | QUÆ IN CŒNOBIO CARTUSIANORUM." B7^r: "MONUMENTA | QUÆ IN MONASTERIO D. CATHA- | rinæ." B8^r: "MONUMENTA | QUÆ IN ÆDE DIVO JACOBO SACRA." B9^r: "MONUMENTA, | QUÆ IN VOSOLOMII SUB SPIRITUS | sancti nomine dedicati Æde sacra | habentur." B11^v: "MONUMENTA | QUÆ IN ÆDIBUS VTIQUE PRIVATIS | habentur." C1^r: "ALTDORFFII | quod Oppidulum cum Academia sub | jurisdictione senatus Norib. | in æde sacra." C7^v: "HERSBRUCCI. | Quod oppidum est Ditionis | Noribergensis." C8^v: "KIRCHSITTENBACHI, | Qui pagus est in territorio Nori- | bergensi." C9^r: "KRAFTSHOFI, | Qui pagus est in territorio Nori- | bergensi." C9^v: "POPPENREUTHI, | Qui pagus est in territorio Nori- | bergensi." C10^r: "STEINBÜHL, | Qui pagus in vicinia statim Urbis | Noribergæ." C10ᵛ: "FÜRTHÆ, | Quod castrum est ad consinia | Territorii Noriberg." C11ʳ: "EBORACI, | Quod est Cœnotium ordinis Bernar- | dini in Franconia." C11ᵛ: "HERRIEDEN, | Quod Castrum est in Episcopata | Aichstadiano." C12ʳ: "BAMBERGÆ, | Quæ Civitas in Franconia." D1ʳ: "FRANCOFURTI AD MŒNUM, | In æde ibidem Divo Petro dicata." D1ᵛ: "AMBERGÆ, | Oppidum in Palatinatu | superiore." D2ʳ: "COBURGI, | Quod oppidum in Thuringia." D2ᵛ: "LIPSIÆ, | in Misnia." D3ʳ: "VITEBERGÆ | in Saxonia." D6ʳ: "MARBURGI IN HASSIA." D6ᵛ: "URATISLAVIÆ | in Silesia." D7ᵛ: "AUGUSTÆ VINDELICORUM." D8ʳ: "AMBERGI. | Quod prœdium est prope Urbem | Augustam Vindelicorum." D8ᵛ: "TUBINGÆ | In ditione Württenberg." D9ʳ: "BASILEÆ | in Helvetia." D10ʳ: "FRIBURGI | in Brisgovia." D10ᵛ: "ŒNIPONTI. | in Tiroli." D11ʳ: "LINZII | in Austria superiore." D12ʳ: "PILSNÆ. | in Bohemia." D12ᵛ: "PRAGÆ | in Bohemia." E1ʳ: "RUTTENBERGI | in Bohemia." E1ᵛ: "IN SILVA DUCIS. | Urbe quadam Brabantiæ." E2ᵛ: "ANTUERPIÆ | in Brabantia." E4ʳ: "BRUXELLIS | Brabantiæ." E4ᵛ: "MACHLINIÆ | in Brabantia." E5ʳ: "LOVANII | in Brabantia." E5ᵛ: "ADVANUM D. AUDOMARI | in Artesia." E6ʳ: "PARISIIS | in Galliis." E6ᵛ: [bl.]. E7ʳ: "LUGDUNI GALLORUM." E8ʳ: "SENIS | in Tuscia." E9ʳ: "PISIS | in Tuscia." E9ᵛ: [bl.]. E10ʳ: "FLORENTIÆ | in Tuscia." E10ᵛ: [bl.]. E11ʳ: "VENETIIS. | In æde D. Sebastiano sacrata:". E11ᵛ: [bl.]. E12ʳ: [bl.]. E12ᵛ: [bl.]. F1ʳ: "Joh. Coclei Norici Relatio de civitate Nori= | bergensi, quae reperitur in suis Natis ad Melæ | Cosmographiam, impressa Norib. 1512 in 4ᵗᵒ. | De Norinbergae Germaniæ centro." F6ʳ: [bl.]. F6ᵛ-7ʳ [double-sided]: "Inscriptio in Gymnasio Ægidiano Norib.". F7ᵛ: [bl.]. F8ʳ: [bl.]. F8ᵛ-9ʳ [double-sided]: "Inscriptiones in dem laboratorio Chemico zu Altdorff." F9ᵛ [bl.].

HT] A3ᵛ SACRARIUM | bonæ memoriæ | NORIMBERGENSIUM | consecratum.

RT] [none]

CW] Only the following: B7ʳ Milles E1ᵛ sequentia F1ᵛ viginti F2ᵛ puos- F3ᵛ Italiæ F4ᵛ vel cunctos

Notes:
Signing: begins A1; only first leaf of each gathering signed (gatherings A-E). Missing: F. 28-32 ll. per p.
Dimensions: t.p. (full): 210 x 170 mm.; MS face ("LECTORI BENEVOLO"): 190 x 135 mm. (inconsistent throughout).
Ornamentation: most tomb inscriptions set off with a small, bold cross. Greek: biblical quotation on D2^v; 12-line poem on D7^r; inscription on D9^v.
Paper: handmade; strong, well preserved, light foxing. Watermark: female figure with wings and letters "H" and "L", 25 mm.

Commentary: Omeis, 60: "[...] collegit Monumenta celebriorum Virorum, cum primis Norimbergensium, in templis et cœmeteriis Norimbb. imo in exteris quoque regionibus exstructa." Will/ *NGL*, 88: "Ist im MScte hinterblieben, und enthält eine Sammlung von Monumenten berühmter Nürnbergere, die ihnen sowol im Vatterlande, als auswärtig errichtet wurden. Schwindel in dem Vorbericht von den *scriptoribus epitaphiorum* gedenkt ihrer nicht; siehe *Catal. Rink.* n. 8642."

Bibliographical data: Herdegen, 244; Omeis, 60; Will/ *NGL*, 88.

Location: Vienna: Österreichische Nationalbibliothek, Handschriften- und Inkunabelsammlung. Sig.: Cod. 12.996. Purchased at auction: Antiquariat Kuppitsch, Vienna 1849. [E]

Recto of letter to Athanasius Kircher (1655)
Pontifica Università Gregoriana

E. Letters

E 1 to Sigmund von Birken
(1650)

"Seinem Vielgeliebten Wiesenfreund und Pegnitzschäfer | FLORIDAN." Regensburg, "den 18. des dritten Blumen Monats. 650", to Nuremberg. 312 x 211 mm. 1 leaf (recto, 29 ll.). Ger.

Location: Nuremberg: Archiv des Pegnesischen Blumenordens. Sig.: C. 135. 1. Condition: relatively well preserved, foxing. Verso: "jh. D. helwig | Viro — Juveni | Præstantiss.° et Literatiss.° | Dr. Sigismundo Betulio | L. L. Candidato, et Poetæ | L. C. dignissimo, amico | plurimum honorando | Regenspurg. | ρʃ A⁰. 1650. M. Majo. | ℞ A⁰. 1651. d. 12. Febr." [wax seal]

E 2 to Athanasius Kircher
(1655)

"Salutem et Felicitatem! | Reverende et Clarissime Domine Pater." Regensburg, 10 January 1655, to Rome. 286 x 193 mm. 1 leaf (recto, 37 ll.; verso, 6 ll.). Lat.

Location: Rome: Università Gregoriana (Kircher Coll.). Sig.: APUG 568 f. 109 r-v. Condition: well preserved, paper clean. Verso: "Reverendo admodum ac Clarissimo Domino Patri | ATHANASIO KIRCHNERO, Presbytero inclytæ | Societatis JESV, Mathematico et Πολυγλόσσῳ | celebratissimo. ρʃ | ROMÆ." [wax seal]

E 3   to Johann Georg Volkamer
       (1662)

"Feliter agere! | Nobilissime et Clarissime Domine Doctor, Collega et Amice dilectissime." Regensburg, 31 January 1662, to Nuremberg. 318 x 219 mm. 1 leaf (recto, 31 ll.; verso, 12 ll.) + address leaf. Lat.

Location: Erlangen: Universitätsbibliothek. Sig.: [Schmidt-Herrling, 272]. Condition: well preserved. A2^r: [bl.]. A2^v: "Viro Nobilissimo et Excellentissimo, Domino GEORGIO | VOLKAMERO, Philosopho et Medico celeberrimo, Præ= | dico felicissimus, Domino Collegæ et Amico filo per= | clarissimo et colendissimo | Noribergam." [wax seal].

F. Other Publications

F 1 Lobgedicht an den Spielenden
(1645)

Title:

XII. | **Folgen** | **Der Pegnitz=Schäfer Lobgedichte** | **an den** | **SPIELENDEN.**
In: Georg Philipp Harsdörffer: *[red]* **GESPRECHSPIELE** | **Fünfter Theil**
[...]. Nürnberg: Wolfgang Endter, 1645:)()()()(1ᵛ-)()()()(4ᵛ. Rpt. Ed. Irmgard Böttcher. Tübingen: Niemeyer, 1969: 46-52.

Collation: 12°:)()()()(1ᵛ-4ᵛ, 3½ leaves; [$4], pp. [rpt. ed.] 46-52.

Contents:)()()()(1ᵛ: title; text begins (prosimetric bucolic text with emblem): "MUntre Bäume dieser Auen.")()()()(3ᵛ: threefold emblem.)()()()(4ᵛ: signed: "Johann Hellwig D."

HT] [none]

RT] [none]

CW] begin)()()()(2ʳ: er

Type: 16 ll. per p. Dimensions: title: 23 x 69 mm.; p. of text: 70 x 113 mm. Style: Frak. Gathering sig.:)(; nos., roman.

Notes:
Signing: begins)()()()(2.
Illustrations:)()()()(3ᵛ: threefold emblem: 1. Indianischer Palm-Baum of the Fruchtbringende Gesellschaft, with motto: "Festgesetzt"; 2. Harsdörffer shield [stone tower], with motto: "Unverletzt"; 3. Harsdörffer emblem [bean plants], with motto: "Wolergetzt".
Ornamentation: three six-pronged stars in middle of headline, except on emblem p. (none) and t.p. (two stars framing "XII."). Orn. initial: t.p. "M".

Commentary: This miniature prose eclogue is the twelfth of fifteen com. pieces in praise of Harsdörffer, "der Spielende," under the title "Ehrengedichte | dem | SPILENDEN | von | Hochanſehlichen Herren und liebwerhten Freunden | zu Ausfertigung | des | Fünften Theils | der | Geſprächspiele | überſendet." Hellwig here invents Noris the nymph: "ein über alle massen schönes Weibsbild; derer Holdseligkeit jedoch mit solchem Heroischen Ansehen vermenget [...]. || Ihre Kleidung war oberhalb des Leibs / und üm die Arme / mit weissem Atlaß beleget / der Unterrokk von rohten Daffet; der gantze Oberrokk gelb und mit schwarzen Adlern eingewirket: Sie hatte auf ihrem Haubt einen von eichenen Laub geflochten Krantz / darunter ein guldenes Stirnblat mit diesen Buchstaben. NORIS. Und in der einen Hand einen weissen Helffenbeinen Richterstab / in der andern einen Palmenzweig haltend: Aus welchem der Schäfer leichtlich schliessen mögen / daß sie etwan eine sonderliche Göttin oder Vorsteherinn dieser Landschaft seyn müste" (pp. 47-48). This description forms the basis for her representation in *Die Nymphe Noris*, p. 63.

Bibliographical data: Herdegen, 244.

F 2   Etliche Hirtengedichte
       (1646)

Title:

VII. | Folgen | **Etliche Hirtengedichte**. In: Georg Philipp Harsdörffer: *[red]* **GESPRECHSPIELE** | **Sechſter Thel** *[sic]* [...]. Nürnberg: Wolfgang Endter, 1646:)()()(4^v-)()()(7^v. Rpt. Ed. Irmgard Böttcher. Tübingen: Niemeyer, 1969: 36-42.

Collation: 12°:)()()(4^v-7^v, 3½ leaves; [$5], pp. [rpt. ed.] 36-42.

Contents:)()()(4^v: title; text begins (prosimetric bucolic text with emblem): "Es hat der Vater Herbst.")()()(7^r: threefold emblem.)()()(7^v: signed: "Montano."

HT] [none]

RT] "VII." (except emblem p.).

CW] begin)()()(4^v: Blätlein

Type: 18 ll. per p. Dimensions: title: 15 x 44 mm.; p. of text: 74 x 111 mm.
Style: Frak. Gathering sig.:)(; nos., roman.

Notes:
   Signing: begins)()()(5.
   Illustrations:)()()(7ʳ: threefold emblem (two winged figures in each frame dance between two palm trees, with resp. mottos: "Künstliches Greifen," "Liebliches Pfeiffen," "Hertzenfreud Heufen"; below, quatrains.
   Ornamentation: two small floral orns. encase RT, except on emblem p.
   Orn. initial: t.p. "E"

Commentary: Like F1, this piece — the seventh of fifteen com. pieces in praise of Harsdörffer, "der Spielende" — is a miniature prose eclogue.

Bibliographical data: Herdegen, 244.

F 3   Schauplatz der Vollkommenheit
       (1647)

Title:

II. | **Schauplatz der Vollkommenheit** | **zu dem VII. Theil der Geſprächſpiele.** | **Beſtehend in ſieben Baumen / nach den ſieben Altern des Menſch= | en geſetzet / und folgender Geſtalt beſchrieben.** In: Georg Philipp Harsdörffer: *[red]* Gesprächspiele | Siebender Theil [...]. Nürnberg: Wolfgang Endter, 1647:)()(4ʳ-)()(7ʳ. Rpt. Ed. Irmgard Böttcher. Tübingen: Niemeyer, 1969: 17-23.

Collation: 12°:)()(4ʳ-7ʳ, 3½ leaves; [$5], pp. [rpt. ed.] 17-23.

Contents:)()(4ʳ: title; text begins (prosimetric bucolic text with emblem): "Die Weide gerne wächst" (first of seven quatrains).)()(5ᵛ: emblem.)()(6ʳ: prose interpretation under the title: "Ausbildung der Vollkommenheit.")()(7ʳ: signed: "Johann Hellwig/D."

HT] [none]

RT] [none]

CW] begin)()(4ʳ: so / so

Type: 15/16 ll. per p. Dimensions: title: 25 x 117 mm.; p. of text: 73 x 106 mm.
Style: Frak. Gathering sig.:)(; nos., roman. Variant:)()(4.

Notes:
Signing: begins)()(4.
Illustrations:)()(5ᵛ: emblem: in middle, before an oak tree, female figure cast in gold, standing upon pedestal of white marble.
Ornamentation: Headline: (*) surrounded by two small floral orns., except on t.p. and emblem p. (none) and)()(7ʳ: (o) instead of (*).

Commentary: This is the second of five com. pieces in praise of Harsdörffer, "der Spielende."

Bibliographical data: Herdegen, 244.

Annotated Bibliography

A Chronological Survey of Notice and Opinion on Johann Hellwig's Life and Works

ENTRIES ARE in short-title form. For complete bibliographical information, bracketed key-words after each entry make reference to the respective section of Bibliographical Resources at front of book. Page numbers indicate only specific references to Hellwig and his works. In the annotation, numbers in parentheses refer to pages in the given entry; those not in parentheses are introduced with p. or pp. and refer to the primary work in question. Cross-references within Annotated Bibliography are noted in square brackets.

001. STAN/ *Rep.*, Bd. 137.108 (1625). [s. II: StAN/ *Rep.*]
   Documents Christoph Hellwig's purchase of house on Zotenberg for 4500 guilder.

002. "ACTA CONSILIARIO" (1634; rpt. 1967), 346, 349-350, 355-56. [s. IV: "Acta consil."]
   Reprint of handwritten record of the Nation of Germany in Padua. Documents Hellwig's nomination and election as *bibliothecarius* of the society (349); his graduation date of 14 August 1634 (355); two books he presented to the library (356).

003. STAN/ *Rep.* (1640), Bd. 153.218. [s. II: StAN/ *Rep.*]
   Hellwig called as a legal witness in Nuremberg (reason unspecified).

004. BIRKEN, SIGMUND VON. *Fortsetzung* (1645). [s. IV: SvB/ *Fortsetzung*]
   Bestowal, whether mythological or real, of a rustic character flower (65-66: "Feld-Negelein") and a monogram (78: "M") on the new Pegnitz Shepherd Montano.

005. HARSDÖRFFER, GEORG PHILIPP. Letter to Birken, 27 September 1646. [s. IV: GPH/ Let. 1646]
Indicates that Hellwig is working on the *Ormund* translation: "Montanus [...] translationem Ormundi adornat."

006. HARSDÖRFFER, GEORG PHILIPP. Letter to Birken, 6 June 1647. [s. IV: GPH/ Let. 1647]
Assumes that *Noris* is complete, including Birken's poetic response there to departure poems, pp. 69-80: "Montano Schäfergedicht ist noch nicht unter der Presse, sol aber ehest angefangen werden, daß also Floridans Beygedicht noch zu recht kommet, wie auch alle seine Abschiedslieder mit eingebracht werden." Gives general description: "Der Inhalt ist von den hiesigen Geschlechten, vielen Bildrheimen und Beschreibungen der Nymphe Noris Herrlichkeit."

007. BIRKEN, SIGMUND VON. *Helden-Beut* (1648), A2^v. [s. IV: SvB/ *Helden-Beut*]
Makes reference to the departure poems and his response in *Noris*, pp. 69-80, and calls the work "die Dritte Fortsetzung" (Book I). Apparently assumes, on this basis and that of the Harsdörffer letter 1647 [006.], that *Noris* is complete as of this writing.

008. STAN/ *Rep.*, Bd. 161.21E, 27F; 163.91-92 (1649). [s. II: StAN/ *Rep.*]
Documents Hellwig as one of two witnesses in real estate transaction: he and sisters Maria and Magdalena sell "Hausanteil am Zotenberg."

009. BIRKEN, SIGMUND VON. *Teutonie* (1652), 16. [s. IV: SvB/ *Teutonie*]
"Ein andrer / Namens Montano / hat jünsthin [sic] die Herrlichkeit dieser Gegend in zweyen Tagen gar herrlich besungen."

010. STAN/ *Rep.*, Bd. 168.166-168 (1654). [s. II: StAN/ *Rep.*]
Documents Hellwig's sister Maria selling family house on Zotenberg in November.

011.-012. KRESS, JOHANN WILHELM. Inscriptions (1655). [s. IV: Kreß/ Inscript.]
[011.; cited in 070.] "Diß Büchlein hatt Herr Johann Helwig der Artzney Doctor, als er sich Anno 1650 von Nürnberg nacher Regenspurg begeben, zum Valet seinem lieben Vaterland trucken lassen, welches Ich Johann Wilhelm

Kress der Elter, meinem lieben Encklein Johann Wilhelm Kress dem Jüngern verehrt, und Ihn damit an Wilhelmtag angebunden, weil darin des Geschlechts der Kressen mit sondern Ehren gedacht wirdt, und es nachrichtlich bey seiner lieben Posteritet zur gedächtnus verbleiben und sich auch wol und Ehrlich halten sollen."

[012.; inside front cover of the copy in GNM: Sig. G. 7877^r.] Indicates that *Noris* is no longer available as of this date. "Dieses Büchlein / weil es dieser Zeit nicht wol mehr zu bekommen ist / soll hinfüro bey meiner lieben Posteritet / wegen der Kreßischen Vorschickung Neunhof / zur Bedächtnus Verbleiben."

013. GEYGER, DANIEL. Letter to a friend (December 1661). [s. IV: Geyger/ Let.]

Accusation of malpractice against Hellwig in the case of the death of Cardinal Franz Wilhelm von Wartenberg, allegedly written only for the eyes of a friend, but circulated throughout court.

014. GEYGER, DANIEL. *Responsum* (1662). [s. IV: Geyger/ *Resp.*]

Lengthy "vindication" in response to Hellwig's own published defense [*Prodromus*] against Geyger's accusation of malpractice in the case of Cardinal von Wartenberg's death [013.]

015. GEYGER, DANIEL. *Sequitur Instrumentum* (1662), D1^r-5^v. [s. IV: Geyger/ *Sequi.*]

Reprint of his libel suit against Hellwig, motivated by publication of *Prodromus*, "Worinnen aber in rei veritate nichts weniger / denn das jenige / was die *Titulatur* mit sich bringt / befindlich / sondern durchgehendts / ein mit allerhandt übel consarcinirten und applicirten sätzen angespickte *famos* Schrift ist" (D2^v).

016. BOHMER, JOHANN CHRISTOPH. Notary report (1662), D5^v-6^r. [s. IV: Bohmer]

Recalls accompanying Daniel Geyger on visit to Hellwig's residence in *Müllersche behausung*; reiterates terms and cause of suit.

017. STAN/ *Rep.*, Bd. 176.17.22b (1663). [s. II: StAN/ *Rep.*]

Documents sale of the house on Fischbach by Johann and Euphrosine Hellwig, together with other heirs.

018. SCHOTTEL, JUSTUS GEORG. *Ausführliche Arbeit* (1663; rpt. 1967), 1183. [s. IV: Schottel]
Acknowledges Hellwig as translator of *Ormund* 1648.

019. KNORR VON ROSENROTH, CHRISTIAN. "Liebe Kinder / etc." (1667), A3^r-7^r. [s. IV: Knorr]
Disparages the 1660 translation (does not mention translator) of Boethius' *Consolatio* as "unverständlich" both in prose and verse and for failing to communicate the true meaning of the original (A3^r). [cf. 124.]

020. STAN/ *Sig.*, Hellwig E1 (1674). [s. II: StAN/ *Sig.*]
Vital statistics: "Dr. Johann Hellwig, Medicus et Physicus | in Nürnberg | nat. 29. Jul. 1609 † 4. Junii 1674 | Conj: a.) Helene Schlüsselfelderin | nat. 1595 | nupt. 1635 † 1641 | b.) ... Köchin".

021. SCHRÖCK, LUCAS. "Lectori Benevolo Salutem!" (1680), a4^v-b1^r. [s. IV: Schröck]
Describes role played by J. G. Volkamer in gathering Hellwig's papers pursuant to his own editing of *Observationes*. [cf. 022.]

022. SCHRÖCK, LUCAS, and JOHANN GEORG VOLKAMER. "Vita Hellwigiana" (1680), b1^v-b2^v. [s. IV: Schröck—Volkamer]
First biographical review of Hellwig. Information provided by Hellwig's friend Volkamer. Contains facts found in no other source, such as position occupied by Hellwig in Collegium Medicum and details of death.

023. LINDEN, JOHANN ANTONIDA. *De scriptis medicis* (1686), 601-602. [s. I: Linden]
Earliest biographical report on Hellwig in an encyclopedia. Lists only the two medical works: *Alphabetum* and *Observationes*. Curiously, calls attention to Geyger's *Responsum* (014.) but fails to mention *Prodromus*.

024. FREHER, PAUL. *Theatrum virorum* (1688), 1414b-1415a. [s. I: Freher]
Fullest account between Schröck—Volkamer [022.] and Herdegen [033.] of Hellwig's life and works; based on Hellwig's funeral sermon [now apparently lost]. Reports his travels and studies between 1631 and 1634. Like Schröck—Volkamer, offers nothing specific for the period 1649-1674. Makes no reference to Hellwig's poetic activities. Lists none of his works, other than an allusion to *Alphabeton*.

025. OMEIS, DANIEL MAGNUS. *De Claris Quibusdam* (1708), 60. [s. I: Omeis]
First bibliography of Hellwig to include both medical and literary works, though still far from complete. Knows *Alphabeton* (as *Medicina Hippocratica*, incorrectly dated 1635), *Noris*, and the "Sacrarium."

026. JÖCHER, CHRISTIAN GOTTLIEB. *Gelehrten-Lexicon* (1715), vol. 2, col. 1480. [s. I: Jöcher]
Derives information from Freher [024.]; lists only *Alphabeton* and *Observationes*.

027. LOTTER, JOHANN GEORG. "Fortsetzung des Verzeichnißes" (1732; rpt. 1970), 447-453. [s. I: Lotter]
Discusses merits of 1667 Knorr von Rosenroth/ van Helmont translation of Boethius' *Consolatio*; does not know identity of 1660 translator, who signed the work with only his initials: "J. H. Dr."; seeks assistance from readership in locating earlier translation mentioned in Knorr's introduction [019.]: "Man würde uns zu vielem Danke verbinden, wenn man uns denselben mit der Zeit näher zu kennen geben wolte; welches einem geneigten Leser ein leichtes wäre, der diese Auflage als eigen besitzet" (449*).

028. TRECHSEL, JOHANN MARTIN. *Erneuertes Gedächtnis* (1735), 870-871. [s. I: Trechsel]
Hellwig family grave (no. 9) listed among those in the chapel courtyard in St. Johannis Friedhof no longer cared for as of 1735, "so in Manglung der Nachkommenschafft ihrer ehemaligen Besitzer" (870). "Auf dem neundten war zu lesen: 'Deß Erbarn Christoff Helwigs, und Frauen Maria seiner Ehewirtin und ihrer beider Leibs Erben Begräbnus, denen GOtt allen genad A. 1625'" (871). Which of the Hellwig children were buried in this plot is not indicated.

029. ZEDLER, JOHANN HEINRICH. *Universal-Lexikon* (1735; rpt. 1961), vol. 12, col. 1328. [s. I: Zedler]
Brief report derived from Freher [024.]. Lists only *Alphabeton*.

030. KESTNER, CHRISTIAN WILHELM. *Medicinisches Gelehrten-Lexicon* (1740), 387. [s. I: Kestner]
Derives information from Linden [023.]; lists same two medical works.

031. GOTTSCHED, JOHANN CHRISTOPH. "Severini Boethii" (1741; rpt. 1970), 491-501. [s. I: Gottsched]

Delivers harsh attack on Hellwig translation (still without knowledge of translator's identity), alleged to contain many of the solecisms for which Gottsched will condemn previous century at large in his 1748 *Grundlegung einer deutschen Sprachkunst*. Assumes its translator was member of Fruchtbringende Gesellschaft. "Aus der Zuschrift selbst sollte man vermuthen, daß er ein Mitglied der fruchtbringenden Gesellschaft gewesen sey" (492-493). "Seine Rechtschreibung, Wortfügung, und die übrigen in die Sprache einfließenden Umstände sind meistentheils so beschaffen, daß sie mit den Regeln der Sprachwissenschaft nicht übereinstimmen.[...]. Und da er [translator] eine grosse Hochachtung gegen diejenigen Muster bezeuget, welche ihm aus der fruchtbringenden Gesellschaft vor Augen lagen, so ist es nicht zu verwundern, daß die meisten ihm den Geschmack gäntzlich verderbet, und er dasjenige für Tugenden angesehen und nachgeahmet, was wir billig nach den Regeln der Sprachlehrer für Fehler und Gebrechen halten. Neugebackene, uneigentliche, und ungewohnte Wörter; kecke, metaphorische, lange und halbe Seiten füllende Perioden; ein hartklingender Gebrauch der Zeitwörter, an statt der Nennwörter; unrichtige Abweichung der Nenn- und Zeitwörter u.s.w. verstellen diese Uebersetzung recht abscheulich" (497-498).

032. GEORGI, THEOPHIL. *Bücher-Lexikon* (1742), 234. [s. I: Georgi]
Lists only *Observationes*.

033. HERDEGEN, JOHANN. *Historische Nachricht* (1744), 242-245. [s. I: Herdegen]

First biographical summary to deal with Hellwig's poetic life in addition to his medical career, for which he was generally more noted. Gives most complete list of Hellwig's works to date, mentioning for first time his German translation of Pirkheimer's Latin description of Neunhof estate, as well as his three important pieces in volumes 5, 6, and 7 of Harsdörffer's *Frauenzimmer Gesprächspiele*. Gives death incorrectly as 24 May (c 4 June). Cites Schröck—Volkamer [022.] in acknowledging role played by Volkamer.

034. BIEDERMANN, JOHANN GOTTFRIED. *Geschlechtsregister* (1748; rpt. 1982), Tabula DCXXII (Schlüßelfelder), Jiii3ᵛ, C. [s. I: Biedermann]

Under "Helena Schlüßelfelderin": born 1595; married to Hellwig 1635; died 1641.

035. VOGT, JOHANNIS. *Catalogus Historico-Criticus* (1753), 132, under "BOETIVS." [s. I: Vogt]
Notes the 1660 translation of Boethius' *Consolatio* is extremely rare, citing Lotter's remark [027.] and Gottsched's article [031.].

036. WILL, GEORG ANDREAS. *Nürnbergisches Gelehrten-Lexicon* (1756), 86-88. [s. I: Will/ *NGL*]
Brief but cogent review of Hellwig's life and works, compiled from comparative accounts of Mercklin [= Linden, 023.], Freher [024.], Omeis [025.], Kestner [030.], and Herdegen [033.]. Does not mention *Ormund* or *Christlich vernünftiges Bedenken*. Maintains that Hellwig was "ein guter Poet" (87). First to draw attention to Hellwig's many Latin occasional poems (87). Incorrectly reports day of death as 24 May (following Herdegen), but notes that Freher gave it as 4 June.

037. BAUER, JOHANN JACOB. *Bibliotheca Librorum Rariorum* (1770), 132. [s. I: Bauer]
Catalogues Hellwig's translation of Boethius' *Consolatio*, but without attribution; cites Vogt [035.].

038. WILL, GEORG ANDREAS. *Bibliotheca Norica* (1772), series I, vol. 2, 322, no. 1483. [s. I: Will/ *BNW*]
Catalogues *Neunhof* 1648.

039. ELOY, N. F. J. *Dictionnaire Historique de la Médecine* (1778; rpt. 1973), 488-489. [s. I: Eloy]
Credits Hellwig's father with having provided "tous les secours possibles pour réussir dans son éducation littéraire" (488).

040. PANZER, G. W. *Verzeichnis von Nürnbergischen Portraiten* (1790), 100. [s. I: Panzer]
Lists three portraits of Hellwig: a) 1655, by Eimart and Sandrart; b) 1674, "mit Denatus" [unverified by editor, MR]; c) [no date], by Rauler and Haffner (in *Observationes*).

041. FREYTAG, FRIEDRICH KARL. "Deutsche Uebersetzungen" (1794), 33-34. [s. I: Freytag]
Remarks, with reference to Vogt [035.], the 1660 translation "kann aber nicht seltner sein, als sie abgeschmackt ist" (33). Still cannot determine identity of translator.

042. WILL, GEORG ANDREAS, and CHRISTIAN CONRAD NOPITSCH. *Nürnbergisches Gelehrten-Lexicon* (1805), part 6, 58. [s. I: Will—Nopitsch]
First to attribute to Hellwig the translation *Christlich vernünftiges Bedenken*: "Am Schlusse der Zueignungsschrift, welche Regenspurg den 1. des Winter=Monats 1659. ausgefertigt und J. H. Dr. unterzeichnet ist, zeigt sichs, daß D. Helwig der Uebersetzer dieses Buches sey [...]."

043. MAYER, MORITZ MAXIMILIAN. *Wilibald Pirkheimer's Aufenthalt zu Neunhof* (1828), vii-viii and 26-31. [s. I: Mayer]
"Es folgt hier eine neue Uebersetzung mit Anmerkungen; auch die poetischen Gedanken Dr. Hellwig's sollen nicht fehlen" (viii). Reprint of Hellwig's original poems (26-31), which had been dropped from the 1758 reprinting.

044. ERSCH, JOHANN SAMUEL, and JOHANN GEORG GRUBER. *Allgemeine Encyclopädie* (1829; rpt. 1978), 254. [s. I: Ersch—Gruber]
Lists only two medical works: *Alphabeton* and *Observationes*. Says that Hellwig's life was "sehr thätig" and "praktisch."

045. GROTTO DELL'ERRI, LUIGI I. *Della Università di Padova* (1841), 115^r. [s. I: Grotto dell'Erri]
Includes Hellwig's honorary plaque at University of Padua. [cf. 105.]

046. TITTMANN, JULIUS. *Die Nürnberger Dichterschule* (1847; rpt. 1965), 67-68. [s. I: Tittmann]
Bases assessment of Hellwig as poet on *Noris*, which he finds inferior to both previous Nuremberg pastorals in that form, Harsdörffer and Klaj's *Pegnesisches Schäfergedicht* (1644) and Birken's *Fortsetzung* (1645). Characterizes the form as "eine poetische Topographie der Stadt Nürnberg" but finds it cumbersome and the language "alterthümlicher, als der der übrigen Pegnitzer. Reim, Quantität und Strophenbau erinnern oft noch an den Meistergesang, der doch sonst dem Kreise fern genug lag" (68).

047. GERVINUS, GEORG GOTTFRIED. *Geschichte der Deutschen Dichtung* (1853), 289. [s. I: Gervinus]
Considers Hellwig within his discussion of Nuremberg *Schäferei*. Expresses astonishment over — but does not disparage — the profusion of themes and forms in *Noris*. First to place literary work of Hellwig and his Nuremberg colleagues in historical and political context.

048. HEYSE, KARL W. LUDWIG. *Bücherschatz* (1854), no. 746. [s. I: Heyse]
Lists only *Noris*.

049. GRAESSE, JEAN GEORG THÉODOR. *Trésor de Livres* (1859), vol. 3, 237a. [s. I: Graesse]
Lists only *Ormund* 1648 and *Ormund* 1666.

050. KOBERSTEIN, AUGUST. *Geschichte der deutschen Nationalliteratur* (1872; rpt. 1974), [s. I: Koberstein]
Includes *Noris* among "lächerlich[e] Beispiele" of onomatopoeic practice of P.Bl.O. (77). Criticizes that school for excessive imitation and singles out Hellwig's Pindaric ode in *Noris*, pp. 55-56, as "besonders künstlich" (104). Also knows *Ormund* 1648.

051. MALTZAHN, WENDELIN VON. *Deutscher Bücherschatz* (1875; rpt. 1966), 358, no. 1907. [s. I: Maltzahn]
Lists only *Ormund* 1648.

052. MENZEL, WOLFGANG. *Geschichte der Deutschen Dichtung* (1875), 332. [s. I: Menzel]
Includes Hellwig's *Noris* among imitations of Opitz' *Hercinie*. [cf. 068.]

053. KAATHOVEN, CORNELIUS WILHELM HENDRIK VAN. *Portraits de médicins* (1882), 283. [s. II: Kaathoven]
Includes 1655 portrait of Hellwig: artist: Jacob Sandrart, after painting by Georg Christoph Eimart d. J.; verse by Georg Philipp Harsdörffer.

054. STAN/ *Personenregister* (1883), 371, ref. no. 1832. [s. II: StAN/ Lochner]
Hellwig's seal. Entry reads: "Hellwig Johann, Dr. phil. et med., Siegel des ... 1637 Aug. 3." Seal of red wax; around it in capital letters: "JOH. HELLWIG PHIL ET MED D."

055. GOEDEKE, KARL. *Grundriß* (1887), ¶183, 58, nos. 1-3; ¶192, 13. [s. I: Goedeke]
Knows only *Ormund* 1666, *Noris*, and *Christlich vernünftiges Bedenken*.

056. HIRSCH, AUGUST. *Biographisches Lexikon*, vol. 3 (1893; 3rd ed. 1962), 149. [s. I: Hirsch]

Incorrectly gives year of birth as 1600 (c 1609). Mentions the two medical works: *Alphabeton* and *Observationes*. Information derived from "Biogr. med. V, pag. 146" [unknown to editor, MR].

057. BISCHOFF, THEODOR. *Georg Philipp Harsdörfer* (1894), 211-212, 218. [s. I: Bischoff]

Describes *Noris* as "eine ansehnlichere Leistung [...] im Geschmacke der Pegnesis und der Nymphe Hercynie gehalten" (218). Gives very brief biographical account after Hellwig's acceptance into P.Bl.O. (211-212).

058. KNOD, GUSTAV C. *Die alten Matrikeln der Universität Strassburg* (1897), 12. [s. I: Knod]

Documents matriculation on 11 May 1631 of "Johannes Hellwigius, Noribergensis Med. Stud."; rector Johann Georg Dorschae.

059. SURGEON GENERAL. *Index-Catalogue* (1901), 1004. [s. I: Surgeon General]

Lists *Alphabeton*.

060. HOLZMANN, MICHAEL, and HANNS BOHATTA. *Deutsches Pseudonym-Lexikon* (1906; rpt. 1961), 186a. [s. I: Holzmann]

Description under "Montano."

061. FRANZ, ALBIN. *Johann Klaj* (1908; rpt. 1968), 22, 25-26, 94, 110. [s. I: Franz]

Mentions several points of connection between Hellwig and Klaj, e.g. Hellwig and Volkamer probably introduced Klaj to social mileau in which he met his bride, daughter of Johann Conrad Rhumelius (25-26); discusses (94) Klaj's "Der Hof ist eine Gedultschuele," which belongs to collection of commendatory poems in Hellwig's *Ormund*, (*)(*)1^v-3^v. Ignores Klaj's poems in *Noris*.

062. STEINMEYER, ELIAS VON. *Die Matrikel der Universität Altdorf* (1912), vol. 1, 200; vol. 2, 280, fn. 18. [s. I: Steinmeyer]

In volume 1, documents matriculation on 31 June 1627 of "Johannes Hellwigius, Norib.", rector Johann Koh. In volume 2, cites Knod [058.].

063. SCHOLTE, JAN HENDRIK. "Nürnberger Dichterschule" (1925; 2nd ed. 1965), 707. [s. I: Scholte]
"Als drittes größeres Schäfergedicht sei noch erwähnt die *Nymphe Noris* (1650) von Montano [...]."

064. MANHEIMER, VICTOR. *Deutsche Barockliteratur* (1927; rpt. 1966), 40, no. 192. [s. II: Manheimer]
Lists only *Ormund* 1648.

065. MÜLLER, GÜNTHER. *Deutsche Dichtung* (1927), 215. [s. I: Müller]
Notes that translation of Italian baroque novels was fashionable in Germany during 1640s and 1650s; cites Hellwig and J. W. von Stubenberg as representatives of the trend.

066. STOLBERG. *Leichenpredigten-Sammlung* (1927-1928). [s. III: Stolberg]
Collects sixteen epicedia by Hellwig.

067. KOSCH, WILHELM. *Deutsches Literatur-Lexikon* (1927; 3rd ed. 1979 ff.), vol. 1, col. 865. [s. I: Kosch]
Lists *Ormund* 1648, *Noris*, and *Christlich vernünftiges Bedenken*.

068. MEYER, HEINRICH. *Der deutsche Schäferroman* (1928; rpt. 1978), 32-34. [s. I: Meyer]
First serious treatment of *Noris* and first to identify kind of pastoral practiced by Pegnitz Shepherds in terms of genre (*Gesellschaftsschäferei*), whose model is Opitz' *Hercinie* [cf. 052.]. Like Gervinus, views P.Bl.O. in functional terms: *Schäferei* fills social purpose. Maintains that realistic representation developed in Nuremberg through the practice of Opitzian pastoral: "Hier merkt man, dass das alles rechte Wirklichkeit ist [...]. Der Zug zu realistischer Selbstdarstellung ist das literarhistorisch Bedeutsame, die Nürnberger haben den Realismus, beinahe den Naturalismus, vorausgenommen" (33). [cf. 069.]

069. KAYSER, WOLFGANG. *Die Klangmalerei* (1932), 238. [s. I: Kayser]
In context of Hellwig's *Noris*, cautions taking too broadly the realism thesis of Meyer [068.]: "Ich betone dieses Ergebnis noch einmal ausdrücklich gegen die andere Deutung H. Meyers [...]. Hinsichtlich der Sprache und des Stiles darf nicht von einem Realismus oder Naturalismus gesprochen werden." Speaks of Hellwig as disciple and friend of Harsdörffer.

070. FRANK ZU DÖFERING, KARL FRIEDRICH VON. *Die Kressen* (1936), cols. 478-483. [s. I: Frank z. D.]

Cites copy of *Noris* in possession of Johann Wilhelm Kreß with handwritten dedication to owner's grandson [s. 011.].

071. LIEGNITZ. *Leichenpredigten-Sammlungen* (1938), 709. [s. III: Liegnitz]

Indexes ten epicedia by Hellwig.

072. SCHWAIGER, GEORG. *Kardinal Franz Wilhelm von Wartenberg* (1954), 86. [s. I: Schwaiger]

Citing letter from Chancellor J. N. Vetterl of 4 December 1661, names Hellwig ("Helbig") as one of the two physicians (the other: Dr. Preßl) who performed autopsy on Cardinal von Wartenberg [cf. 013., 014.].

073. WALLER, ERIK. *Bibliotheca Walleriana* (1955), vol. 1, 197, no. 4291. [s. I: Waller]

Catalogues *Alphabeton*.

074. NEWALD, RICHARD. *Die deutsche Literatur* (1957), 211. [s. I: Newald]

Recognizes Hellwig mainly as translator: "Als Übersetzer von *Francesco Ponas* Heldengedicht Ormund (1646) [c 1648] und *Boethius* (1660) bewegte er sich im Umkreis der gefährlichen höfischen Welt und des Stoizismus."

075. FABER DU FAUR, CURT VON. *German Baroque Literature*, vol. 1 (1958), 149b-150b. [s. II: Faber du Faur]

Collection holds three major works by Hellwig: *Ormund* 1648, *Noris*, and *Christlich vernünftiges Bedenken*. Credits Hellwig as "one of the most active members" of P.Bl.O. but sees him mainly as an imitator: "[W]hat attracted him to the Shepherds of the Pegnitz was precisely their predilection for verse play, to which he too was a zealous addict.[...] But even he could produce nice imitations of Klaj's and Birken's style" (149b). Claims that Hellwig "corresponded continuously with Birken who advised him and checked his material" (150a), an assertion that is possible but unverified.

076. *AUKTIONSPREISE* (1960 ff.). [s. I: *Auktionspreise*]

Offers *Noris*: vols. 11 (1960), 18 (1967), 20 (1969).

077. SPAHR, BLAKE LEE. *Archives of the Pegnesischer Blumenorden* (1960), 13 and 98 (no. 113). [s. II: Spahr]
First cataloguing of Hellwig's papers in P.Bl.O. archives, as 49-5a [one letter to Birken; new P.Bl.O. sig.: C.135.1]. Uncovers written note from Harsdörffer to Birken [6 June 1647], important for reconstructing genesis of *Noris*: "Montano Schäfergedicht ist noch nicht unter der Presse, sol aber ehest angefangen werden, daß also Floridans Beygedicht noch zu recht kommet, wie auch alle seine Abschiedslieder mit eingebracht werden" (13).

078. SCHULTHEISS, WERNER. "Woher stammt die Bezeichnung 'Noris'?" (1963/1964), 551-553. [s. I: Schultheiß]
Credits Hellwig with having coined the term "Noris." Vredeveld [107.] corrects this assumption.

079. GARBER, KLAUS. "Nachwort" (1966), 19*-20*. [s. I: Garber/ 1966]
Mentions Hellwig only as one of the first members of P.Bl.O.

080. ROSSETTI, LUCIA. *Acta Nationis Germanicae Artistarum* (1967). [s. IV: "Acta consil."]
[s. 002.]

081. MANNACK, EBERHARD. *Die Pegnitz-Schäfer* (1968; 2nd ed. 1988), 157, 230-233. [s. I: Mannack]
Reprinting of two items from *Noris*: "Sanduhr," p. 90, attributed to Hellwig (c Johann Sechst); "Es hat die HimmelsGnad die Schäfer so begabt," pp. 12-15. [s. also 101.]

082. SZYROCKI, MARIAN. *Die deutsche Literatur des Barock* (1968; 2nd ed. 1979), 169. [s. I: Szyrocki]
Categorizes Hellwig primarily as translator.

083. DÜLMEN, RICHARD VAN. "Sozietätsbildungen in Nürnberg" (1969), 176. [s. I: Dülmen]
Mentions Hellwig only as an early member of P.Bl.O. Ignores him in discussion of Nuremberg *Schäferdichtung*.

084. HEFNER, OTTO TITAN VON. *Die Wappen bürgerlicher Geschlechter* (1971), plate 87. [s. I: Hefner]
Hellwig's shield described: Justitia with bound eyes, holding sword and scale; colors not known. [cf. 109.]

085. FLETCHER, JOHN E. "Georg Philipp Harsdörffer" (1972), 206. [s. I: Fletcher]

Mentions letter from Hellwig to Kircher [Regensburg, 10 January 1655] located in Archives of Pontificia Università Gregoriana, Rome, in which he describes how he had accompanied the great polymath by ship between Marseilles and Genoa in September 1633. Letter occasioned by the imminent staging in Nuremberg of Kircher's *Oedipus Aegypticus*.

086. WARNOCK, ROBERT G., and ROLAND FOLTER. "The German Pattern Poem" (1970). [s. I: Warnock—Folter]

Interest in Hellwig as composer of pattern poems. Reprint from *Noris*, pp. 85, 87, 90: "Nußbaum" (68); "ein kleine Oergelein" (58); "eine Sanduhr" (59); and from *Ormund*, p. 116: "Egyptische flammenseule" (54). Regard Hellwig somewhat reluctantly as innovator in pattern poetry: "the poems become more elaborate in form, if not always more artistic as poetry" (48), but primarily as a dilettante, or apologist of the form (44), an opinion echoed by Kühlmann [122.]. Claim (51) that Hellwig's "Nußbaum" is "a precise parallel" to emblem no. 39 of Andreas Alciatus' "In fertilitatem sibi ipsi damnosam" [cf. 095.].

087. KIRCHNER, GOTTFRIED. *Fortuna in Dichtung und Emblematik* (1970). [s. I: Kirchner]

Uses Hellwig's translation of Boethius' *Consolatio* in discussion of that work's importance for the question of *fortuna* in Baroque.

088. DENCKER, KLAUS-PETER. *Text Bilder* (1972). [s. I: Dencker]

Interest in Hellwig as composer of pattern poems. Reprint from *Noris*, pp. 86, 87, 89: "Reichsapfel" (43); "ein kleines Oergelein" (43); "Quell" (45).

089. JANTZ, HAROLD. *German Baroque Literature* (1974), vol. 1. [s. II: Jantz]

Includes *Ormund* 1648 (no. 1326) and *Noris* (no. 1325). Concludes his remarks on *Noris* with a reference to America that editor (MR) finds inscrutable: "One of the classic Nürnberg pastorals on the Pegnitz, with the full virtuosity of poetic melody & shape: sounds of nature, picture poems, emblems, even various on America" [sic] (168b).

090. GARBER, KLAUS. *Der locus amoenus* (1974), 129 (fn.), 136-137, 142 (fn.). [s. I: Garber/ 1974]
Serious treatment of *Noris* in terms of Garber's reconstruction of Nuremberg *Schäferei* as "Prosaekloge." Finds that *Noris* employs technique of allusion to greater extent than the two earlier — more "realistic" — prose eclogues of Harsdörffer, Klaj, and Birken. [cf. 068., 069.]

091. PETIT, MARC. *Poètes baroques allemands* (1977), 136. [s. I: Petit]
Interest in Hellwig as composer of pattern poems. Reprint of "eine Sanduhr" from *Noris*, p. 90.

092. D'ORS, MIGUEL. *El caligrama* (1977), 33-34, 83-84. [s. I: D'Ors]
Ranks Hellwig highly among seventeenth-century German composers of figured poetry (33-34). Reprint from *Noris*, pp. 87 and 89: "ein kleines Oergelein" (83); "Quell" (84).

093. HERZOG-AUGUST-BIBLIOTHEK. *Deutsche Drucke des Barock* (1977-1989). [s. II: H-A-B]
Ormund 1648: A 166.
Die Nymphe Noris: A 4803.
Christlich vernünftiges Bedenken: B 601.
Ormund 1666: B 602.

094. PEIGNOT, JEROME. *Du caligramme* (1978), 53. [s. I: Peignot]
Interest in Hellwig as composer of pattern poems. Reprint of "eine Sanduhr" from *Noris*, p. 90.

095. DALY, PETER M. *Literature in the Light of the Emblem* (1979), 127-132. [s. I: Daly]
Interest in Hellwig as composer of pattern poems. Argues that Hellwig's "Nußbaum" (*Noris*, p. 85) is structually more emblematic than the poem upon which it is modeled in Alciatus' *Emblematum liber* [cf. 086.]. Finds Hellwig's version particularly interesting in that it reveals a bipartite structure characteristic of word-emblem: first half of poem is pictorial, second half interpretive (127, 132). Reprint of "Nußbaum", with English translation (128-129).

096. RYPSON, PIOTR. "La Tradición de la poesia visual" (1980), 53-58. [s. I: Rypson]
Interest in Hellwig as composer of pattern poems. Reprint of "Nußbaum" in *Noris*, p. 85 (56).

097. MACHÉ, ULRICH, and VOLKER MEID. *Gedichte des Barock* (1980; 2nd ed. 1986), 160, 371. [s. I: Maché—Meid]
Reprint of "eine Sanduhr" in *Noris*, p. 90 (160).

098. EMRICH, WILHELM. *Deutsche Literatur der Barockzeit* (1981), 53. [s. I: Emrich]
Reprint of "M" ("Der Stumme stummt") attributed to Hellwig in Birken's *Fortsetzung*, p. 78.

099. GRAN, ULF. "Studier i manierism" (1981), fig. 8. [s. I: Gran]
Interest in Hellwig as composer of pattern poems. Reprint of "Nußbaum" in *Noris*, p. 85.

100. DÜNNHAUPT, GERHARD. *Bibliographisches Handbuch* (1980-1981). [s. I: Dünnhaupt]
Noris: (331, no. 42; also, 800, no. 56; 1027, no. 48). *Ormund* 1648: (327, no. 22; also, 796, no. 45; 1025, no. 37). [1990 ed.: no additions.]

101. LOHMEIER, ANKE-MARIE. *Beatus ille* (1981), 451, 479-481. [s. I: Lohmeier]
Reproduces "Es hat die HimmelsGnad die Schäfer so begabt" from *Noris*, pp. 12-15 (479-481), as example of *laus ruris*, viz. of the type "Lob des Schäferlebens." [cf. 081.]

102. ERNST, ULRICH. "Europäische Figurengedichte" (1982), 327-328. [s. I: Ernst]
Interest in Hellwig as composer of pattern poems. Reprint from *Noris*, p. 8: "Pyramis" (328); from *Ormund*, p. 116: "Egyptische flammenseule" (327).

103. KREBS, JEAN-DANIEL. *Georg Philipp Harsdörffer* (1983). [s. I: Krebs]
Includes *Noris* in discussion of rural temple or grotto in *Schäferei* (447). Considers Hellwig an important poet of figured verse: "J. Hellwig/ *Montano*, avec la *Nymphe Noris* qui ne compte pas moins de douze poèmes figuratifs, s'est particulièrement distingué, dans l'entourage de Harsdörffer, dans un genre encore cultivé avec succès plus tardivement par J. Geuder/ *Rosidan*" (590).

104. SEVERIN, KARL. *Fünfundzwanzig Figurengedichte* (1983). [s. I: Severin]
Interest in Hellwig as composer of pattern poems. Reprint from *Noris*, pp. 8, 86, 91: "Pyramis" (59); "Reichsapfel" (35); "Ehrengebäu" (21).

105. ROSSETTI, LUCIA. *Gli Stemmi dello Studio di Padova* (1983), 19, no. 58. [s. I: Rossetti]
Photo and description of Hellwig's bronze honorary plaque in atrium of University of Padua. *Scudo* [Hellwig's family shield]: "Azzurro: La Giustizia, con veste [rossa], impugnante 1 bilancia [...] nella mano sinistra e 1 spade [...], la punta all'insu, nella destra, accostata da 6 stelle [d'oro], 3 a ciascun fianco, l'una sull'altra." Legend: "IOHANnes HELLVIG / NORICUS Inclytæ Nationis Germanicæ Artistarum BIBLIOTHECarius ET / CONSiliarius BOHEMicus." On Hellwig's escutcheon: "ULTRAMONTANA." [cf. 045.]

106. NEWMAN, JANE OGDEN. "Institutions in the Pastoral" (1983), 297-302. [s. I: Newman/ 1983)
Interprets *Noris* as a key text in the mythologization and institutionalization of P.Bl.O. as poetic society. Places it in European context.

107. VREDEVELD, HARRY. "Zur Herkunft des Wortes 'Noris'" (1984), 208-211. [s. I: Vredeveld]
Corrects Schultheiß [078.], demonstrating that the allegorical word "Noris" was probably the invention of Eobanus Hessus more than one hundred years earlier; Hellwig, who was familiar with neo-Latin tradition, merely borrowed the word for his purpose of inventing the female deity.

108. W.D. "Nymphe 'Noris'" (1985). [s. I: W.D.]
Reviews contribution of Vredeveld [107.] to understanding history of the word "Noris."

109. NEUBECKER, OTTFRIED. *Großes Wappen-Bilder-Lexikon* (1985). [s. I: Neubecker]
Hellwig's shield (124) [description, s. 084. and 085.]. Koch family shield (111): man holding up cooking spoons. The two shields can be seen together on Hellwig's 1655 portrait.

110. TREW-SAMMLUNG. *Gelegenheitsgedichte* (1985). [s. III: Trew]
From the Altdorfian collection at Universitätsbibliothek, Erlangen; richest collection of Hellwig's occasional verse. Twenty-two poems in Latin and German to seventeen addressees.

111. ADLER, JEREMY. "Pastoral Typography" (1986), 127-135. [s. I: Adler]
Argues that Hellwig's innovative use of figured poetry made him a leader, perhaps surpassing even Birken, in revival of pattern poetry as aesthetic novelty. Demonstrates complexity of Hellwig's "verbal-visual" poetry (131) and the dynamic, even "theatrical quality" of the cycle of ten pattern poems in *Noris*, pp. 83-91. Reprinting of entire set from *Noris*. One of the first studies to regard early modern German figured poetry as other than manneristic and trivial; evaluates Hellwig's contribution as genuinely poetic. [cf. 117.]

112. HIGGINS, DICK. *Pattern Poetry* (1987), 76-77. [s. I: Higgins]
Describes the twelve pattern poems from *Noris* [no. 1 incorrectly given as p. 72 (c p. 7)] as well as the one from *Ormund*, p. 116, "Egyptische flammenseule." Reprint (77) of "Sanduhr" in *Noris*, p. 90, properly attributing it to Johann Sechst. Surveys previous studies of pattern poetry that adduce Hellwig. [cf. 086., 088., 091., 092., 094., 095., 096., 097., 099., 102., 104.]

113. REINHART, MAX. "An Annotated Edition" (1987). [s. I: Reinhart/ 1987]
Reset text of *Noris* with commentary; simplified bibliographical description.

114. PAAS, JOHN ROGER. *Effigies et Poesis* (1988), 396-399. [s. I: Paas]
Includes the Sandrart—Eimart portrait of Hellwig from 1655 and a later copy of it.

115. JAITNER, KLAUS. "Der Pfalz-Sulzbacher Hof" (1988), 301-302. [s. I: Jaitner]
Shows that Hellwig accompanied Francis van Helmont to Sulzbach in May 1651 (301). In the same context, quotes a report by Johann Kaspar Gundermann to Philipp Wilhelm of Pfalz-Neuburg, 31 May 1651, that Helmont and his "Begleiter" [= Hellwig?] came into bodily danger at the hands of men who disapproved of Helmont's influence on Duke Christian August (302).

116. JÖNS, DIETRICH, and HARTMUT LAUFHÜTTE. *Sigmund von Birken* (1988), 37. [s. I: Jöns—Laufhütte]

Reprint of Hellwig's departure poem to Birken, "Sind dann künftig unsre Auen," from their edition of Birken's *Biographia*. Original publication in *Noris*, p. 70. Birken emended text slightly; use of the poem in *Guelfis* (1669) shows further variants.

117. ADLER, JEREMY, and ULRICH ERNST. *Text als Figur* (1988), 75a, 145b, 152, 165a. [s. I and II: Adler—Ernst]

Consider Hellwig one of the outstanding seventeenth-century German practitioners of pattern poetry. The theoretical statement in *Noris*, pp. 82-83, "dürfte zu den wichtigsten poetologischen Aussagen über das Figurengedicht im Barock gehören" (75a) [cf. 086.). Comment on the structure of the cycle of twelve [this passage mistakenly says thirteen] pattern poems in *Noris*: "Es entsteht eine ganze Fülle von Entsprechungen, welche die Gedichte thematisch und ästhetisch verbinden" (145a) [cf. 111.].

118. SAMMONS, CHRISTA. Exhibit: "German Baroque Literature" (1988). [s. II: Sammons]

Noris one of six books on exhibit of pattern poetry. Others: Birken's *Fortsetzung* and *Guelfis*; Klaj's *Der leidende Christus*; Schottel's *Teutsche Vers- oder Reim Kunst*; Geuder's *Der Friedseligen Irenen Lustgarten*.

119. REINHART, MAX. "The Privileging of the Poet" (1988), 229-243. [s. I: Reinhart/ 1988]

Maintains that *Noris*, by contrasting the literary idea of true nobility with that of inherited nobility, is a representative text in the changing consciousness of learned German *Bürgertum*.

120. NEWMAN, JANE OGDEN. *Pastoral Conventions* (1990), 228-232. [s. I: Newman/ 1990]

Argues that there occurred a mythical transformation of Nuremberg's seventeenth-century landscape into the new home of pastoral poetry. Regards *Noris* as unique among early pastorals of P.Bl.O. because of its "power to make the ideal real in the text" (230).

121. REINHART, MAX. "Historical, Poetic and Ideal Representation" (1990), 41-66. [s. I: Reinhart/ 1990]

Demonstrates the interplay in a typical prose eclogue of literary form and real-world process and how, in the case of *Noris* — composed during the final war years — the utopian intent of the genre and the peaceful outcome of hostilities mesh in a unique literary and historical synchronism.

122. KÜHLMANN, WILHELM. "Kunst als Spiel" (1991), 509 and 517. [s. I: Kühlmann]

Interest in Hellwig as composer of pattern poems. Asserts, as Warnock and Folter [086.], that Hellwig is mainly a mannerist, or trivializer of pattern poetry, overly concerned with emphasizing its psychological effect on readers.

123. REINHART, MAX. "Poets and Politics" (1991), 217-228. [s. I: Reinhart/ 1991]

Presents social evolution of early modern Nuremberg as a clash of estatist interests, in which the professionals challenge patrician monopolization in law courts while poets seek to do the same by disguised social messages, particularly in the "anmuhtige Schreibart" of prose eclogue.

124. REINHART, MAX. *"De Consolatione Philosophiae"* (1992). [s. I: Reinhart/ 1992]

Evaluates Hellwig's German translation of Boethius' *Consolatio*; considers the critical response to it and compares the new translation by Knorr and Helmont, 1667 [cf. 019.]; reviews its negative reception in the German Early Enlightenment [027., 031.].

125. REINHART, MAX. *Johann Hellwig: A Descriptive Bibliography* (1993). [s. I: Reinhart/ *DB*]

Descriptive and exhaustive history of Hellwig's books and other writings, introduced with a detailed biography. Includes annotated and other bibliographies and indexes.

126. REINHART, MAX. *Johann Hellwig's "Die Nymphe Noris"* (1993). [s. I: Reinhart/ 1993]

Historical-critical edition. Includes introduction, word glossaries, and indexes.

127. GARBER, KLAUS. "Der Hirten- und Blumenorden an der Pegnitz" (forthcoming), 131-151. [s. I: Garber/ forthcom.]
Examines *Noris* within its social and historical context. Finds it an exemplary work of carefully guarded social criticism. "In den Augen dieses Autors ist die Gattung der Pastorale offensichtlich von Nimbus des Hermetischen und des Kritischen umgeben [...]. Helwig gehört zu den Autoren, denen sich im Gegensatz zu den vielen bukolischen Versifikatoren des Jahrhunderts ein Bewußtsein von der latenten negativen Potenz der Gattung erhalten hat" (145).

Supplemental Bibliography

THE FOLLOWING list supplements the Bibliographical Resources. It offers a selection of studies that are relevant to the broader context of Hellwig's life and works.

Abbreviations and short-titles:

Alewyn = *Deutsche Barockforschung: Dokumente einer Epoche*. Ed. Richard Alewyn. 4th ed. Neue Wissenschaftliche Bibliothek, 7. Köln: Kiepenheuer, 1970.
Bircher and van Ingen = *Sprachgesellschaften, Sozietäten, Dichtergruppen: Vorträge und Berichte*. Eds. Martin Bircher and Ferdinand van Ingen. Wolfenbütteler Arbeiten zur Barockforschung, 7. Hamburg: Hauswedell, 1978.
Blühm = *Hof, Staat und Gesellschaft in der Literatur des 17. Jahrhunderts*. Eds. Elger Blühm, Jörn Garber, and Klaus Garber. Amsterdam: Rodopi, 1982.
Garber = *Europäische Bukolik und Georgik*. Wege der Forschung, 355. Ed. Klaus Garber. Darmstadt: Wissenschaftliche Buchgesellschaft, 1976.
GRM = *Germanisch-Romanische Monatsschrift*
JdSg = *Jahrbuch der deutschen Schillergesellschaft*
Pfeiffer = *Nürnberg — Geschichte einer europäischen Stadt*. Ed. Gerhard Pfeiffer. 1971. Rpt. München: Beck, 1982.
MVGN = *Mitteilungen des Vereins für Geschichte der Stadt Nürnberg*
Smith = *Nuremberg: A Renaissance City, 1500-1618*. Ed. Jeffrey Chips Smith. Austin: University of Texas Press, 1983.
Voßkamp, *Schäferdichtung* = *Schäferdichtung: Referate*. Dokumente des Internationalen Arbeitskreises für Barockforschung, 4. Hamburg: Hauswedell, 1977.
Voßkamp, *Utopieforschung* = *Utopieforschung: Interdisziplinäre Studien zur neuzeitlichen Utopie*. 3 vols. Stuttgart: Metzler, 1982.
Wiedemann = *Literatur und Gesellschaft im deutschen Barock: Aufsätze*. Ed. Conrad Wiedemann. *GRM*, Beiheft 1. Heidelberg: Winter, 1979.

Baader, Joseph, ed. *Nürnberger Polizeiordnungen aus dem XIII bis XV Jahrhundert*. Bibliothek des litterarischen Vereins in Stuttgart, 63. 1861. Rpt. Amsterdam: Rodopi, 1966.

Barner, Wilfried. *Barockrhetorik: Untersuchungen zu ihren geschichtlichen Grundlagen*. Tübingen: Niemeyer, 1970.

Berbig, Hans Joachim. *Das Nationalgefühl in Nürnberg nach dem Dreissigjährigen Krieg*. Diss. München 1960.

Berns, Jörg Jochen. "Zur Tradition der deutschen Sozietätsbewegung im 17. Jahrhundert." In Bircher and van Ingen, 53-73.

Bleeck, Klaus, and Jörn Garber. "Nobilitas: Standes- und Privilegienlegitimation in deutschen Adelstheorien des 16. und 17. Jahrhunderts." In Blühm, 49-114.

Bog, Ingomar. "Reichsverfassung und reichsstädtische Gesellschaft: Sozialgeschichtliche Forschungen über reichsständische Residenten in den Freien Städten, insbesondere in Nürnberg." *Jahrbuch für fränkische Landesforschung* 18 (1958): 325-340.

Böschenstein-Schäfer, Renate. *Idylle*. Sammlung Metzler, 63. Stuttgart: Metzler, 1967.

Böttcher, Irmgard. "Der Nürnberger Georg Philipp Harsdörffer." In *Deutsche Dichter des 17. Jahrhunderts: Ihr Leben und Werk*. Eds. Harald Steinhagen and Benno von Wiese. Berlin: Schmidt, 1984: 289-346.

Breuer, Dieter. "Zur Rolle Nürnbergs im literarischen Leben des katholischen Oberdeutschland." In *Oberdeutsche Literatur 1565-1650: Deutsche Literaturgeschichte und Territorialgeschichte in frühabsolutistischer Zeit*. Zeitschrift für bayerische Landesgeschichte (Reihe B), Beiheft 11. München: Beck, 1979: 37-43.

Brunner, Horst. *Literatur in der Stadt: Bedingungen und Beispiele städtischer Literatur des 15. bis 17. Jahrhunderts*. Göppinger Arbeiten zur Germanistik, 343. Göppingen: Kümmerle, 1982.

Conermann, Klaus. "Der Poet und die Maschine: Zum Verhältnis von Literatur und Technik in der Renaissance und Barock." In *Teilnahme und Spiegelung: Festschrift für Horst Rüdiger*. Eds. Beda Allemann and Erwin Koppen. Berlin: de Gruyter, 1975: 173-192.

Conrady, Karl Otto. *Lateinische Dichtungstradition und deutsche Lyrik des 17. Jahrhunderts*. Bonn: Bouvier, 1962.

Diepgen, Paul. *Geschichte der Medizin: die historische Entwicklung der Heilkunde und des ärtzlichen Lebens*. Vol. 1: *Von den Anfängen der Medizin bis zur Mitte des 18. Jahrhunderts*. Berlin: de Gruyter, 1949.

Dyck, Joachim. "Das Selbstverständnis des Dichters: ein Argumentationssystem." In *Ticht-Kunst: Deutsche Barockpoetik und rhetorische Tradition*. 3rd ed. Tübingen: Niemeyer, 1991: 113-134.

Eisenbart, Liselotte Constanze. *Kleiderordnungen der deutschen Städte zwischen 1350 und 1700: Ein Beitrag zur Kulturgeschichte des deutschen Bürgertums*. Göttinger Bausteine zur Geschichtswissenschaft, 32. Göttingen, Berlin, and Frankfurt a. M.: Musterschmidt, 1962.

Ellinger, Friedrich Wolfgang. "Die Juristen der Reichsstadt Nürnberg vom 15. bis 17. Jahrhundert." In *Genealogica, Heraldica, Juridica: Reichsstadt Nürnberg, Altdorf und Hersbruck*. Freie Schriftenfolge der Gesellschaft für Familiengeschichte in Franken, 6. Nürnberg: Kommissionsverlag Egge, 1954: 130-222.

Ellinger, Georg. *Geschichte der neulateinischen Literatur Deutschlands im sechzehnten Jahrhundert*. Vol. 2. 1929. Rpt. Berlin: de Gruyter, 1969.

Empson, William. *Some Versions of Pastoral: A Study of the Pastoral Form in Literature*. 1935. Rpt. New York: New Directions, 1974.

Endres, Rudolf. "Endzeit des Dreißigjährigen Krieges." In Pfeiffer, 273-279.

———. "Sozialstruktur Nürnbergs." In Pfeiffer, 194-199.

Evans, R. J. W. "Learned Societies in Germany in the Seventeenth Century." *European Studies Review* 7 (1977): 129-151.

Fischer, Ludwig. *Gebundene Rede: Dichtung und Rhetorik in der deutschen literarischen Theorie des Barock in Deutschland*. Tübingen: Niemeyer, 1968.

Freitag-Stadler, Renate. "Herrensitze im Bereich der Reichsstadt Nürnberg: unter Berücksichtigung des Problems der Weiherhäuser." Diss. Erlangen/Nürnberg 1972.

———. "Neunhof bei Kraftshof, ein Nürnberger Patriziersitz." *MVGN* 61 (1974): 129-160.

Fürstenwald, Maria. "Letztes Ehren=Gedächtnis und Himmel=klingendes SCHAEFER SPIEL: Der literarische Freundschafts- und Totenkult im Spiegel des barocken Trauerschäferspiels." *Daphnis* 2 (1973): 32-53.

Garber, Klaus. "Der Autor im 17. Jahrhundert." *Lili* 42 (1981): 29-45.

———. "Die Friedens-Utopie im europäischen Humanismus: Versuch einer geschichtlichen Rekonstruktion." *Modern Language Notes* 101/3 (1986): 516-552.

———. "Gelehrtenadel und feudalabsolutistischer Staat: Zehn Thesen zur Sozial- und Mentalitätsgeschichte der 'Intelligenz' in der Frühen Neuzeit." In *Kultur zwischen Bürgertum und Volk*. Ed. Jutta Held. Argument-Sonderband, AS 103. Berlin: Argument, 1983: 31-43.

———. "Gibt es eine bürgerliche Literatur im 17. Jahrhundert?" *GRM* 31 (1981): 462-470.

———. "Skizze zur Sozialgeschichte der Schäferdichtung als utopischer Literaturform Europas." In Voßkamp, *Utopieforschung*, 37-81.

———. "Sozietäten, Akademien, Sprachgesellschaften." In *Europäische Enzyklopädie zu Philosophie und Wissenschaften*. Vol. 4. Ed. Hans Jörg Sandkühler. Hamburg: Meiner, 1990: 366-384.

———. "Zur Statuskonkurrenz von Adel und gelehrtem Bürgertum im theoretischen Schrifttum des 17. Jahrhunderts." In Blühm, 115-143.

Garrison, Fielding H. *An Introduction to the History of Medicine with Medical Chronology, Suggestions for Study and Bibliographic Data*. 4th ed. 1929. Rpt. Philadelphia and London: Saunders, 1960.

Gerteis, Klaus. *Die deutschen Städte in der Frühen Neuzeit: Zur Vorgeschichte der "bürgerlichen Welt."* Darmstadt: Wissenschaftliche Buchgesellschaft, 1986.

Goldmann, Karlheinz. *Nürnberger und Altdorfer Stammbücher aus vier Jahrhunderten: Ein Katalog*. Beiträge zur Geschichte und Kultur der Stadt Nürnberg, 22. Nürnberg: Selbstverlag des Stadtrats Nürnberg, 1981.

Grant, William Leonard. *Neo-Latin Literature and the Pastoral*. Chapel Hill: University of North Carolina Press, 1965.

Grimm, Gunter. *Literatur und Gelehrtentum in Deutschland: Unternehmungen zum Wandel ihres Verhältnisses vom Humanismus bis zur Frühaufklärung*. Studien zur deutschen Literatur, 75. Tübingen: Niemeyer, 1983.

Grimm, Reinhold R. "Arcadia und Utopia: Interferenzen im neuzeitlichen Hirtenroman." In Voßkamp, *Utopieforschung*, 82-100.

Hable, Guido. *Geschichte Regensburgs: Eine Übersicht nach Sachgebieten*. Studien und Quellen zur Geschichte Regensburgs, 1. Regensburg: Mittelbayerische Druckerei- und Verlags-Gesellschaft, 1970.

Haendler, Carl Gottfried, comp. "Register über die Nürnbergischen Mandate nach chronologischer Ordnung von Anno bis 1800." In StBN, Sig.: Amb.309.2°.

Haller von Hallerstein, Helmut Freiherr. "Nürnberger Geschlechterbücher." *MVGN* 65 (1978): 212-235.

Hamm, Berndt. "Humanistische Ethik und Reichsstädtische Ehrbarkeit in Nürnberg." *MVGN* 76 (1989): 65-147.

Hansmann, Wilfried. *Gartenkunst der Renaissance und des Barock*. Köln: Du Mont, 1983.

Hardison, O. B., Jr. *The Enduring Monument: A Study of the Idea of Praise in Renaissance Literary Theory and Practice*. Chapel Hill: University of North Carolina Press, 1962.

Harper, Anthony John. "In the Nürnberg Manner? Reflections on a 17th. Century Parody." *Neophilologus* 58 (1974): 52-65.

Hartmann, Fritz, and Rudolf Vierhaus, eds. *Der Akademiegedanke im 17. und 18. Jahrhundert.* Wolfenbütteler Forschungen, 3. Bremen: Jacobi, 1977.

Hausberger, Karl. *Geschichte des Bistums Regensburg.* Vol. 1: *Mittelalter und frühe Neuzeit.* Regensburg: Pustet, 1989: esp. 332-346.

Henne, Helmut. "Deutsche Lexikographie und Sprachnorm im 17. und 18. Jahrhundert." In *Deutsche Wörterbücher des 17. und 18. Jahrhunderts: Einführung und Bibliographie.* Ed. Helmut Henne. Hildesheim: Olms, 1975.

Hildebrandt, Reinhard. "Rat contra Bürgerschaft: Die Verfassungskonflikte in den Reichsstädten des 17. und 18. Jahrhunderts." *Zeitschrift für Stadtgeschichte* 2 (1974): 221-241.

Hirsch, Arnold. "Die Entstehung der modernen Seelenlage im Schäferroman." 1957. Rpt. in Garber, 306-328.

Hirschmann, Gerhard. "Das Nürnberger Patriziat." In *Deutsches Patriziat 1430-1740: Büdinger Vorträge 1965.* Ed. Hellmuth Rössler. Schriften zur Problematik der deutschen Führungsschichten in der Neuzeit, 3. Limburg/Lahn: Starke, 1968: 257-276.

Hoffmeister, Gerhart. *Die spanische Diana in Deutschland: Vergleichende Untersuchungen zu Stilwandel und Weltbild des Schäferromans im 17. Jahrhundert.* Philologische Studien und Quellen, 68. Berlin: Schmidt, 1972.

Huebner, Alfred. *Das erste deutsche Schäferidyll und seine Quellen.* Diss. Königsberg 1910.

Ingen, Ferdinand van. "Die Erforschung der Sprachgesellschaften unter sozialgeschichtlichem Aspekt." In Bircher and van Ingen, 9-26.

Iser, Wolfgang. "Spencers Arkadien: Fiktion und Geschichte in der englischen Renaissance." 1970. Rpt. in Garber, 231-265.

Jöns, Dietrich. "Literaten in Nürnberg und ihr Verhältnis zum Stadtregiment in den Jahren 1643-1650 nach den Zeugnissen der Ratsverlässe." In *Stadt — Schule — Universität — Buchwesen und die deutsche Literatur im 17. Jahrhundert.* Ed. Albrecht Schöne. München: Beck, 1976: 84-98.

———. "Literatur und Stadtkultur in Nürnberg im 17. Jahrhundert: Bericht über ein Forschungsprojekt an der Universität Mannheim." In Bircher and van Ingen, 217-221.

Krauss, Werner. "Über die Stellung der Bukolik in der ästhetischen Theorie des Humanismus." 1938. Rpt. in Garber, 140-164.

Krautter, Konrad. *Die Renaissance der Bukolik in der lateinischen Literatur des XIV. Jahrhunderts: von Dante bis Petrarca.* Theorie und Geschichte der Literatur und der schönen Künste, 65. München: Fink, 1983.

Krummacher, Hans-Henrik. "Das barocke Epicedium: Rhetorische Tradition und deutsche Gelegenheitsdichtung im 17. Jahrhundert." *JdSg* 18 (1974): 89-147.

Kühlmann, Wilhelm. *Gelehrtenrepublik und Fürstenstaat: Entwicklung und Kritik des deutschen Späthumanismus in der Literatur des Barockzeitalters.* Studien und Texte zur Sozialgeschichte der Literatur, 3. Tübingen: Niemeyer, 1972.

Kunstmann, Heinrich. *Die Nürnberger Universität Altdorf und Böhmen: Beiträge zur Erforschung der Ortbeziehungen deutscher Universitäten.* Köln: Böhlau, 1963.

Lange, Hermann. "Vom Adel des Doctor." In *Das Profil des Juristen in der europäischen Tradition.* Eds. Klaus Luig and Detlef Liebs. Ebelsbach: Gremer, 1980: 279-294.

Lorenz, Bernd. "Nürnberger Ärtze als Büchersammler: Medizinische Privatbibliotheken des 15.-18. Jahrhunderts." *MVGN* 72 (1985): 75-83.

Lytle, Guy Fitsch. "The Renaissance, the Reformation, and the City of Nuremberg." In Smith, 17-22.

Mannack, Eberhard. "Realistische und metaphorische Darstellung im *Pegnesischen Schäfergedicht* (1644)." *JdSg* 17 (1973): 154-165.

Martino, Alberto. "Barockpoesie, Publikum und Verbürgerlichung der literarischen Intelligenz." *Internationales Archiv für Sozialgeschichte der deutschen Literatur* 1 (1976): 107-144.

Meyer, Julie. "Die Entstehung des Patriziats in Nürnberg." *MVGN* 27 (1928): 1-96.

Müller, Arnd. "Zensurpolitik der Reichsstadt Nürnberg." *MVGN* 49 (1959): 66-169.

Müllner, Johannes. *Die Annalen der Reichsstadt Nürnberg von 1623.* Teil I: *Von den Anfängen bis 1350.* Teil II: *Von 1351 bis 1469.* Ed. Gerhard Hirschmann. Quellen zur Geschichte und Kultur der Stadt Nürnberg, 8 and 11. Nürnberg: Selbstverlag des Stadtrats, 1972 and 1984.

Mulzer, Erich. *Vor den Mauern Nürnbergs: Kunst und Geschichte der Vorstädte.* Nürnberg: Spindler, 1961.

Neuburger, Max, and Julius Pagel. *Handbuch der Geschichte der Medizin.* Jena: Fischer, 1902-1905.

Neumann, Friedrich. *Geschichte des neuhochdeutschen Reimes von Opitz bis Wieland: Studien zur Lautgeschichte der neuhochdeutschen Gemeinsprache.* Berlin: Weidmann, 1920.

Oestreich, Gerhard. *Strukturprobleme der frühen Neuzeit: Ausgewählte Aufsätze.* Ed. Brigitta Oestreich. Berlin: Duncker & Humblot, 1980.

Otto, Karl F. *Die Sprachgesellschaften des 17. Jahrhunderts*. Sammlung Metzler, 109. Stuttgart: Metzler, 1972.

Paas, John Roger. "Poeta incarcerata: Georg Philipp Harsdörffers Zensurprozeß 1648." In Wiedemann, 155-164.

Peters, Herrmann. *Aus pharmazeutischer Vorzeit in Bild und Wort*. Nürnberg: Springer, 1886.

Pfeiffer, Gerhard, ed. (with assistance of Wilhelm Schwemmer). *Geschichte Nürnbergs in Bilddokumenten*. München: Beck, 1970.

Pitz, Ernst. *Die Entstehung der Ratsherrschaft in Nürnberg im 13. und 14. Jahrhundert*. Bayerische Landesgeschichte, 55. München: Beck, 1955.

Recktenwald, Horst Claus. *Die fränkische Universität Altdorf*. 2nd ed. Nürnberg: Spindler, 1990.

Rössler, Hellmut, and Günther Franz, eds. *Universität und Gelehrtenstand 1400-1800: Büdinger Vorträge 1966*. Deutsche Führungsgeschlechten in der Neuzeit, 4. Limburg/Lahn: Starke, 1970.

Rusterholz, Peter. "Nachwort." In *Schäfferey von der Nimfen Hercinie*. Universal-Bibliothek, 8594. Stuttgart: Reclam, 1969: 71-79.

———. "Schäferdichtung — Lob des Landlebens." In *Zwischen Gegenreformation und Frühaufklärung: Späthumanismus, Barock 1572-1740*. Ed. Harald Steinhagen. Vol. 3 of *Deutsche Literatur: Eine Sozialgeschichte*. rororo, 6252. Hamburg: Rowohlt, 1985: 356-366.

Schall, Kurt. *Die Genannten in Nürnberg*. Nürnberger Werkstücke zur Stadt- und Landesgeschichte, 6. Nürnberg: Schriftenreihe des Stadtarchivs Nürnberg, 1971.

Schelenz, Hermann. *Geschichte der Pharmazie*. Berlin: Springer, 1904.

Schöne, Albrecht, and Arthur Henkel, comps. *Emblemata: Handbuch zur Sinnbildkunst des XVI. und XVII. Jahrhunderts*. Stuttgart: Metzler, 1967.

Segebrecht, Wulf. *Das Gelegenheitsgedicht: Ein Beitrag zur Geschichte und Poetik der deutschen Lyrik*. Stuttgart: Metzler, 1977.

Simon, Matthias. *Nürnbergisches Pfarrerbuch: Die evangelisch-lutherische Geistlichkeit der Reichsstadt Nürnberg und ihres Gebietes 1524-1806*. Einzelarbeiten aus der Kirchengeschichte Bayerns, 41. Nürnberg: Selbstverlag des Vereins für Bayerische Kirchengeschichte, 1965.

Sinemus, Volker. *Poetik und Rhetorik im frühmodernen deutschen Staat: Sozialgeschichtliche Bedingungen des Normenwandels im 17. Jahrhundert*. Palaestra, 269. Göttingen: Vandenhoeck & Ruprecht, 1978.

Snell, Bruno. "Arkadien: Die Entstehung einer geistigen Landschaft." 1945. Rpt. in Garber, 14-43.

Spahr, Blake Lee. "Nürnbergs Stellung im literarischen Leben des 17. Jahrhunderts." In *Problems and Perspectives: A Collection of Essays on German Baroque Literature*. Europäische Hochschulschriften, Reihe 1, 423. Frankfurt a. M.: Lang, 1981: 271-284.

———. "The Pastoral Works of Sigmund von Birken." Diss. Yale University 1952.

Staber, Josef. "Die geistliche Barockkultur." Chapter 5 of *Kirchengeschichte des Bistums Regensburg*. Regensburg: Habbel, 1966: esp. 138-151.

Steinbach, Franz. "Geburtsstand, Berufsstand und Leistungsstand: Studien zur Geschichte des Bürgertums II." *Rheinische Vierteljahrsblätter* 14 (1949): 35 ff.

Stockinger, Ludwig. "Entwicklungsprobleme der Schäferpoesie vom 17. zum 18. Jahrhundert im Lichte zeitgenössischer poetologischer Äußerungen." In Voßkamp, *Schäferdichtung*, 141-160.

Stolleis, Michael. *Staat und Staatsräson in der frühen Neuzeit: Studien zur Geschichte des öffentlichen Rechts*. stw, 878. Frankfurt a. M.: Suhrkamp, 1990.

Strauss, Gerald. *Nuremberg In the Sixteenth Century*. New Dimensions in History: Historical Cities. New York: Wiley, 1966.

Strich, Fritz. "Der lyrische Stil des 17. Jahrhunderts." 1916. Rpt. in Alewyn, 229-259.

Stromer, Wolfgang von. "Reichtum und Ratswürde: Die wirtschaftliche Führungsschicht der Reichsstadt Nürnberg 1348-1648." In *Führungskräfte der Wirtschaft in Mittelalter und Neuzeit 1350-1850. Büdinger Vorträge 1968-1969*. Ed. Herbert Helbig. Deutsche Führungsschichten in der Neuzeit, 6. Limburg/Lahn: Starke, 1973: 1-50.

Sudhoff, Karl. *Kurzes Handbuch der Geschichte der Medizin*. Berlin: Karger, 1922.

Thorndike, Lynn. *A History of Magic and Experimental Science: The Seventeenth Century*. Vols. 7 and 8. New York and London: Columbia University Press, 1958.

Trunz, Erich. "Der deutsche Späthumanismus um 1600 als Standeskultur." 1931. Rpt. in Alewyn, 147-181.

Verweyen, Theodor. "Dichterkrönung: Rechts- und sozialgeschichtliche Aspekte literarischen Lebens in Deutschland." In Wiedemann, 7-29.

Viëtor, Karl. "Vom Stil und Geist der deutschen Barockdichtung." 1926. Rpt. in Alewyn, 39-71.

Wagman, Frederick Herbert. *Magic and Natural Science in German Baroque Literature: A Study in the Prose Forms of the Later Seventeenth Century*. 1942. Rpt. New York: AMS Press, 1966.

Waldersdorf, Hugo Graf von. *Regensburg in seiner Vergangenheit und Gegenwart*. 4th ed. 1896. Rpt. Regensburg: Pustet, 1973.

Weisz, Jutta. *Das deutsche Epigramm des 17. Jahrhunderts*. Germanistische Abhandlungen, 49. Stuttgart: Metzler, 1979.

Wiedemann, Conrad. "Druiden, Barden, Witdoden: Entwurf eines Identifikationsmodells." In Bircher and van Ingen, 131-150.

———. "Heroisch — Schäferlich — Geistlich: Zu einem möglichen Systemzusammenhang barocker Rollenhaltung." In Voßkamp, *Schäferdichtung*, 96-122.

Wightman, William P. D. "Myth and Method in Seventeenth-Century Biological Thought." *Journal of the History of Biology* II/2 (1969): 321-336.

Zeller, Rosmarie. *Spiel und Konversation im Barock: Untersuchungen zu Harsdörffers "Gesprächspielen."* Quellen und Forschungen zur Sprach- und Kulturgeschichte der germanischen Völker, N. F. 58 (177). Berlin and New York: de Gruyter, 1974.

Zink, Fritz. "Die Entdeckung des Pegnitztales." *MVGN* 50 (1960): 271-285.

Zorn, Wolfgang. "Die soziale Stellung der Humanisten in Nürnberg und Augsburg." In *Die Humanisten in ihrer politischen und sozialen Umwelt*. Eds. Otto Herding and Robert Stupperich. DFG, Kommission für Humanismusforschung, Mitteilung III. Boppard: Boldt, 1976: 35-49.

Index of Libraries

THE INDEX, organized alphabetically by city (American spellings), consists of the seventy-three libraries represented in Descriptive Bibliography, under the heading "Copies." Items belonging to special collections are included under respective city and library, e.g. Trew = Erlangen: Universitätsbibliothek.

A
Amberg:
 Staatliche Provinzialbibliothek: A4/1
Augsburg:
 Staats- und Stadtbibliothek: A4/2-3

B
Bamberg:
 Staatsbibliothek: A2/1; B1.1/1
Basel:
 Universitätsbibliothek: A1/1; A4/4
Berkeley:
 Bancroft Library: A2/2
Berlin:
 Staatsbibliothek zu Berlin - Preussischer Kulturbesitz: A2/3-4; A3/1; C1.49
Berlin:
 Stadtbibliothek: A2/33
Berlin:
 Universitätsbibliothek: B1.2/1
Bethesda:
 National Library of Medicine: A1/2; A4/5

C
Chicago:
 University of Chicago Library: A2/5
Coburg:
 Landesbibliothek: B3/1

D
Darmstadt:
 Hessische Landes- und Hochschulbibliothek: A4/6
Darmstadt:
 Zentralarchiv Evangelische Kirche: C1.49
Donaueschingen:
 Fürstliche Fürstenbergische Hofbibliothek: A2/6
Dresden:
 Sächsische Landesbibliothek: A4/7

E
Edinburgh:
 National Library of Scotland: A3/2; A4/8
Eichstätt:
 Katholische Universität, Universitätsbibliothek: A3/3
Einsiedeln:
 Stiftsbibliothek: B3/2
Erlangen:
 Universitätsbibliothek: A1/3; A2/7; A4/9; B2.2/1-2; C1.1; C1.3-4; C1.5; C1.6-7; C1.8-9; C1.10; C1.23-24; C1.26-27; C1.28; C1.36; C1.37; C1.42; C1.43; C1.44; C1.46; C1.49; E3

F
Firenze:
 Biblioteca Nazionale Centrale: A4/10
Frankfurt a. M.:
 Senkenbergische Bibliothek: A4/42
Freiburg:
 Universitätsbibliothek: A1/4

G

Glasgow:
University Library: A4/11
Gotha:
Forschungsbibliothek: A4/12
Göttingen:
Niedersächsische Staats- und Universitätsbibliothek: A1/5; A2/8; A4/13; B3/3
Greifswald:
Ernst-Moritz-Arndt Universitätsbibliothek: A4/14

H

Heidelberg:
Universitätsbibliothek: A2/9-10

I

Innsbruck:
Universitätsbibliothek: A2/11

K

Krakow:
Uniwersytet Jagielloński, Biblioteka Jagiellońska: A4/15

L

Laubach:
Gräflich Solms-Laubachsche Bibliothek: C1.52; C1.53
Leipzig:
Universitätsbibliothek: A2/12; A4/16; B3/4; C1.11-12; C1.23-24; C1.39; C1.48
Lodz:
Biblioteka Uniwersytecka: A2/13
London:
British Library: A1/6; A2/14; A4/17; B1.1/2
Lüneburg:
Ratsbücherei: A2/15

M

Madison:
University of Wisconsin, Memorial Library: A2/16
Mainz:
Universitätsbibliothek (Medizinhistorisches Institut): A1/7
Marburg:
Universitätsbibliothek: A4/18

Munich:
Bayerische Staatsbibliothek: A2/17; A4/19-20; B1.1/3; B3/5; C1.56
Munich:
Stiftsbibliothek Abtei St. Bonifaz: B1.1/8
Munich:
Universitätsbibliothek: A1/8

N

New Haven:
Beinecke Rare Book and Manuscript Library: A2/18; B1.1/4; B3/6; C1.13; C1.21-22; C1.47
Nuremberg:
Archiv des Pegnesischen Blumenordens: E1
Nuremberg:
Germanisches National Museum: A1/9; A2/19-22; B2.1/1-2; B2.2/3; C1.3-4; C1.10; C1.26-27; C1.34-35
Nuremberg:
Landeskirchliches Archiv: C1.10; C1.11-12; C1.26-27
Nuremberg:
Stadtbibliothek: C1.2; C1.14-15; C1.17-18; C1.29-30

O

Oslo:
Universitetsbiblioteket: A4/21
Oxford:
Bodleian Library: A4/22
Oxford:
Queen's College Library: A4/23

P

Padua:
Museo Civico, Biblioteca: A4/24
Paris:
Bibliothèque Nationale: A1/10; A4/25
Philadelphia:
The Library Company: A4/26
Philadelphia:
Thomas Jefferson University (Jefferson Medical College): A4/27
Prague:
Národní v Praze: A4/28
Princeton:
University Library: A2/23

Index of Libraries

R

Regensburg:
Fürst Thurn und Taxis, Zentralarchiv, Hofbibliothek: A3/4
Regensburg:
Staatliche Bibliothek: A4/29
Rome:
Biblioteca Apostolica Vaticana: A4/30
Rome:
Università Gregoriana (Kircher Collection): E2

S

St. Petersburg:
Biblioteka Akademii Nauk: A4/31
Salzburg:
Universitätsbibliothek: A4/32
Schwerin:
Mecklenburgische Landesbibliothek: A4/33
Strasbourg:
Bibliothèque Nationale et Universitaire: A2/24-25; A4/34

T

Tübingen:
Universitätsbibliothek: A4/35

U

University Park:
Pennsylvania State University Library: A2/32
Uppsala:
Universitetsbibliotek: A1/11; A4/36

V

Vienna:
Österreichische Nationalbibliothek: A4/37; B1.1/5; D1
Vienna:
Universitätsbibliothek: A2/26; A3/5; A4/38

W

Winterthur:
Stadtbibliothek: A4/39

Wolfenbüttel:
Herzog August Bibliothek: A2/27; B1.1/6; B1.2/2; B3/7; C1.23-24; C1.28; C1.36; C1.39; C1.40; C1.41; C1.44; C1.45; C1.46; C1.48; C1.49; C1.50-51; C1.52; C1.53; C1.54
Wroclaw:
Biblioteka Uniwersytecka: A2/28-30; A4/40; B1.2/3; B3/8
Würzburg:
Universitätsbibliothek: A2/31

Z

Zurich:
Zentralbibliothek: A1/12; A4/41; B3/9
Zwickau:
Ratsschulbibliothek: B1.1/7; B3/10

Index of Names

INCLUDED HERE are the personal names (except for Johann Hellwig) that are mentioned in the chapters, General Introduction and Descriptive Bibliography. When both maiden and family names of women appear in the text they are cross-listed here, e.g. Bärnbeck, Elena (∞Kob). If only a family name and first initial are known, the attempt is made to attach some identifying word, such as profession or city, e.g. Graff, J. (artist). Spellings of names reflect documentary form(s). Superscripted numbers refer to footnotes. Individuals bearing the same names are distinguished by date of death.

Adelmann
  Bernhard von Adelmannsfeld: 15^{70}, 15^{71}, 63
Adler
  Jeremy: 12, 13, 23, 34, 54
Agricola
  Catharina Barbara (née Donauer): 82
  Hieronymus: 82
Albert
  Freiherr von Törring, Bishop of Regensburg: 17
Albrecht
  Margrave: 91
Amalfi
  Duke Georg von: 37
Ammon: 99
Andreae
  Johann: 17
Anton Ulrich
  Duke of Braunschweig-Lüneburg: 14, 14^{69}, 52, 53, 57, 58, 78
Arnold
  Christoph (Lerian): 7, 12, 14, 94, 101
Aufseß
  Hans Freiherr von: 64
August
  Duke of Braunschweig-Lüneburg: 39

Bältingslawia
  B. von: 68
Bamberger: 38
Barbeck
  Hugo: 38
Bärnbeck
  Elena (∞Kob): 71, 72
Bauer
  Johann Jacob: 13^{62}
Baumgartner: 88
  Conrad: 96
  Hieronymus (†1551): 37
  Hieronymus (†1565): 98
  Hieronymus (†1602): 98
Beheim (Böheim, Behaim): 89
  Lucas Friderich: 36, 37, 78, 99
  Martin: 96
Bellovallius: 3
Bernegger
  Matthias: 17
Besler
  Catharina Barbara (née Rosa): 74
  Michael Ruprecht: 74
Betulius
  Sigmund [s. Birken, Sigmund von]
Bezzel
  Christoph: 35
Biedermann
  Johann Gottfried: 5^{30}, 6^{40}
Birken (also: Sigmund Betulius)
  Sigmund von (Floridan): 7, 7^{43}, 7^{44}, 8, 8^{46}, 9, 9^{52}, 11, 12, 13^{61}, 14, 14^{69}, 32, 38, 76, 86, 87, 94, 108
Boccaccio
  Giovanni: 7^{42}

Boethius
  Anicius Manlius Severinus: 13, 13[64], 15, 18, 66, 67
Bohmer
  Johann Christoph: 17[82]
Bosl
  Karl: 1[3], 20[94]
Böttcher
  Irmgard: 110, 111, 112
Bowers
  Fredson: 21[99]
Bruno
  Jacob: 2
Brunsterer: 99
Burdach
  Konrad: 34

Cämmerer: 92
Celtis
  Conrad: 9, 9[50], 10
Christian August
  Duke of Sulzbach: 17
Chytraeus
  Nathan: 9, 9[51]
Citharæda
  Anna Nicodemus: 10
Clerford
  Heinrich: 6[36]
Cocleus [Cochläus]
  Johannes: 105
Comenius
  Johann: 18

Dalnsteiner
  Paul: 85
David
  Johann: 68
Deissinger
  L. (Vienna): 39
Delort: 3
Dieterichs
  Georg Septimus: 42
Dietherr: 92
  C. L.: 66
Dilherr
  Johann Michael: 18, 80, 82, 84
Donauer
  Catharina Barbara (∞Agricola): 82
  Christoff Sig(is)mund: 81, 82, 83, 85
Dörrer: 89
  Wilhelm: 97

Dresserus
  Matthaeus: 9, 9[51]
Dümler
  Jeremia: 32, 72, 77
Dünnhaupt
  Gerhart: 23, 34, 54
Dürr
  Johann Conrad: 81

Ebner: 89
  Hieronymus: 97
Ehinger: 38
Ehrenberg
  Richard: 1[5]
Eloy
  N. F. J.: 2[14], 4[26], 4[27]
Elsener
  Ferdinand: 10[53]
Endter
  Johann: 82, 84
  Michael: 83
  Wolf(f)gang: 27, 74, 75, 76, 78, 81, 82, 84, 86, 110, 111, 112
Ernst
  Ulrich: 12, 13, 23, 34, 54
Ersch
  Johann Samuel: 34, 54, 67
Eschnloher: 38
Eyßvogel: 99

Faber du Faur
  Curt von: 8[46], 11[58], 36, 75, 83
  Emma von: 36
Faltzner: 99
Felwinger
  Paul: 77
Ferdinand Albrecht
  Duke of Braunschweig-Lüneburg: 54
Fischer
  Christoff: 81, 82, 85
Flechsdörffer: 99
Fleckenstein
  P. Mauritius von: 68
Folter
  Roland: 12[59], 12[60]
Fonseca
  Rodericus a: 3
Fräntzel
  Bartholomaeus: 84
Freher
  Paul: 2[9], 2[11], 2[12], 3[20], 4[26], 17[80], 18[86], 20[94], 29

Index of Names

Friedrich
  Duke of Saxony: 47
Fü(h)rer: 89
  Anna Elisabeth (née Schlüsselfelder): 75
  Christoff (†1610): 35, 37, 98
  Johann Leonard: 75
Füterer: 99
  Jacob: 98
Fütter
  Sebastian: 10

Gandolf
  Cardinal Archbishop Max von Kuenburg: 49
Garber
  Klaus: 10[53]
Gebhardt
  Johann: 83
Geissenhausser
  Anna Rosina (∞Heberlein): 81
Georgi
  Theophil: 46
Gerhard
  Christoff: 66
Gervinus
  Georg Gottfried: 34
Geuder
  Martin: 97
  Philipp: 98
Geyger
  Daniel: 18, 18[86], 19[91], 19[92], 20, 41, 42
Gilhofer: 54
Gil Polo
  Gaspard: 83
Goebel
  Theophil: 45
Goedeke
  Karl: 13[62], 20[94], 23, 34, 58, 67
Goldast
  Melchior: 15, 15[71], 61, 63
Göring
  Simon: 83
Gottsched
  Johann Christoph: 16, 16[77]
Grabner: 100
Graesse
  Jean Georg Théodor: 13[62], 54, 58
Graff
  J. (artist): 35
Graser: 100
Gravius
  Johann: 74

Grimm
  Jacob: 58
  Wilhelm: 58
Groeter
  Friedrich: 34
Groland: 89
  Leonhard: 97
Groß (-ss): 100
  Conrad: 96
  Sebastian: 97
Grotto dell'Erri
  Luigi I.: 3[19]
Gruber
  Erasmus: 82
  Johann Georg: 34, 54, 67
Grundherr: 89
  Ulrich: 96
Grunhagen
  (Pastor, Höchst/Nidda): 48
Grünwald
  Susanna (∞Sechst): 86
Gugel: 92
Gundermann
  Johann: 74
Gutbrod
  Wolfgang Achatz: 66
Guttmann: 58
Gyger
  Dr. J. R.: 30

Haf(f)ner
  Melchior: 46
Hagelsheimer: 92
Hagen
  Georg: 80
Haller: 89
  Anna Felicitas (∞Tetzel): 73
  Johann Albert: 73
  Ruprecht: 96
  Wilhelm: 96
Hammer
  William: 9[50]
Harsdörffer: 89
  Georg Philipp (Strephon; der Spielende): 7[45], 8, 8[46], 8[47], 9[52], 10, 10[56], 11, 13, 13[64], 14, 14[67], 15, 15[74], 18, 52, 57, 75, 82, 83, 86, 87, 88, 94, 101, 110, 111, 112, 113
  Johann: 97
  Paul(us): 99
  Paul: 39
Hayden [s. Heiden]

Heberlein
  Anna Rosina (née Geissenhausser): 81
  Johann Paul: 81
Hefner
  Otto Titian von: 2[7]
Hegner: 38
Heiden (Hayden): 92, 100
Heigel
  Dr. D. (Regensburg): 20, 20[93]
Heinrich: 5, 5[28], 19[93]
Hellwig (Helwig, Helbig)
  Anna: 2[7]
  Blasius: 2, 2[7]
  Christoph d. Ä.: 1, 1[4], 2, 2[7], 2[14], 4, 4[23], 6[37]
  Christoph d. J.: 1[2]
  Euphrosina (née Koch): 5, 6, 6[38]
  Georg Andres: 1[2]
  Hans Georg: 1[2]
  Helena (née Schlüsselfelder): 5, 5[29], 5[30]
  Helena ("H. H."): 1[2], 6[37], 88
  Helena Sabina: 6, 6[37]
  Magdalena: 1[2], 17[81]
  Maria (née Mörl): 1, 1[2], 2
  Maria d. J.: 1[2], 1[4], 17[81]
Helmont
  Francis Mercurius van: 16, 17, 18, 18[85]
  Jan Baptist van: 17
Hennemann
  Wilhelm: 49
Herdegen
  Johann: 3[16], 7[45], 20[94], 29, 34, 46, 61, 106, 111, 112, 113
Hesekiel
  Ludovici: 37, 38
Hessus
  Eobanus: 8, 9, 9[50]
Heyse
  Karl W. Ludwig: 34
Hilling
  Gregor: 5, 5[28]
Hipprocates: 27
Hirsch
  August: 1[3], 4[26], 29, 46
Hirschvogel: 100
Hoffmann
  Caspar: 2
Hoffmen
  Helena (∞Leutkirchner): 1[2]
Hofmann
  Hanns Hubert: 1[5]
  Moritz: 10

Holtzschuher: 90
Hieronymus: 97
  Sigmund Gabriel: 36, 37, 99
Homburg
  Ernst Christoph: 76
Horn
  Dr. Franz Philipp: 39
Hostwitz
  der Marcomanner Fürst: 101
Hund
  Samuel: 14
Hunter
  Dr. William: 47
Hütter
  Johann: 54

Imhof(f) (ImHoff) (Im Hoff): 90
  Andreas (†1579): 37, 98
  Andreas (†1597): 98
  Andreas (†1637): 27, 36, 37, 99
  Anna Katharina (∞Koch): 5[34]
  Jacob: 95
  Maria Helena (née Pömer): 77
  Wilhelm d. Ä.: 77
  Wilhelm d. J.: 5[34], 77

Jaitner
  Klaus: 17[84]
Jantz
  Harold: 34, 54
Jenisch: 15, 95
  Ferdinand: 6, 6[37], 60, 66, 77
  Georg Paul: 84
  Maria Sabina (née Koler): 6, 6[37], 60, 77
  Paul: 77
Jöcher
  Christian Gottlieb: 23, 29, 46
Jöns
  Dietrich: 76

Kahlert
  Prof. Dr. August: 39
Kapp
  C. E.: 48
Katterbeck: 38
Kayser
  Wolfgang: 8[46]
Kerscher
  Johann Jacob: 45

Index of Names

Kestel: 38
Justus Hieronymus: 80
Kestner
  Christian Wilhelm: 4[26], 29, 46
Kircher
  Athanasius: 3, 3[17], 107, 108
Klaj
  Johann (Klajus): 8, 12, 14, 38, 87, 94, 101
Kleewein
  Joachim: 5[34]
  Margaretha Katharina (∞Koch): 5[34]
Knod
  Gustav C.: 2[9], 2[15]
Knorr
  Christian von Rosenroth: 16, 16[75], 18
Kob
  Elena (née Bärnbeck): 71, 72
  Johann: 2, 72, 80
  Maria Müllich (née Trammel): 72
Koburger: 38
Koch
  Anna Katharina (née ImHoff): 5[34]
  Esther: 5[34]
  Euphrosina (née Steininger): 5, 5[34]
  Euphrosina (∞Hellwig): 5, 5[33], 6, 6[38]
  Herbert: 73
  Jacob: 5, 5[34], 6, 66
  Konrad: 5[34]
  Margaretha Katharina (née Kleewein): 5[34]
Kojsiewicz
  Ferdynand: 48
Kolde
  Dr. Theodor: 64
Koler (Coler): 6, 15, 90, 95
  Anna Philipina: 60, 77
  Christoff: 97
  Georg Seyfried: 6, 60, 77
  Maria Sabina (∞Jenisch): 6, 6[37], 60, 77
  Paul: 61
König
  Georg: 72, 80, 81, 82
Koppmayer
  Jacob: 45, 84
Kosch
  Wilhelm: 13[62], 34, 54, 67
Kötzler: 93
Kraus
  J. (artist): 35
Krauter: 100
Kreß (von Kressenstein): 33, 38, 90, 101
  Antoni: 37, 38, 102
  Caspar: 37, 38, 102
  Christoff (-ph) (†1535): 35, 36, 38, 97
  Christoff (†1537): 102
  Conrad: 38, 101
  Friderich (fl 1291): 101
  Friderich (†ca. 1406): 101
  Hanns: 102
  Hieronimus (-ymus): 35, 37, 38, 98, 102
  Hupold: 38, 101
  Jobst Christoff: 35, 37, 38, 95
  Johann Wilhelm: 37
  Otto: 101
  Sebald: 102
Kronauer
  Dr. Johann H.: 50
Kueffstein
  Johann Ludwig Freiherr von: 83

Lang
  Johann Georg: 84, 85
Langmann: 100
Lassberg
  Joseph Freiherr von: 34
Laufhütte
  Hartmut: 75
Lehner
  Johann: 85
Leutkirchner
  Elisabeth (∞Mörl): 1[2]
  Helena (née Hoffmen): 1[2]
  Matthaeus: 1[2]
Licetus
  Fortunatus: 3
Linden
  Johann Antonida: 17[80], 29, 46
Lochner
  Friedrich (Periander): 7, 12, 14, 94, 101
  Jakob: 14
Löffelholtz: 90
  Christoff: 99
  Johann Friderich: 36, 37, 72, 73, 99
Logan
  Dr. William: 49
Lotter
  Johann Georg: 16, 16[76]
Ludwell
  Wilhelm: 10, 78
Ludwig Rudolf
  Duke of Braunschweig-Lüneburg: 58

Maltzahn
  Wendelin von: 13[62], 54
Manheimer
  Victor: 13[62], 34, 54
Marci
  Cornelius: 35, 37, 73, 88
Martino
  Alberto: 16[78]
Matthias
  Emperor: 37, 92
Mauricius
  Georg: 2
Mayer
  Moritz: 15, 15[73], 64
Meichsner: 38
Meisterlin
  Sigismund: 9[50]
Memminger
  Paul: 66
Mendel: 100
  Marquard: 96
Menzel
  Albert: 29
Meusebach
  K. H. G.: 34
Meyer
  Heinrich: 10[53]
Michaelis
  Georg Philipp: 48
Monte-Major
  Jorge de: 83
Mörl
  Elisabeth (née Leutkirchner): 1[2]
  Konrad (Cunrad): 1[2]
  Maria (∞Hellwig): 1, 2
Mücke
  Benjamin Gottfried: 47
Muffel: 90
  Gabriel: 96
Müller
  Günther: 13[62], 14[65]
Mummenhof
  Ernst: 4[24]
Münzmeister: 38

Neubecker
  Ottfried: 2[7]
Neumärker: 38
Newald
  Richard: 13[62]
Neydecker
  Johann: 54

Nicolai
  Christoph: 5, 5[28]
Niefert
  J. (Lodz): 35
Noessler
  Georg: 2, 2[11], 79, 80
Nopitsch
  Christian Conrad: 2[9], 67
Nützel: 91
  Carl: 9, 9[51]
  Caspar: 97

Oelhafen: 93
Oertel: 93
Omeis
  Magnus Daniel: 2[13], 10[54], 20[94], 29, 34, 106
Opitz
  Martin: 8, 9
Örber
  Ludovicus (Ludwig): 3[18]
Ortlieb: 100

Pasmann
  Cardinal of Bratislava: 18[86]
Pechlin
  J. N.: 48
Peucerus
  Caspar: 9, 9[51]
Pfann
  Johann: 85
Pfintzing: 91
  Sebald: 96
Piccart
  Michael: 9, 9[51]
Pilgram von Eib: 38
Pipenburg
  Joachim: 87
  Magdalena: 87
Pirckheimer: 100
  Wil(l)ibald: 6, 13, 15, 15[70], 15[71], 60, 61, 63, 97
Pömer: 91
  Albert: 77
  Albrecht: 73
  Bartholm: 98
  Christoph Jacob: 73
  Maria Helena (∞Imhof): 77

Pona
  Francesco (-isco): 13, 14, 14[66], 52, 53, 57, 58, 78
Portner
  Peter: 82
Preßl
  Dr. (Regensburg): 18[87]
Prükel
  Job. Peter: 47
Pucher: 93
Puck: 100

Queck
  Georg: 85

Ranchinus: 3
Rauler
  J. Z.: 46
Rehdiger
  V. (Breslau): 58
Rehlinger: 38
Reicke
  Emil: 4[22], 4[24]
Reinhart
  Max: 3[20], 9[52], 10[53], 13[64], 15[74]
Rhau
  Caroline: 61
Rhodius
  Johannis: 3
Rhumel
  Johann Conrad: 27, 28
Riet(h)er: 91
  Johann: 35, 37, 38, 98
Rinder
  Johann Leonhard: 83
Rittershausen
  Nicolaus: 72
Röder
  Johann: 86
  Maria Rosina (née Schmid): 86
Roggenbach: 93
Rosa
  Catharina Barbara (∞Besler): 74
  Johann: 74
Rossetti
  Lucia: 3[19]
Roth
  Johann Ferdinand: 2[6]
Rüdel
  Dr. Sigismund: 4

Rüden
  Christoff Adam: 81
Rudolf
  Emperor: 90

Sachs: 100
Sala
  Johannis: 3[20]
  Julius: 3, 3[20]
Sammons
  Christa: 34
Sartorius (printer): 75
Satzinger
  Walter: 1[4]
Saubert
  Adolf: 84
  Johann: 18, 76
Scarpius: 3
Schedel: 93
Scheffel
  Christian Stephan: 48
Scheibel
  Johann Ephraim: 68
Scheres (a.k.a. Zieritz)
  Johann Conrad von: 67
Scherffen
  Balthasar: 72
Scheurl: 93
Schiltel
  Isabella Jacobe (∞Syroth): 85
Schlaudersbach: 93
Schlegel
  J. W.: 48
Schleicher: 93
Schlüsselfelder: 91
  Anna Elisabeth (∞Führer): 75
  Carl: 5, 73
  Catharina (née Tucher): 5
  Helena (∞Hellwig): 5, 5[29], 5[30]
  Hieronymus Wilhelm: 73
  Johann Christoph: 80, 81
  Maria Salome (née Tetzel): 73
  Wilhelm: 97
  Wilibald: 98
Schmid
  Maria Rosina (∞Röder): 86
Schmidmajer (-mair): 93
  Johann Jodoc: 77
Schmidt-Herrling
  Eleonore: 109
Schmoll
  Matthaeus: 81

Schmuggenhof: 100
Schönigk
  Johann: 77
Schopper: 100
Schorer
  Anna Maria (née See): 83
  Rupprecht: 83
Schottel
  Justus Georg: 13, 13^{62}, 54
Schreyer
  Sebald: 10
Schröck
  Lucas: 2^{12}, 4^{23}, 4^{26}, 5^{28}, 6^{37}, 20, 20^{93}, 20^{94}, 20^{96}, 20^{97}, 20^{98}, 45, 46
Schuler
  Johann: 35
Schultheiß
  Werner: 8^{48}
Schupp
  Johann Baltasar: 68
Schürstab: 91
Schützer: 38
Schwaiger
  Georg: 17^{80}, 18^{87}
Sechst (Sext)
  Johann (Alcidor): 7, 12, 14, 86, 94, 101
  Susanna (née Grünwald): 86
See
  Anna Maria (∞Schorer): 83
Seubold: 100
Sext [s. Sechst]
Sieber
  Justus: 67
Siebmacher
  Johann: 6^{39}
Sleidanus
  Johann: 9, 9^{51}
Sloane
  Sir Hans: 29
Spahr
  Blake Lee: 34
Spindler
  Paul(us): 3^{18}
Stark: 91
  Johannes: 98
von Stein: 38
Steinbürger: 38
Steininger
  Euphrosina (∞Koch): 5^{34}
  Johann: 5^{34}
Steinmeyer
  Elias von: 2^9, 2^{10}, 64
Stern: 38

Stetten
  Anna Maria (∞Winckler): 84
Stöberlin
  Wolfgang: 75
Stokhamer: 93
Stolle
  Gottfried: 68
Strandberg
  Zacharias Johansson: 50
Stromer: 91
  Peter: 96
  Ulrich d. Ä.: 96
  Ulrich d. J.: 96
Stubenberg
  Johann Wilhelm von: 14
Surgeon General
  United States Army: 29
Sylvaticus
  Benedictus: 3
Syroth
  Emmeran: 85
  Isabella Jacobe (née Schiltel): 85
Szyrocki
  Marian: 13, 13^{62}

Tauber
  Johann: 66
Tetzel: 92
  Anna Felicitas (née Haller): 73
  Carl Erasmus: 73
  Jobst: 98
  Johann Jacob: 4, 36, 37, 73, 74, 88, 99
  Maria Salome (∞Schlüsselfelder): 73
Teufel: 100
Tilly
  Werner: 29
Tittmann
  Julius: 11^{57}
Tomasinus
  Jacobus: 3
Toppler: 92
Tozzetti
  Targioni: 47
Trammel
  Maria Müllich (∞Kob): 72
Trechsel
  Johann Martin: 4^{23}
Trew
  Christoph Jacob: 47
Troschel
  Peter: 35, 67

Tucher: 92
   Andreas: 97
   Antoni: 97
   Barthold: 96
   Catharina (∞Schlüsselfelder): 5

Vergil
   Publius Maro: 7[42]
Veslingius
   Johannis: 3
Vogel
   Egidius: 57
Vogt
   Johannis: 13[62], 16, 16[79]
Volkamer (Volckamer): 36, 92
   Berthold: 96
   Georg: 27, 35, 37, 38, 99
   Guido von: 36
   Johann Georg (Helianthus): 4[23], 4[26], 5, 5[28], 6[37], 7, 12, 14, 19, 20, 20[93], 20[94], 20[97], 42, 88, 92, 94, 95, 101, 109
Volckert
   G. (Berlin): 34
Von Thill: 93
Vorchtel: 100
Voyt: 93
Vredeveld
   Harry: 8[48]

Wagner: 100
Waldstromer: 93
Walish: 39
Wallenstein
   Albrecht Wenzel Eusebius von: 35, 37, 92
Waller
   Erik: 29
Waltzahn
   Freiherr von: 38
Warnock
   Robert G.: 12[59], 12[60]
Wartenberg
   Count Franz von, Bishop and Cardinal of Regensburg: 17, 17[80], 18, 18[89], 19[90], 19[92], 41, 42, 83
Weber
   Michael: 76
   Philipp: 77
Weigel: 38
Weihern
   Freiherr von: 64

Welsch
   Georg Hieronymus: 20, 20[96]
Welser: 92
   Sebald: 98
Widt
   Johann Reinhardt: 29
Will
   Georg Andreas: 2[9], 2[11], 3[20], 4[24], 10, 10[54], 11[57], 29, 34, 46, 61, 64, 67, 106
Winckler
   Anna Maria (née Stetten): 84
   Benedict von Döliz: 84
Wolff: 38

Zedler
   Johann Heinrich: 29
Zenner: 101
Zieritz (s. Scheres)
Zingel: 101
Zollner: 38
Zunner
   Johann David: 14, 52, 57, 58